Advaita Vedānta and

Advaita Vedānta and Zen Buddhism

Deconstructive Modes of Spiritual Inquiry

Leesa S. Davis

continuum

Continuum International Publishing Group
The Tower Building
11 York Road
London SE1 7NX

80 Maiden Lane
Suite 704
New York NY 10038

www.continuumbooks.com

First published 2010
Paperback edition first published 2011

British Library Cataloguing-in-Publication Data
A catalogue record for this book is available from the British Library.

ISBN: HB: 978-0-8264-2068-8
ISBN: PB: 978-1-4411-2109-7

Library of Congress Cataloging-in-Publication Data
Davis, Leesa S.
Advaita Vedanta and Zen Buddhism : deconstructive modes of spiritual inquiry / Leesa S. Davis.
p.cm.
Includes bibliographical references and index.
ISBN 978-1-4411-2109-7 (pbk.)
1. Advaita. 2. Zen Buddhism. 3. Deconstruction. I. Title.

B132.A3D38 2011
181′.482--dc23

2011022986

Typeset by Free Range Book Design & Production Limited
Printed and bound in Great Britain

In Memoriam

Patricia Mary Davis
1930–1987

Contents

Acknowledgements ix
Abbreviations xi
Introduction: Experiential Deconstructive Inquiry xiii

Part One:
Foundational Philosophies and Spiritual Methods

1. Non-duality in Advaita Vedānta and Zen Buddhism 3
   Ontological differences and non-duality 3
   Meditative inquiry, questioning, and dialoguing as a means to spiritual insight 8
   The 'undoing' or deconstruction of dualistic conceptions 12
2. Advaita Vedānta: Philosophical Foundations and Deconstructive Strategies 18
   Sources of the tradition 18
      Upaniṣads: 'That art thou' (*tat tvam asi*) 18
      Gauḍapāda (c. 7th century): 'No bondage, no liberation' 22
      Śaṅkara (c. 7th–8th century): 'there is no apprehender different from this apprehension to apprehend it' 27
   Modern and contemporary masters 47
      Ramana Maharshi (1879–1950): 'Who am I?' 49
      H. W. L. Poonja (1910–1997): 'You have to do nothing to be who you are!' 58
      Gangaji (b. 1942): 'You are That!' 65
   Advaita Vedānta summary: 'Nothing ever happens' 69
3. Zen Buddhism: Philosophical Foundations and Deconstructive Strategies 71
   Sources of the tradition 73

The *Laṇkāvatāra Sūtra* and the *Vajracchedikā Prajñāpāramitā Sūtra*: 'All things … are not independent of each other and not two' 73
Nāgārjuna (c. 113–213): '*Saṃsāra* is nothing essentially different from *nirvāṇa*. *Nirvāṇa* is nothing essentially different from *saṃsāra*' 80
Eihei Dōgen (1200–1253): 'If I am already enlightened, why must I practice?' 93
Contemporary masters 106
Ekai Korematsu (b. 1948): 'Return to the spine' 107
Hōgen Yamahata (b. 1935): 'Why not now?' 109
Zen Buddhism summary: 'Neither being nor non-being is to be taken hold of' 111

Part Two:
Deconstructive Techniques and Dynamics of Experiential Undoing

4. Four Deconstructive Techniques Common to Both Traditions 117
The teacher–student dynamic 118
Four key deconstructive techniques 123
Unfindability analysis 123
Bringing everything back to the here and now 133
Paradoxical problems 139
Negation 146
5. Dynamics of Experiential Undoing 156
Non-dual experiential 'space' 157
Experiential mapping: Practitioners in the space 159
Experiential undoing in Advaita Vedānta 160
Experiential undoing in Zen Buddhism 169

Conclusion: Deconstruction of Reified Awareness 186
Notes 191
Bibliography 207
Index 213

Acknowledgements

I take great pleasure in acknowledging those who have supported this project along the way. Many thanks to the Advaita *satsang* communities and Zen groups in Melbourne, Australia. In particular I am grateful to Ekai Korematsu-oshō and the Jikishōan Zen Buddhist community for their assistance in collecting information on contemporary Sōtō Zen practice. The willingness of Jikishōan practitioners to discuss their practice and Ekai-oshō's commentaries on key aspects of Sōtō thought and practice have provided me with an invaluable database for part two of this book.

Warm thanks to Dr Peter L. Nelson for his friendship, moral support and critical feedback through all stages of this project. I am also much indebted to Professor Kaisa Puhakka for her enthusiastic support and encouragement. Dominik and Hildegard Wieser of Basel provided much needed moral and financial support at a critical time and Kirsty Schaper at Continuum has also been most supportive. David Godman's work on Sri Ramana Maharshi and H. W. L. Poonjaji has been a vital source of information and inspiration for many years now – to him goes my admiration and thanks.

Special thanks and gratitude to my long-suffering husband, Olivier Burckhardt, a paradigm of unremitting patience and exasperation, who has helped and supported me at all levels throughout the long process of this book's development.

The preparation of this book was generously supported by a grant from The Hermann and Marianne Straniak Foundation and I am happy to take this opportunity to thank them.

Acknowledgement is made to the following for kind permission to quote from works written, edited, or published by them: Professor Eliot Deutsch for quotations from Deutsch, E. and Van Buitenen, J. A. B., eds (1971), *A Source Book of Advaita Vedānta*, The University Press of Hawaii, Honolulu; Sri V. S. Ramanan, President, Board of Trustees, Sri Ramanasramam for quotations from Sri Ramana Maharshi (1984), *Talks With Sri Ramana Maharshi*, Sri

Ramanasramam, Tiruvannamalai, India; Ekai Korematsu-oshō for quotations from his unpublished teachings and commentaries.

Abbreviations and Conventions

Bṛ. UB.	Bṛhad-āraṇyaka Upaniṣadbhāṣya
Bṛ. Up.	Bṛhad-āraṇyaka Upaniṣad
BSB	Brahmasūtrabhāṣya
Ch. Up.	Chāndogya Upaniṣad
GK	Kārikās on the Māṇdūkya Upaniṣad a.k.a. the Gauḍapādīya-kārikā
Laṇkā	Laṇkāvatāra Sūtra
MMK	Mūlamadhyamakakārikās
Mu. Up.	Muṇḍaka Upaniṣad
Upad.	Upadeśasāhasrī
Vajra	Vajracchedikā Prajñāpāramitā Sūtra

C.	Chinese
J.	Japanese
K.	Korean
Skt.	Sanskrit

Conventions

For reasons of consistency, all Chinese names and terms have been rendered into pinyin transliteration. Chinese names in book and article titles remain as published.

In all dialogues the teacher's name is given once in square brackets, e.g. [*Ramana Maharshi*], and thereafter identified by the initial of the first name, e.g., [*R*]. All questioners are first referred to as '[*Student*]' and '[*S*]' thereafter.

Every attempt has been made to use non-discriminatory language; however the use of masculine pronouns in the classical dialogues has not been changed because in these traditions spiritual seekers were almost always male. In modern and contemporary dialogues where the name is given or known, corresponding male or female pronouns are used. In all other cases, male and female pronouns are alternated or, whenever possible, plurals are used.

Introduction

Experiential Deconstructive Inquiry

What is the knowledge by which I may find my true nature?

Spiritual Aspirant to Śaṅkara[1]

Spiritual practice is, above all, an experiential journey. Upon beginning this journey, a spiritual aspirant, to a greater or lesser degree, enters into a potentially life-changing engagement with a tradition, a teacher, and a practice. This engagement reflects one of the most powerful notions in religion: the idea that spiritual practice can lead to an experience of insight or a 'knowledge', which, in its profoundest aspect, can bring about a hitherto unknown or unrealized relationship to self and world.

The two traditions that this study will consider – the Upaniṣadic tradition of Advaita Vedānta, emanating from the seventh- to eighth-century Indian sage Śaṅkara, and the Buddhist path of Zen (C. Chan), especially the Sōtō practice lineage emanating from the thirteenth-century Japanese Master Eihei Dōgen, both of which are now widely practised in the West – offer forms of spiritual inquiry that, it is claimed, can lead a practitioner to liberating realization of the 'true nature' of self and world.

According to Advaita and Zen philosophies, reality is fundamentally unconditioned and non-dual in nature, and that realization of this 'true nature' of things is the aim and goal of human life. As a corollary to this, both traditions claim that our ordinary dualistic way of experiencing the world does not give us true or direct knowledge of 'the nature of things', as our experience of reality is somehow distorted or filtered by conditions and structures that we falsely identify with reality itself.

To this end, a common instruction of Zen masters and Advaitin sages is the admonishment to 'look directly', and in many respects the entire spiritual endeavour in these traditions appears to hinge on this: that is, for the student to remove, or at least lessen, the distortions, filters and various kinds of conditionings through which he or she normally views the world. Both maintain that if their instructions are carried out then delusion in the form of misplaced identification will be overcome and the insight will be 'direct', that is, free from conditioning factors and outside of dualistic structures.

Following this, the key question for the spiritual aspirant is 'How?' and it is the 'how' of these practice traditions that we will explore here. If, as these traditions claim, our 'everyday' dualistic structures of being and knowing do not give us 'true' knowledge, what must we do to see through them or remove them? 'What is the knowledge or what is the method by which I may find my true nature?' 'What do I have to know and what do I have to do?'

Taking the perspective of the questioning student, the above questions will be asked of Advaita and Zen masters and texts with the aim of exploring the liberative logic and semantic power of Advaita and Zen teachings and instructions through the experiential impact on the student. Thus, the primary objective of this study is to clarify how language and other communicative techniques are used in selected spiritual practices of Advaita Vedānta and Zen Buddhism and how the boundaries and barriers of conceptual thought and personal dualistic experiencing are subverted, reconfigured and experientially deconstructed to disclose a purported non-dual knowing that both traditions claim is somehow innate but unrecognized.

Both Advaita and Zen make the claim that spiritual awakening does not involve 'adding anything new' to the practitioner's experience. Both claim that there is nothing to be attained or gained from spiritual practice but, nevertheless, both traditions also claim that there is a fundamental non-dual realization as to the 'nature of things' that is obscured or mistaken by the 'everyday' dualistic structures that we live by. Hence, the dualistic thought processes and dichotomizing habits that are unrecognized in the practitioner's 'commonsense' 'everyday' experiencing must be recognized and 'seen through' in a process of 'experiential undoing' of the thought-constructed unquestioned dualistic assumptions which, according to these traditions, cause seekers to objectify and reify reality. In this sense, both spiritual paths, in practice, can be read as offering forms of deconstructive spiritual inquiry designed to recognize, work with, and overcome in significant ways the mediated or constructed quality of human experience and ascriptions. In both traditions, 'authentic' being and 'real' knowing are intimately related and are claimed to be disclosed through engagement with a spiritual practice.

In this context, the Advaita and Zen experiential spiritual quest can be said to be similarly framed. Both traditions posit an ontological quest through epistemological investigations based on a theory of error. That is, the core operational assumption of both traditions is that our experience of reality is obscured or hindered by conditioned ontological boundaries and epistemological filters that we habitually mistake for reality itself. Hence, the 'goal' of spiritual practice in these traditions is to disclose these mistaken ontological and epistemological categories to the practitioner and to 'undo', 'see through' or deconstruct erroneous ontological objectifications and epistemic reifications that obscure or distort what tradition claims to be 'reality-as-it-is'.

Although Advaita and Zen launch their respective 'reality-as-it-is' on differing ontologies, in the deconstructive meditative inquiries that Sōtō Zen and Advaita Vedānta advocate the key dualistic barriers and dichotomized conceptual categories that spiritual aspirants struggle with fall under the same general headings: self and other (subject and object), ends and means (cause and effect) and linear dualistic conceptions of space and time. In the course of this study, we shall examine how these deconstructive practices are taught in Zen and Advaita, and how unquestioned adherence to these dualistic constructs are thrown into question in the personal experiencing of the practitioner and experientially undone.

It should be noted, and will become clear in the course of our discussion, that this study does not address philosophical deconstruction in the French sense but rather identifies a process of experiential deconstruction in certain Buddhist and Hindu non-dual philosophies and practice instructions. This mode of deconstruction targets dualistic frames of being and knowing and is ignited via certain non-dual spiritual practices that aim to 'undo', or at least lessen, dualistic either/or structures that, according to these traditions, obscure our direct experience of 'things as they are'.

What is proposed here is to carefully consider the practice instructions given by Zen and Advaita texts and teachers and the accompanying exchanges with students offered in these spiritual traditions, with the aim of clarifying the liberative intent and deconstructive implications of such instructions in relationship to the core doctrinal and philosophical tenets of each tradition. In this way, possible distinctions in approach and technique between various deconstructive spiritual strategies can be identified and the experiential dynamics of the deconstructive process can be approached. As stated above, the experiential impact of these teachings will be explored from the viewpoint of the questioning student as the nature of the questions generated are indicative of the key dualistic constructions that have to be experientially undone.

The point here is that the well-known 'paradoxical' and 'puzzling' statements and practice instructions of Zen Buddhism and Advaita Vedānta will yield to a fuller exploration of their meaning and dynamics if the experiential dimension is taken into account. In other words, in examining the experiential tensions, existential doubts and (often) radical questioning that manifests in the experience of the student when confronted by these 'paradoxical' and 'puzzling' statements and instructions, we can begin to identify the conditioned structures that the student is struggling against and a window on the inner logic and workings of these practices may be opened. For example, such instructions as Chan master Hongzhi Zhengjue's[2] 'simply drop off everything' (Hongzhi, 1991, p. 10) and a contemporary Advaita practitioner's description of his spiritual practice as the 'practice of no practice' (InterviewDO2, 2002) can appear to be either facile advice or mere word games if the master's non-dual deconstructive liberative intent and the student's dualistic doubts and difficulties are not taken into account.

To such statements and instructions the questions that this book asks is not only 'What do they mean?' but also, and perhaps more importantly, 'What are they doing?' and what happens in the experiential worlds of practitioners as a result. To explore Advaita and Zen deconstructive spiritual practices in this way, a multi-dimensional methodological approach that opens an analytical window on the experience of practitioners is needed: an approach that is flexible enough to identify and trace the experiential trajectory of practice, and precise enough to allow critical appraisal of the phenomenological data with some philosophical accuracy.

The primary method of experiential data collection for this study was participant-observation fieldwork in which I actively took part in Advaita and Zen practice communities for over three years: going on intensive practice retreats; attending teachings and public talks; interviewing teachers and practitioners; and, in the case of Zen, receiving a commentary from a contemporary Zen teacher especially for this research. This approach placed me in a dynamic insider/outsider position in which maintaining awareness of a shifting sense of active participation versus critical overview was extremely important.[3] For this reason, the observed material was not rigorously classified until the participant-observation stage of the research was completed and some distance from the practice situation was attained. This distance, coupled with careful analysis of the philosophical underpinnings and master–student dialogues from foundational and contemporary Advaita and Zen texts, served as a check and balance to the phenomenological data collected in 'live' practice situations.

To explore the 'how' of these practice traditions from the viewpoint of the questioning student, we are thus working within two frameworks: the spiritual methods or practices of tradition and the investigative methodologies of research. To take both these frameworks into account, and to be able to move conceptually between them, the most suitable methodological approach proved to be heuristic in design and transpersonal in orientation. In addition to this, to analyse the 'live' experiential material gathered in practitioner interviews with more philosophical precision, a hermeneutical-phenomenological strategy was also developed and employed in part two of this study.[4]

Briefly, heuristic research design offers a methodological framework that can both parallel and critically appraise the liberative spiritual methods (practice) of Advaita and Zen, as it centres on qualitative methods and 'seeks to obtain qualitative depictions that are at the heart and depths of ... experience' in which the investigator '... gathers detailed descriptions, direct quotations, and case documentations ... [that] enable the researcher to derive the raw material of knowledge and experience from the empirical world' (Moustakas, 1990, p. 38).

Furthermore, heuristic inquiry provides appropriate conceptual tools for entering into the more intuitive, experiential frameworks of spiritual methods in the sense that the concerns and procedures of heuristic research and spiritual methods interface and overlap in many key areas. In heuristic inquiry, the researcher immerses him- or herself in active experience and works through experiential and analytical stages such as self-dialogue, tacit knowing, focusing, and inner attention, all of which parallel the kind of engagement, attention and intention that is required of a spiritual practitioner. In spiritual practice, the 'workshop' is one's own self; while one can never 'get inside' another person's experiencing, the need to recognize the phenomenal world of the experiencing persons is an important orientation to any empirical investigation that works towards understanding and explicating experiential data in a philosophical framework.

Engaging with a spiritual practice in which previously unquestioned dualistic structures and overlays are thrown into question involves 'shifts' or 'movements' in the practitioner's internal frames of experiencing; here, a transpersonal orientation is useful for identifying the shifts in awareness that practitioners report. Based on studies of meditative awareness by transpersonal theorists Valle and Mohs (1998, pp. 100–101), eight key characteristics of transpersonal awareness that are 'often recognized in the practice of meditation' were realigned for the purposes of this study from the perspective of non-duality that is central to both Advaita and Zen practice and philosophies. These non-dual characteristics were identified directly from foundational texts and contemporary practitioner reports and, for conceptual purposes, are representative of the kind of shifts that practitioners experience. The eight non-dual characteristics of meditative awareness are:

1 The stillpoint of being: I am not this or that, I simply *am*.
2. All-accepting compassion: Things *are* perfect and complete just as they *are*.
3. Pure Being: Subject–object dichotomy dissolves.

4. Dissolution of spatial boundaries: Being is all-space.
5. Dissolution of categories of time: There is only Now.
6. Non-dual knowledge: Immediate knowing.
7. Non-dual action: Direct action without premeditation or consequence.
8. Deconstruction of constructed conceptions of self and world.

These qualities or characteristics of meditative awareness highlight the multi-dimensionality of meditative experience and provide a useful framework for isolating and analysing the static dualistic conceptual structures that deconstructive spiritual practice throws into question and experientially 'undoes'.

It should be noted that the key non-dual characteristics of meditative awareness and the phases of heuristic inquiry are considered separately for analytical purposes; in the actual practice situation they are interlinked and presuppose each other.

This study naturally falls into two parts. Part one, 'Foundational Philosophies and Spiritual Methods', outlines the foundational philosophical tenets and spiritual methods (practices) of tradition and identifies their deconstructive thrust. This is done by examining teacher–student dialogues in traditional sources and contemporary teachings in each tradition, and hermeneutically clarifying and explicating the deconstructing or 'undoing' of the student's unquestioned dualistic experiencing structures (ontological and epistemological).

The second part of this study, 'Deconstructive Techniques and Dynamics of Experiential Undoing', builds on the above by first identifying four deconstructive techniques common to both traditions, and second, phenomenologically exploring the dynamics of such 'experiential undoing' through the reported experience of actual cases of contemporary Advaita and Zen practitioners. By mapping practitioners' reported practice experience against the philosophical underpinnings of tradition we can see these experientially deconstructive philosophies 'in action' in contemporary practice situations and gain some insight into the shifts in worldviews that these practices ignite.

In chapter one, 'Non-duality in Advaita Vedānta and Zen Buddhism', the respective ontological orientations of Zen and Advaita are described and compared and their experiential modes of approach to spiritual insight (meditative inquiry, questioning, and dialoguing) are outlined. The discussion goes on to offer preliminarily descriptions of the undoing or deconstruction of dualistic conceptions in Advaita and Zen spiritual inquiry. The approach here is broad and the discussion general, with the aim of laying the foundations for the more in-depth analysis of the traditions in chapters two and three and the more phenomenological thrust of part two.

Chapters two and three, 'Advaita Vedānta: Philosophical Foundations and Deconstructive Strategies' and 'Zen Buddhism: Philosophical Foundations and Deconstructive Strategies', deal directly with the foundational philosophical tenets and spiritual methods employed in the practice traditions of Advaita Vedānta and Zen Buddhism. In keeping with the emphasis on the experiential impact of these teachings, these chapters take an 'old masters' approach to tradition wherein the reported spiritual experience of lineage founders and key teachers is shown to be paradigmatic for the practice tradition that follows. Thus, the line of inquiry taken here focuses on the individual experiential aspects of spiritual practice and its relationship to doctrine rather than the more community-based collective expressions of Advaita and Zen practice.[5] In this context, the core non-dual teachings and key philosophical tenets of each tradition are outlined from traditional source texts and presented 'in action' through the teacher–student exchanges of lineage founders. The teachings of modern and contemporary Advaita and Zen are also presented through teacher–student exchanges that highlight their links to, and points of divergence from, key traditional teachings.

In part two, four key deconstructive techniques are identified, described and analysed in the context of the practice situation. Following this, the dynamics of deconstructive practice experience are explored. Central to the exploration of the dynamic process(es) of deconstructive spiritual inquiry in part two is the need to posit a suitable conceptual framework in which practitioners' reported experiential data can be explored and mapped against the liberative claims of tradition.

To this end, working from the perspective of the experiential impact of these teachings, and 'suspended' (as it were) between the insider and outsider positions, a hermeneutical-phenomenological strategy is employed that reads Advaita and Zen teacher–student exchanges as a dialectic between the two levels of reality or the 'two truths' that are a philosophical mainstay of each tradition. The absolute non-dual standpoint (*pāramārthika*) of the teacher and the relative dualistic standpoint of the pupil (*vyavahāra*) are shown to be a shifting dynamic in which the student is pushed to different levels of understanding until finally the idea of levels or understandings dissolves. This strategy also brings to light how Advaita and Zen masters employ the two truths as a deconstructive device to expose the interplay and ultimate non-duality between opposites and dichotomies.

In addition to this, a standard Indian philosophical 'formula,' found in both Buddhist and Advaita dialogues – the four-cornered negation or tetralemma – is identified as a deconstructive rubric that is employed to shift the practitioner into a non-dual experiential 'space' in which seemingly contradictory assertions can coexist in the practitioner's awareness without apparent contradiction.

Through the above analytical approach we can then identify practitioners' reported experiential deconstructive 'shifts' or 'openings' in awareness as movement into a non-dual 'space' in which experiential undoing unfolds and an attempt to integrate the philosophical, observational and phenomenological data in a description and analysis of the dynamics of deconstructive spiritual inquiry and the phenomenology of experiential undoing.

Chapter four, 'Four Deconstructive Techniques Common to Both Traditions', outlines the techniques of deconstructive spiritual inquiry by discussing the practice situation and the role of the teacher in Advaita and Zen. Four key deconstructive techniques that are common to both traditions are then identified and described. These are:

1. unfindability analysis;
2. bringing everything back to the here and now;
3. paradoxical problems;
4. negation.

This chapter utilizes the above described heuristic analytical framework to show how these techniques are employed, individually and in combination, in Advaita and Zen practice instructions and in the context of teacher–student dialogues. These deconstructive 'moves' are then related to the core philosophical tenets of each tradition as explicated in chapters two and three. To this end, emphasis is placed on showing how these deconstructive techniques are wielded to expose previously unquestioned inconsistencies in the structures of the practitioner's personal experiencing and how they are 'worked' to experientially undo key conceptual dualisms of self and other (subject and object), ends and means (cause and effect), and linear dualistic conceptions of space and time to instigate the process of experiential undoing; that is, the experiential deconstructive 'shift' or 'movement' in the *actual* experience of the practitioner.

Chapter five, 'Dynamics of Experiential Undoing', employs a hermeneutical-phenomenological strategy to parallel practitioners' experiential reports (empirical study) with philosophical analysis. That is, the reported experiential impact of these deconstructive practices is phenomenologically 'mapped' against the key philosophical and experiential tenets of tradition and previously identified deconstructive 'moves' of Zen and Advaita teachers, with the aim of making some observations on the similarities and differences in each tradition's approach and unpacking the deconstructive dynamics that underlie the process.

To this end, chapter five expands on the previous chapter's analysis of the practice situation and the techniques of deconstructive spiritual inquiry by attempting to describe the process of experiential undoing and its underlying dynamics. This description proceeds in two ways. First, experiential 'shifts' or 'movements' reported by practitioners are posited as a phenomenological 'space' in which experiential undoing unfolds. To enable a more rigorous entry into the experiential dynamics two key non-dual categories, the Advaitin 'empty moment' between thought and thought and the Zen 'turning space' of 'non-thinking' (*hishiryō*) previously identified from the dialogues and practice instructions in chapters two and three are used as a rubric to map practitioners' experiential reports of moving into non-dual awareness.

Secondly, the philosophical, observational and phenomenological data are integrated by mapping the reported experiential impact of deconstructive spiritual inquiry on two veteran Advaita and Zen practitioners against the key philosophical tenets of tradition and previously identified deconstructive strategies employed by teachers. Aside from highlighting differences and similarities in the deconstructive dynamics, the multi-dimensional nature of this mapping aims to bring the intra-psychic dynamics of the ontological shifts that these practices generate for practitioners into relief and thereby gain some insight into the transformation of identity and worldview that practitioners experience.

The study concludes by summarizing the differences and highlighting the similarities in each tradition's use of deconstructive techniques. What comes to the surface is that despite their almost diametrically opposed ontologies, the deconstructive point in both traditions is that the choice between any dichotomous pairing (doing/not-doing, self/other and so on) is only binding as long as there is attachment to either/or patterns of thought. Once the attachment to either/or patterns of thought that support dichotomous epistemic framings and objectified ontologies is weakened, the seeming contradictions of non-dual understandings dissolve. Furthermore, when the diametrically opposed ontologies of Zen and Advaita are viewed in a dialectical relationship based on their shared deconstructive techniques and dualistic 'targets', the phenomenology of experiential shifts into non-dual awareness exhibit striking similarities.

Part One

Foundational Philosophies and Spiritual Methods

Chapter 1

Non-duality in Advaita Vedānta and Zen Buddhism

Ontological Differences and Non-duality in Advaita Vedānta and Mahāyāna Buddhism

T. R. V. Murti summarizes the philosophical differences between the Buddhist and Brāhmaṇic-Hindu paths to liberation thus:

> There are two main currents of Indian philosophy – one having its source in the atma doctrine of the Upanishads and the other in the anatma doctrine of the Buddha. They conceive reality on two distinct and exclusive patterns.
>
> The Upanishads and the systems following the Brahmanical tradition conceive reality on the pattern of an inner core or soul (atman), immutable and identical amidst an outer region of impermanence and change, to which it is unrelated or but loosely related. This may be termed the Substance-view of reality …
>
> The other tradition is represented by the Buddhist denial of substance (atman) and all that it implies. There is no inner and immutable core in things; everything is in flux. Existence (the universal and the identical) was rejected as illusory; it was but a thought construction made under the influence of wrong belief. This may be taken as the Modal view of reality.
>
> (Murti, 1955, pp. 10–11)

Murti's description of two patterns of reality, one conceived on an 'inner core [*ātman*], immutable and identical amidst an outer region of impermanence and change' and the other conceived on the 'denial' of such an 'immutable and identical inner core' with the assertion that 'everything is in flux' is an apt evaluation of the core ontologies of the Upaniṣadic-based tradition of Advaita Vedānta and the Mahāyāna tradition of Buddhism.

Viewed from the perspective of the *ātman* doctrine, or the ontology of 'all-self', the Advaitin's equation of *ātman* (self) with the nature of ultimate reality (*brahman*) is a statement of the ontological 'fullness' of things.[1] All phenomena are not-different from *brahman* because, ultimately there are no distinctions or differentiation within *brahman*.[2] The self, like reality, is unlocalized and stable. Fundamentally, all *is brahman*.

While viewed from the Buddhist *anātman* doctrine or the (non-) ontology of 'no-self', especially how it developed in the *Prajñāpāramitā* texts of the Mahāyāna tradition, the denial of any such permanent, changeless, substantial self and the assertion that all phenomena share this lack of substantial self-nature (*svabhāva*) represents the fundamental ontological 'emptiness' (*śūnyatā*) of things. All phenomena arise and fall on an interdependent, contingent, continuum (*pratītyasamutpāda*) and are impermanent (*anicca*) 'flashings in the vast phenomenal world'.[3] The self, like reality, is uncentred and unstable. Fundamentally, all is empty (*śūnya*).

Hence, from the differing perspectives of the substance-view and the modal-view (or the all-self and no-self doctrines), different metaphysical systems are derived that are, as Richard King points out, diametrically opposed. In comparing the foundational Advaita commentarial text *Kārikās on the Māṇḍūkya Upaniṣad*, also known as the *Gauḍapādīya-kārikā* (*GK*) attributed to Gauḍapāda, with the fundamental Mahāyāna Buddhist text the *Mūlamadhyamaka-kārikā* (*MMK*) by the second-century-CE founder of the Mādhyamika school, Nāgārjuna, King offers the following:

> In a sense one might say that the authors of the MMK and the GK are looking at the same picture from opposite sides of the mirror. Their presuppositions (and therefore their conclusions) are thus diametrically opposed. Paradoxical as this may seem, it is because of 'the directly facing nature' of the two systems that the Mahayana and the Advaita traditions are so often confused; in many respects their discussions and conclusions are mirrored in the views of the other. Mirror images are, of course, reversals of the things which they reflect …
>
> (King, 1995, p. 238)

Although King goes on to say that we should 'not take [the mirror image] analogy too seriously' and that he holds the position 'that the prima facie similarity of Advaita and Mahayana ideas, in actuality, reflects their direct incommensurability' (King, 1995, p. 238), the mirror image analogy and the 'directly facing nature' of the substance and modal systems are of interest and relevance to this discussion when taken in the context of the claimed non-dual nature of reality and the non-dual experience that is posited as the liberative 'end point' (as it were) of both traditions.

Before discussing the relevance of the 'directly-facing' nature of Mahāyāna and Advaita ontology to the experience of non-duality, it is useful to clarify exactly what each tradition means by describing the 'highest knowledge as being beyond all traces of duality' (Murti, 1955, p. 217) and the nature of Ultimate Reality as non-dual.

Śaṇkara's Advaita and the Mahāyāna tradition of Mādhyamika[4] are described as *advaitavāda* and *advayavāda* respectively (Loy, 1988a, pp. 28–29 and Murti, 1955, p. 217). *Advaitavāda* (the theory of non-difference, i.e., the non-difference between, or identity of, subject and object) and *advayavāda* (the theory of not-two, i.e., neither of the two extreme views) presents us with a nuanced distinction of non-duality as posited by the Advaitin and non-duality in the general Mahāyāna sense and the particular Mādhyamika Buddhist sense.[5]

T. R. V. Murti, following Bhattacharya (Murti, 1955, p. 217, fn. 1), describes the distinction between *advaya* and *advaita* thus:

> A distinction must ... be made between the advaya of the Mādhyamika and the advaita of the Vedānta although in the end it may turn out to be one of emphasis of approach.
>
> Advaya is knowledge free from the duality of the extremes (antas or dṛṣṭis) of 'Is' and 'Is not', Being and Becoming etc. It is *knowledge freed* of conceptual distinctions.
>
> Advaita is knowledge *of* a differenceless entity – Brahman (Pure Being) ...
>
> (Murti, 1955, p. 217, his italics)

For the purposes of this discussion, the *advaya* and the *advaita* distinction is important in recognizing the nuances in Vedāntic and Mahāyāna articulations of non-duality. In comparing Mādhyamika and Advaita in terms of the *advaya* and *advaita* distinctions, the orientation of their respective non-dual philosophical projects becomes clear: Advaita Vedānta offers a theory of *advaitavāda*, a theory of non-difference; Mādhyamika, can be described as offering a theory of *advayavāda*, a theory of 'non-two', i.e., neither of the two extremes of the existence and nonexistence of reality as such.

Following on from this, if we take the non-dual philosophical orientation of each tradition from the viewpoint of practice, i.e., the 'how' of these spiritual paths, the *advaya/advaita* distinction can be seen in 'operation' in instructional discourses and is indicative as to how these philosophical orientations underpin deconstructive instructional discourse.

For example, the respective *advaya/advaita* orientations can be seen in the differing descriptions of non-duality found in Advaita and Zen literature: in the *Bṛhad-āraṇyaka Upaniṣad* (IV:5.15) Yājñavalkya asks Maitreyī the deconstructive question 'where everything has become just one's own self, by what and whom should one see … by what and whom should one know? By what should one know him by whom all this is known?' 'When everything has become just one's own self' is a statement of non-difference, and in asking 'by what should one know him by whom all this is known?' Yājñavalkya is challenging Maitreyī to find *something*, anything, outside of this differenceless self that is, according to Advaita, 'everything'.

Zen (K. Sŏn) master Kusan describes non-duality as 'the very Buddha dharma itself' and goes on to state that fundamentally non-duality means non-two, i.e., neither of any opposing categories; 'no coming or going, no birth or death, no being a man or a woman, no being an ordinary person or an accomplished one', and so on. He then asserts, following the insights of the Mādhyamika, that this 'not this nor that' negation of dichotomies 'should be understood to be the essence of the Buddha dharma' (Kusan, 1985, p. 92).

In the simplest terms, the soteriological or liberative aim of the spiritual paths of Advaita Vedānta and Mahāyāna Buddhism is to awaken the practitioner to a full experiential understanding of reality as tradition claims it to be – fundamentally non-dual. In Śaṇkara's Advaita, following his interpretation of the Upaniṣads, a core non-dual tenet is the non-difference or the identity of *brahman* (reality) and *ātman* (self): 'This Brahman is the self (*ayam ātmā brahma*)' (*Bṛ. Up.* II:5.19).[6] In Zen, following the insights and analysis of the purported fourteenth patriarch of Zen, Nāgārjuna, one of the key 'non-two' pairings is the negation of difference between *saṃsāra* (relative, conditioned reality) and *nirvāṇa* (absolute, unconditioned Reality): '*Saṃsāra* … is nothing essentially different from *nirvāṇa*. *Nirvāṇa* is nothing essentially different from *saṃsāra*' (*MMK* XXV:19).[7]

Based on this, the Advaita practitioner seeks to realize that ultimate reality (*brahman*) and self (*ātman*) are in essence, not different. From the Zen practitioner's point of view, practice consists of realizing that, in essence, conditioned reality (*saṃsāra*) and unconditioned reality (*nirvāṇa*) are 'not two'. In both cases, it is asserted that, in essence, there is no duality between the conditioned and the unconditioned or the relative and the absolute.

As noted in the above discussion, there is, however, a crucial difference: the 'essence' or ontology that the Advaitin and the Buddhist are referring to. The Advaitin 'essence' is the all-pervading universal substratum of *brahman*: permanent, unchanging and indivisible. The Buddhist, on the other hand, is referring to the 'essenceless' essence of no substantializing ontology. For the Mahāyāna, both *saṃsāra* and *nirvāṇa*, taken as categories placed in opposition, are merely views about reality and cannot be representative of reality which admits no conceptual distinctions.

In a more sophisticated analysis of Advaita and Buddhist ontologies, David Loy discusses the mirror-like opposition of these two systems and their resultant ontological disagreements in terms of dialectic relationship rather than diametrical opposition. To this end, Loy examines the Advaita and Zen deconstruction of dualisms in several key disputed issues: 'all-self versus no-self; only-modes versus all-Substance; impermanence versus immutability; all-conditionality versus no-causality; and all path versus no path, under the categories of self, substance, time, causation, and the "Path"' (Loy, 1988a, p. 202).

From this 'nondualist approach' Loy concludes that 'the surface conflict of categories conceals a deeper agreement regarding the phenomenology of the nondual experience' for, in both cases, 'what is more important than the choice between the denial of subject or object is the denial, common to both systems, of any bifurcation between self and non-self and so on' (Loy, 1988a, p. 12).

One of the key areas of exploration of this study is the phenomenology of the deconstruction of dualities in the experience of the practitioner. To this end, Loy's dialectical approach and insight into the phenomenology of the non-dual experience provides a fruitful orientation to Advaita and Mahāyāna ontologies. In practice, regardless of their denial or affirmation of substance, both systems deny any bifurcation between categories, because they both deny, for different reasons, the dualistic thought processes and structures that create oppositional categories in the first place.

For the practitioner, who is in the experiential trajectory of deconstructive spiritual practice, the deconstruction of dualisms, whether it be presented to the student in the form of the negation of dualistic thinking or the non-difference of subject and object, displays a similar phenomenology which hinges on the experiential undoing of the same general dualistic categories. Misunderstanding or misinterpretation of duality as the 'real' is the agreed-upon 'problem' and whether the experience of non-duality involves 'the Self of Advaita swallowing the not-self of Buddhism or the not-self of Buddhism eliminating the Advaitin Self' (Loy, 1988a, p. 204) the deconstructive process of these practices are reacting against the same thing: the bifurcation between dualistic categories and structures of thought – and that is the key issue that is to be addressed here, both theoretically and phenomenologically.

Experientially speaking, the crucial realization in both traditions is the undoing of dualistic conceptual structures and bifurcated oppositional ways of thinking that obscures direct non-dual insight. Non-duality is both the fundamental characteristic of reality and the realization to be had in order to attain a 'liberated' state. According to both traditions, it is our dualistic view of the world that stops us from experiencing 'things as they are' i.e., non-dual. As stated earlier, Loy identifies the key categories to be deconstructed as 'self, substance, time, causation, and the "Path"' (Loy, 1988a, p. 202). In this study, following Loy, we will concentrate on how the respectively prescribed deconstructive spiritual practices in Advaita Vedānta and Zen Buddhism work to undo the dualisms of self and other (subject and object), ends and means (cause and effect) and linear conceptions of space and time, in the experience of the practitioner.

Loy notes that 'all philosophy is an attempt to understand our experience, but here the critical issue is the type of experience that we accept as fundamental, as opposed to the type of experience that needs to be "explained"' (Loy, 1988a, p. 8). Experience structured and explained in dualistic categories appears self-evident, the non-dual claims of Advaita Vedānta and Mahāyāna Buddhism 'feel' counterintuitive and require explanation. The point seems to hinge on what we take as real and what we take as appearance. Gauḍapāda illustrates this point when he asserts that there is no real conflict between dualists and non-dualists, it is merely a matter of correct recognition of the 'real':

> Although dualists may think that they disagree with us, there is no real conflict; we both admit duality, but we, unlike them, hold that duality is confined to the realm of appearances and is not found in reality.
>
> (*GK* III, 17–18; summarized in Potter, 1981, p. 109)

Spiritual instruction in these traditions hinges on the practitioner moving away from dualistic structures of thought, and in the closer examination of master/student exchanges in part two we shall see how the different nuances or dimensions of non-duality are put into practice. In the practice situation, the overcoming of the subject/object dichotomy and the 'non-two' orientation are not only non-dual doctrinal orientations but also two key deconstructive strategies employed by both Advaita and Zen teachers to move the student away 'from appearance to reality'.

Meditative Inquiry, Questioning, and Dialoguing as a Means to Spiritual Insight in Advaita Vedānta and Zen Buddhism

Much of spiritual literature depicts the existential problems and doubts of spiritual aspirants as they come up against a doctrine or practice that is both intellectually and experientially inconsistent with their worldview. In the traditions under consideration here, the respective spiritual searches of two key masters, Sri Ramana Maharshi (1879–1950) and Eihei Dōgen Zenji (1200–1253) were each brought to a head by the urgent need to resolve a deeply troubling existential question.

In the case of the Advaita master Ramana Maharshi, for example, the undeniable fact of bodily death led him to a radical questioning of 'what is it that dies?' By questioning exactly 'who or what he was' (*ātman vichara*), Ramana realized that identification with the form of the body was an erroneous identification and 'who he really was' was the non-dual self (*ātman*): permanent, unchanging and not subject to birth and death.

In the case of Sōtō Zen master Eihei Dōgen, his deep doubt over the necessity of practice in the light of intrinsic Buddhahood forced him to question the duality between spiritual practice as a means and Buddhahood or realization as an end, and through contact with the 'correct' teacher and the 'authentic' practice of 'just sitting' (*shikantaza*), he resolved his question in the non-dual realization that practice and enlightenment are one.

Ramana asking 'Who am I?' and Dōgen asking 'Why must I practice if I am already enlightened?' so focused their energies and inquiries that their respective spiritual breakthroughs and methods of inquiry became paradigmatic for the Advaita Vedāntic and Sōtō Zen Buddhist lineages that followed. In a broader sense, the import of these questions is central to any spiritual practitioner for they succinctly reflect two fundamental spiritual doubts: 'who am I really?' and 'what am I doing?'

In contemporary Advaita, meditative inquiry is focused on the deconstructive question 'Who am I?' which is augmented and extended by questioning and dialoguing with a teacher. In Sōtō Zen, the deconstructive practice of *shikantaza*, an objectless yet physically precise form of meditative inquiry, is the core of spiritual practice and is also augmented and extended by questioning and dialoguing with a teacher either in private interviews (*dokusan*), or at formal or informal dharma talks (*teishō* and *chōsan*).

The interaction of Zen and Advaita teachers with their students is presented in the literature and is carried out in contemporary practice situations as a one-to-one encounter in which a 'live' spiritual issue is addressed.[8] The teacher 'reads' the students' questions according to the particular difficulty that the student is displaying and tailors his or her response to counter the problem that is blocking or hindering the student. The difficulties and the 'stumbling blocks' that a seeker encounters in practice are therefore indicative of the kinds of unquestioned dualistic conditionings that need to be overcome. These dualisms can be loosened or undone in the experience of the practitioner by the deconstructive responses of a teacher whose 'answers' often disclose the previously unquestioned dualistic assumptions inherent in the question.

In the case of Ramana Maharshi, it was noted that he 'worked' directly and, in the view of this analysis, deconstructively with aspirants' questions. As the scholar and Ramana devotee T. M. P. Mahadevan observed:

> Sri Ramana's teachings were not given in general. In fact, the sage had no use for 'lectures' or 'discourses'. His words were primarily addressed to the particular aspirant who felt some difficulty in his spiritual path and sought to have it resolved ... he has [sic] often to get behind the words that constitute a question and correct the questioner even in the manner of the questioning. Sri Ramana does not leave the interlocutor in the place where he was.
>
> (Maharshi, 1984, p. iii)

Ramana's responses were tailored to shift the practitioner out of whatever doubt or problem was impeding him. By dealing directly with the individual in front of him, Ramana sought to move the questioner away from explanation and into a direct experience of the 'answer'. In this way the questioning process itself becomes a deconstructive forum within which the dualistic cognitions of the student can be exposed and experientially undone.

Shunryu Suzuki-rōshi (1904–1971)[9] a Sōtō master in Dōgen's lineage, worked with his students in a similar way. His disciple and *dharma*-heir Richard Baker comments on Suzuki-rōshi's manner of responding to questions:

> Suzuki's responses to my questions were various, sometimes brushing me off, sometimes definitely and clearly answering. It was a study in how to ask questions. I often couldn't look to his responses as answers in the usual sense, so I accepted them as foils, mirrors, changes in energy, or sometimes as hints. Sometimes he'd answer with his body. If I asked him about breathing, he might change the way he breathed.
>
> (Chadwick, 1999, p. 257)

Once again, the teacher works with the individual problem presented by the student's question. Answers are not set lectures or explanations but immediate and direct responses or demonstrations as to how the student should proceed. Richard Baker notes that working with Suzuki-rōshi was 'a study in how to ask questions' and Ramana would 'correct the questioner even in the manner of the questioning' indicating that both traditions have little or no use for explicating abstract philosophical points in the practice situation, but seek rather to push the student to 'question the question' itself and orientate him or her towards the necessary inner inquiry in which the 'answer' is revealed or where the question itself dissolves.

In the following two Advaita examples Ramana Maharshi is quite clear on this point:

> [*Ramana Maharshi*]: What is it that persists through all these states? Find it out. That is your Self.
> [*Student*]: Supposing it is found, what then?
> [*R*]: Find it out and see. There is no asking hypothetical questions.
> [*S*]: Am I then one with Brahman?
> [*R*]: Leave Brahman alone. Find who you are. Brahman can take care of Himself.
>
> (Maharshi, 1984, p. 567)

> [*Student*]: I think that the soul is the light within. If after death it becomes one with Brahman how can there be transmigration of soul?
> [*Ramana Maharshi*]: Within whom? Who dies?
> [*S*]: I shall then frame my question in a different way.
> [*R*]: Dialectics are not wanted. Consider the answer and see.
>
> (Maharshi, 1984, p. 568)

And the contemporary Sōtō master Ekai Korematsu-oshō leaves no doubt as to 'where the student should look':

> [*Student*]: What if I am ill or physically incapacitated; how can I do this practice then?
> [*Ekai*]: Are you ill or handicapped now?
> [*S*] No, but …
> [*E*]: Don't worry about things you don't have, actualize what you are!
>
> (Korematsu, 1999c)

For the practitioner, the lived experience of a spiritual path is an ongoing process of applying oneself in and to a form of inquiry in which fundamental dimensions of human existence are claimed to be revealed. The inquiry usually consists of two aspects: the 'internal' meditative inquiry in which the seeker practices in the prescribed form, and the 'external' interaction of questioning and dialoguing with a teacher. Questions and doubts can be generated in the student's practice experience in two main ways; by difficulties generated in the internal meditative inquiry or from study of traditional texts and dialogues. As stated above, abstract speculation and hypothetical questions from spiritual aspirants are not encouraged. In fact, in order to be 'answered' at all the students' questions must be judged to reflect a genuine spiritual difficulty. In this approach, students' questions tend to reflect their 'live' spiritual problems, a factor that contributes to the urgency of the inquiry and the potency of the response.

Generally speaking, the master–student dialogues and teaching strategies of Zen and Advaita are rhetorically structured and semantically geared for maximum experiential impact, and this is reflected in the dynamic 'charge' of student–teacher encounters. Writing on the experiential impact of Zen dialogues, Stephen Clark makes the comment that a 'better account [of the meaning of the exchange] can be given by simply considering the subjective aspects of the event' (Clark, 1986, p. 220). From this point of view, it is not some idea or abstract philosophical concept that is being 'undone' or rendered insubstantial; rather, from the subjective viewpoint of the practitioner, 'it is *actually me*!' (InterviewKC9901, 2000). This practitioner response well illustrates the challenge to constructs of personal identity that these practices ignite. By calling into question the practitioner's 'me' that has always unquestioningly been thought of as 'I', Advaita and Zen deconstructive practices push practitioners to test the substantiality of the 'I-notion' and to test the veracity of unquestioned concepts that their own life-worlds are grounded upon.

The 'Undoing' or Deconstruction of Dualistic Conceptions in Advaita Vedānta and Zen Buddhism

Building on the above preliminary description of the modes of deconstructive spiritual inquiry in Advaita and Zen, this section will broadly introduce the use of dialogues in the practice situation by looking at some Zen and Advaita teaching methods, as these are recorded in texts and observed in contemporary practice.

First, let us consider Korean Sŏn (J. Zen) master Kusan Sunim's practice instructions given to a group of practitioners at the beginning of the traditional three-month summer meditation retreat:

> The Dharma taught by the Buddhas and patriarchs is medicine prescribed according to the kind of disease. What would be the use of medicine if there were no disease to fight? The darkness of the mind is due to your delusive thoughts and emotions alone. When you find yourselves in good or bad circumstances, you neglect your true mind and surrender to the power of conditions. To be swayed by circumstance and to indulge in rash, ill-considered actions causes the mind to be diseased. For the great truth to appear, stop all this now. Throw it away! To awaken your mind, press your face against the wall and ask with all your strength, 'What is it?'
>
> (Batchelor, 1990, p. 22)

Thus, according to Zen master Kusan Sunim, the 'true' mind and the 'great' truth are realized by ceasing to be swayed by circumstance and overcoming the power of conditions. For this great truth to appear we simply need to throw away the hold that conditioning factors have on us by turning our faces to the wall and engaging all our strength in the question: 'What is it?'

For the Zen student three main questions immediately present themselves. What has to be stopped? What has to be thrown away? And what exactly is the 'it' in the question 'What is it?' Clearly, the master is not seeking an actual answer to these questions, at least not in the 'ordinary' sense. Indeed the very attempt to 'answer' these questions produces a kind of circular reasoning that triggers trains of thought such as 'Stop what?' 'What is what?' 'Is it stopped?' and then back to 'What is it?' and on and on. Since the retreat participants are going to spend thirteen hours a day for the next three months on their meditation cushions wrestling with these questions it can be inferred that the response the master is attempting to actualize is somehow to be found or revealed in the mounting frustration of the student and the accompanying destabilization of commonsense notions of certainty that such engagement produces.

In short, it appears that in this form of inquiry, commonsense notions of a solid questioning subject and a certain objectified answer are difficult to sustain. The very nature of the Zen master's approach undermines any idea of answering his questions in an ordinary manner. Even at a surface glance, this form of spiritual inquiry 'feels' counterintuitive; it simply does not make sense within ordinary structures of thought and, according to Zen literature, that is precisely the point: our ordinary, commonsense ontological and epistemological constructions of identity and certainty are, at base, not representative of 'reality-as-it-is'. Consequently, in Zen practice these constructions of self and identity are seen as a structure that the spiritual aspirant needs to deconstruct in order to realize and actualize spiritual awakening.

In a similar vein, when asked how to realize the Self (i.e. awakening) the Advaitin sage Sri Ramana Maharshi offered the following instructions:

> [*Student*]: How to realise Self?
> [*Ramana Maharshi*]: Whose Self? Find out.
> [*S*]: Who am I?
> [*R*]: Find it yourself.
> [*S*]: I do not know.
> [*R*]: Think. Who is it that says 'I do not know?' What is not known? In that statement, who is the 'I'?
> [*S*]: Somebody in me.
> [*R*]: Who is that somebody? In whom?

[*S*]: Maybe some power.
[*R*]: Find it.
[*S*]: How to realize Brahman [i.e. Ultimate Reality]?
[*R*]: Without knowing the Self why do you seek to know Brahman?
[*S*]: The *sastras* [scriptures] say Brahman pervades all and me too.
[*R*]: Find the 'I' in me and then there will be no time to think of Brahman.
[*S*]: Why was I born?
[*R*]: Who was born? The answer is the same for all of your questions.
[*S*]: Who am I then?
[*R*]: (smiling) Have you come to examine me and ask me? You must say who you are.

(Maharshi, 1984, pp. 60–61)

In attempting to isolate a separate, solid, foundational 'I' the spiritual seeker runs up against seemingly unanswerable questions that spiral in on themselves: Who is it that says 'I do not know?' What is not known? Who is the 'I'? Here, a tension is produced by the injunction 'Find out' which can trigger a round of circular reasoning along the lines of: How can I not know who I am and when I look, why can't I immediately find out? Who am I and why don't I know? And on and on. The implication of this form of spiritual inquiry is that we do not have 'real' knowledge of whom or what we 'actually' are. Accordingly, it appears that what is commonly identified as 'me' cannot be located within this deceptively simple set of questions. The experience that the spiritual aspirant encounters when he or she looks for the 'I' that is normally taken as 'me' and cannot find anything resembling it feels counterintuitive. How can I not find myself? This line of inquiry simply does not make sense within the structures and boundaries of our ordinary notions of self, and this is Ramana's point. By repeatedly challenging the seeker to find this 'I' that is so loosely talked about he is indicating the limited and limiting nature of this conditioned conception of self.

According to Vedāntic thought, our ordinary commonsense knowledge of 'I' is a kind of structure or framework superimposed on our true nature that prevents us from seeing ourselves and reality as 'they really are'. To 'find out' the spiritual aspirant must engage in an inner inquiry into the structures and boundaries that constitute our ordinary notions of self. Furthermore, 'finding out' does not entail bringing anything new into the inquiry; rather, as Ramana emphasizes, it is a process of removal; 'to make room anywhere it is enough that things are removed from there. Room is not brought in afresh' (Maharshi, 1984, p. 199).

Zen masters tell their students to 'look directly'. Advaitin sages admonish seekers to 'find out'. Both maintain that if their instructions are carried out, then delusion in the form of misplaced identification will be overcome. Both these forms of spiritual inquiry are pointing to the idea that our ordinary way of being in the world does not give us true knowledge. Our experience of reality is somehow distorted or filtered by conditions and structures that we falsely identify as reality itself. As stated in the introduction, in many respects the entire endeavour appears to hinge on the injunction to 'look directly', that is, to do away with the distortions, filters, and the various kinds of conditioning through which we normally view and perceive the world.

Given the fact that the forms of spiritual inquiry briefly outlined above begin with somehow disclosing and acknowledging the conditioned and mediated nature of our experience, the thesis that human knowledge and experience is constructed and/or mediated by background concepts and concerns does not appear to be in question here. However, according to the religious traditions of Advaita Vedānta and Zen Buddhism, this recognition is only the starting point on the path to liberation; the real work is in the undoing or the deconstructing of the various ontological structures and epistemological filters that separate us from 'real' being and knowing. The counterintuitive nature of non-dualistic Buddhist and Vedāntic claims as to 'how things really are' produces an experiential tension that brings the seeker 'up against something' that cannot easily be reconciled within everyday structures of knowing and being, and this experiential tension is the beginning of the deconstructive process that this form of spiritual inquiry initiates.

One of the classic Zen examples of this experiential tension comes from Dongshan Liangjie,[10] founder of Chinese Caodong Chan (J. Sōtō Zen)[11] who upon first hearing the Heart Sūtra's[12] 'There is no eye, no ear, no nose, no body, no mind' immediately responded by feeling his face with his hand and then said to his tutor, 'I have eyes, ears, a nose, a tongue, and so on; why does the sutra say that they don't exist?' (Powell, 1986, p. 23).[13] Unless the *sūtra* is dismissed as pure nonsense, the question remains, 'Why does this contradict the way I experience myself?' and, if curiosity, or 'deep doubt', is really aroused, 'How to find out?' This exact question was echoed in practitioner interviews for this study where a Zen practitioner described her response to first hearing the Heart Sūtra's radical negations as 'This is stupid!' and further reporting that: 'The first time I went for an interview with [the teacher] I told him that I was interested in Zen meditation and he said "Zen is not about meditation." I just thought *What!?*' but something, she didn't know what, made her 'stick around' (InterviewH10, 2000).

Both Dongshan Liangjie and the Zen student are reacting against the deconstructive moves of these teachings. Clearly, the fact of eyes, noses and tongues cannot be denied and *zazen* (seated meditation) is the *sine qua non* of Zen Buddhist practice; these are obvious facts. But to *practice* Zen, attachment to self as a solid, static entity and preconceived conceptualizations concerning the nature of meditation practice must be 'undone' and this is what the *sūtra* and the master are pointing to. More formally, it is the habitual reification and objectification of entities and concepts and the tendency of the mind to fall into polarizing dichotomies and dualisms that must be deconstructed, but not only intellectually; given the Zen priority of experience, our habitual 'misreadings' of reality must be experientially recognized and hence experientially and *directly* 'undone' at their source.

In Advaita, a clear example of the student's experiential tension comes from Ramana Maharshi's negation of the dualistic projection that the teacher can somehow confer awakening upon a student:

> [*Ramana Maharshi*]: The jivanmukta [the enlightened one] can have no sankalpa [the ability to act with a particular goal in mind] whatsoever. It's just impossible.
> [*Student*]: Then what is the fate of all of us who pray to you to have grace on us and save us? Will we not be benefited or saved by sitting in front of you or coming to see you? What is the use of people like me coming to see you?
> (Godman, 1998c, p. 334)

'What is the use of people like me coming to see you?' is a question that occurs to most students at one time or another. Variations of it are numerous: 'What good is this doing me?' 'Am I making progress?' 'Should I continue with this practice? Should I stop?' 'Should I be doing something else?' The dilemma of the student in the above dialogue is provoked by Ramana's negation of acting with any preconceived plan or goal. His questioner, who is operating on the assumption that Sri Ramana is receiving questions with the 'aim' or 'intention' of guiding his students to liberation, interprets this statement as a denial of the possibility of his teacher taking any active role in his or anyone's spiritual 'progress'. Ramana's negation of the ability to act with a particular goal in mind (*sankalpa*) is immediately perceived by this student as a denial of the possibility of there being anything to be gained through or by the *guru*'s 'grace'. From the practitioner's point of view, there is suddenly the unsettling idea that sitting with Ramana is not going to be of any benefit or even use to his spiritual path, a notion that suddenly calls into question his entire relationship to the teacher.

In experiential terms, Ramana's statement has challenged the student by throwing his dualistic projections into question: 'How can a teacher teach with no planned aims or goals yet Sri Ramana is sitting there and I am sitting before him and it is all to no benefit?' The student's objectification of a 'saviour' teacher is exposed by the student's own response.

It must be remembered that the *guru* is of central importance to Advaita (indeed to Hinduism as a whole) and, judging by the emphasis that Ramana places on the *guru*'s grace in many other teachings[14] we can infer that he is not simply denying that importance. From the seeker's standpoint, however, what is being 'undone' is the dualistic concept that the teacher affects or imparts a liberated state of being. This implies a separation of a present state of being (unenlightened) that can be changed or transformed into a future state of being (enlightened); a separation that Advaita rejects.

In another instance, a contemporary Advaitin teacher 'undoes' a similar conceptual problem when she answers a student thus:

> [*Student*]: I'm so happy! I've seen Isaac, Vartman[15] and now you!
> [*Gangaji*]: Have you seen your self?
>
> (Gangaji, 1999)

This deconstructive instruction is pure Advaita: 'It is the Self alone that is to be meditated upon' (*Bṛ. Up.* I:4.7). In one pivotal sentence, Gangaji has shifted the questioner away from objectifying relationships with teachers and back to the beginning and end of the inquiry: the self.

In this form of inquiry, ordinary ways of thinking and experiencing do not seem to hold. The point here is that these experiences are not non-ordinary in the sense of being supernatural – both Zen and Advaita claim to work with a kind of innate human capacity – nor are they non-ordinary in a trivial sense, i.e., merely self-contradictory or absurd, a view that is corrected by the liberative drive behind these traditions. Rather, the experiences that these spiritual processes ignite are non-ordinary in that they do not 'make sense' within our 'everyday' unquestioned epistemological and ontological structures. In other words, their impact springs from the fact that they appear to contradict and undermine the 'given-ness' of our everyday knowing. Hence, it is precisely this unquestioned habitual dualistic 'structuring' and static conceptual 'filtering' that the practices of Advaita and Zen aim to experientially deconstruct.

Chapter 2

Advaita Vedānta: Philosophical Foundations and Deconstructive Strategies

The non-dual experiential path of Advaita Vedānta has occupied the dominant position in Indian philosophy from the time of Śaṅkara (c. 7th–8th century) to the present day. Although it is not the only school of Vedānta,[1] its influence has been such that the very term 'Vedānta' is often made synonymous with it. In this chapter our discussion will focus on Śaṅkara's lineage and his non-dual exposition of Vedānta with its subsequent manifestations in contemporary Advaita. The emphasis will be on outlining key philosophical tenets and tracing practice instructions and teachings that serve to shift the questioner away from dualistic perceptions of the world and dichotomous ways of thinking. In other words, practice instructions and teachings that serve to deconstruct or experientially 'undo' our 'erroneous' fragmented perception of reality and experientially disclose reality (*brahman*) to the seeker as Advaita claims it to be: devoid of any real distinctions, not constituted by parts, and in essence, not different from the self (*ātman*).

Sources of the Tradition

Upaniṣads: 'That art thou' (*tat tvam asi*)

The Upaniṣads represent the culmination of a great shift in Vedic thought from the external, ritualistic worship of *brahman* to an internal, subjective quest for and subsequent inner identification with *brahman*. In the philosophical speculations and pedagogical conclusions of the Upaniṣads the spiritual quest is ultimately posited as an inner quest for reality in which the seeker explores the dimensions and ramifications of three primary spiritual questions that can be framed as:

- What is the nature of *brahman*?
- What is the nature of the self?
- How can we know *brahman*?

One of the simplest ways to approach these questions is to consider the *mahāvākyas*[2] or 'great sayings' of the Upaniṣads that succinctly articulate the nature and relationship of *brahman* and the self and which are traditionally believed to encapsulate the full spiritual potency of the text.[3]

First, to illustrate the uncompromising non-dual primacy of *brahman*, the *Chāndogya Upaniṣad* VI:2.1 states that *brahman* is 'One without a second';[4] second, according to the *Aitareya Upaniṣad* III:1.3, '*brahman* is intelligence'.[5] In terms of the self, the *Bṛhad-āraṇyaka Upaniṣad* declares the identity of *brahman* and the self with 'This *brahman* is the self' (II:5.19)[6] and posits the subjective affirmation of this identity with 'I am *brahman*' (I:4.10).[7] While in Uddālaka's instruction to Śvetaketu in the *Chāndogya Upaniṣad* VI:13.1, which culminates in perhaps the most experientially potent Upaniṣadic equation of *ātman* and *brahman*, we are unequivocally told: 'That art thou' (*tat tvam asi*).

Thus, according to Upaniṣadic definitions, *brahman* admits of no distinctions or divisions ('One without a second'); is both being (One) and knowing (intelligence) and is identical with the self, in both the objective sense ('This *brahman* is the self') and the subjective sense ('I am *brahman*'). Hence, we can know *brahman* by the realization that *That*, i.e., *brahman*, is what we are.

From the seeker's point of view, the questions concerning the nature of *brahman* and the nature of the self can be collapsed into the epistemological question: 'How can we know *brahman*?' which can then be reframed as the fundamental experiential question for all spiritual practitioners: 'How can liberation (*mokṣa*) be attained *by me*?' In the master–student dialogues of the Upaniṣads this question is addressed in many different contexts, but, from the Advaita perspective, always with the conclusion that liberation is the realization of the identity of self (*ātman*) and reality (*brahman*). As we shall see in later Advaita teachings and dialogues, this identification is simple to state but, for the experiencing practitioner, devastating in its implications for unquestioned 'everyday' notions of 'I'.

Traditional Vedāntic *sādhana* (spiritual practice) proceeds by affirmation and negation: the practitioner either takes the *via negativa*, as in the great Upaniṣadic negative injunction, *neti, neti* (not this, not this),[8] to negate any and all identifications with the bodily form or meditates on the positive *mahāvākyas*, thereby constantly affirming identification with *brahman* and disidentifying with his body and by extension all misidentifications with 'name and form' (*nāma rūpa*). The interplay between affirmation and negation is a feature of spiritual instruction in Advaita and in these Upaniṣadic dialogues we see this interplay in prototypical form.

In some instances, a seeker is first instructed in the affirmative that he or she *is brahman* and then, if there is some conceptual barrier to an immediate realization, the teacher will employ a deconstructive move in the negative, often with a series of paradoxical questions to shift questioners out of the dualistic structures of thought that are blocking them. In other deconstructive moves, the questioner will be plunged into a series of seemingly paradoxical or self-contradictory questions and declarations that directly challenge his or her dualistic experience of self and world.

To illustrate the deconstructive moves of the Upaniṣads, a key dialogue from one of the older and most important Upaniṣads, the *Bṛhad-āraṇyaka Upaniṣad*,[9] will be examined. The dialogue involves the *ṛṣi* Yājñavalkya and is a teaching on the theoretical unknowability of *brahman* given to the seeker Uṣasta Cākrāyaṇa. In this dialogue (*Bṛ. Up.* III:4.1–4.2), Yājñavalkya masterfully deconstructs Uṣasta Cākrāyaṇa's projection of *brahman* as an object that can be conventionally explained and grasped. In the beginning of the dialogue, the seeker Uṣasta Cākrāyaṇa requests Yājñavalkya 'to explain the brahman that is immediately present and directly perceived, who is the self in all things' and is given the pure Advaita answer: 'This is your self. That is within all things.' Uṣasta Cākrāyaṇa continues: 'Which is within all things, Yājñavalkya?'

> He who breathes in with your breathing in is the self of yours which is in all things … He who breathes up with your breathing up is the self of yours which is in all things. He is your self which is in all things. (*Bṛ. Up.* III:4.1)

When asked for an explanation of the 'immediately present and directly perceived *brahman* who is the self in all things' Yājñavalkya immediately and unequivocally gives the first and only answer: 'This is your self. That is within all things.' *Ātman* is none other than *brahman*. As Uṣasta Cākrāyaṇa's next question indicates, he was not receptive to the 'direct' teaching, so Yājñavalkya elaborates, once again in the positive, that is, by stressing the identification of *brahman* and the essence of all things which is nothing other than the self which is none other than all things; 'He who breathes in with your breathing in is the self of yours which is in all things' and so on.

Uṣasta Cākrāyaṇa has heard the words but they have no more significance for him than mere naming; that is, merely naming the self as 'that which is in all things' has not brought him any closer to realizing 'that which is immediately present and directly perceived'. From Uṣasta Cākrāyaṇa's point of view, it is as if Yājñavalkya has said 'this is a cow', 'this is a horse'. Yes, but so what?

Uṣasta Cākrāyaṇa asks 'for the *brahman* that is ... the self in all things' to be explained to him again. Once again he is told 'this is your self which is within all things' which prompts the question 'which is within all things, Yājñavalkya?' And Yājñavalkya answers:

> You cannot see the seer of seeing, you cannot hear the hearer of hearing, you cannot think the thinker of thinking, you cannot understand the understander of understanding. He is your self which is within all things ... Thereupon Uṣasta Cākrāyaṇa kept silent. (*Bṛ. Up*. III:4.2)

After repeating the positive 'This is your self which is within all things' Yājñavalkya then presents Uṣasta Cākrāyaṇa with a teaching in the negative in which he uses paradoxical statements to show Uṣasta Cākrāyaṇa that 'the *brahman* that is immediately present and directly perceived, that is the self in all things', cannot be comprehended or grasped by our usual conceptual faculties of sense and perception. In other words, the questioner cannot 'work it out' or 'work it through' intellectually. If the pure Advaita answer is not experientially seen or 'felt' then a deconstructive 'move' to confound, or, better, to confront the barrier that the intellect is presenting, is required: 'You cannot see the seer of seeing, you cannot hear the hearer of hearing, you cannot think the thinker of thinking, you cannot understand the understander of understanding.' That which is inherent, ungraspable, unknowable in the 'ordinary' conceptual sense cannot be 'explained'; indeed Uṣasta Cākrāyaṇa has already mistaken the direct teaching in the positive for an exercise in *nāma rūpa*, a mere naming, so Yājñavalkya is forced to employ a deconstructive correction to experientially undo Uṣasta Cākrāyaṇa's conceptualizing barriers.

The positive implication of Yājñavalkya's teaching is that 'the seer of seeing, the hearer of hearing, the thinker of thinking and the understander of understanding' *is* exactly that '*brahman* that is immediately present and directly perceived, that is the self in all things'. The *brahman* that Yājñavalkya is pointing out, the *brahman* 'that is immediately present', is thus not an external creator that can be conceptualized by objectified definitions and differentiated by qualitative analysis but is the self, and as such is always directly and immediately present.

In this interaction between Yājñavalkya and his questioner we see what this research regards as prototypical forms of deconstructive spiritual inquiry: the seeker is requesting non-dual knowledge while remaining mired in the structures and polarizations of personal dualistic experience, experience that these teachings aim to experientially undo.

Gauḍapāda (c. 7th century): 'No bondage, no liberation'

Gauḍapāda is said to be the first Advaitin, and his masterwork, the commentarial text *Kārikās on the Māṇḍūkya Upaniṣad* or the *Gauḍapādīya-kārikā*[10] (*GK*) is said to be the first Advaita commentary. Traditionally, Gauḍapāda is believed to be Śaṅkara's *paramaguru* (that is, the teacher of Śaṅkara's teacher, Govinda). According to Dasgupta, Śaṅkara attributed the founding of Advaita Vedānta to Gauḍapāda by making the 'confession that the absolutist (*advaita*) creed was recovered from the Vedas by Gauḍapāda' (Dasgupta, 1992b, p. 422).

Little is known of Gauḍapāda's life and the name 'Gauḍapāda' may well have been used for a school of authors beginning in the seventh century. The historical ambiguity of its author notwithstanding, the *GK* serves to establish many of the key tenets of classical scholastic Advaita and sets forth what would become cornerstones of later Advaita teachings. In the *GK,* Gauḍapāda puts forward the key Advaita teachings that '*brahman*, or reality is non-dual (*a-dvaita*), the world is false (*mithyā*), the result of illusion (*māyā*) and essentially self (*ātman*) is not different from non-dual *brahman*' (Deutsch and Van Buitenen, 1971, p. 118).

In this section, Gauḍapāda's uncompromising non-dualistic position on the nature of *brahman* will be examined by drawing out and explicating his main non-dualistic contentions and indicating their importance to the dynamics of deconstructive spiritual inquiry in the tradition that follows. Of primary interest to this discussion is Gauḍapāda's theory and explanation of the non-origination of all phenomena (*ajātivāda*).

The main thrust of Gauḍapāda's teaching is his core theory of non-origination (*ajātivāda*). According to *ajātivāda* the entire world of duality is merely an appearance: nothing ever really comes into being, for nothing other than *brahman* really exists. To support his teaching of *ajātivāda*, Gauḍapāda employs the metaphysical principle that 'That which is non-existent at the beginning and in the end, is necessarily so (non-existent) in the middle. The objects are like the illusions we see, still they are regarded as if real' (*GK* II, 6; Nikhilananda, 1987, p. 92). By rephrasing the above, we can now say that that which originates (is nonexistent in the beginning) and that which is destroyed (is nonexistent in the end) is by nature completely nonexistent (is necessarily nonexistent in the middle). Nonexistence cannot produce existence. That which is unreal by its very nature cannot ever be real. Gauḍapāda's basis for this point is a standard presupposition in Indian thought – that the nature of a thing cannot change: 'The immortal cannot become mortal, nor can the mortal ever become immortal. For, it is never possible for a thing to change its nature' (*GK* III, 21; Nikhilananda, 1987, p. 171).

Reality (*brahman*) is by nature non-originated and undifferentiated, 'One without a second' (*Ch. Up.* VI:2.1). *Ātman*, by its very nature, is, according to Advaita teachings, identical with *brahman*: 'This *brahman* is the self' (*Bṛ. Up.* II:5.19). This identity is not produced by any change in the nature of *brahman* or *ātman*, for a thing cannot change its nature; hence, to be identical, the nature of reality (*brahman*) and the nature of *ātman* must always be the same. (Perhaps it is better to say that there is only one nature to things, that of *brahman*.)

For reality to 'really' be manifold and differentiated, as commonly experienced, the fundamental characteristics of its nature would have to undergo some form of change, and this, according to Gauḍapāda, cannot happen. Change presupposes the characteristics of beginning and ending, which in this case would require the undifferentiated nature of reality (and by extension all phenomena) to end and suddenly begin to differentiate into the world of multiplicity and differentiation that we commonly experience. Gauḍapāda consistently operates from the standpoint of *brahman*, expressing the 'true' and 'real' nature of things in identity with *brahman*. From this standpoint, all distinctions and differentiation are originated and therefore unreal.

The radical denial of differentiation, multiplicity and change raises empirical questions that Gauḍapāda answers in terms of reality and appearance. To establish *brahman* as the sole reality, Gauḍapāda is concerned to show the empirical world as it is commonly experienced, as mere appearance. That is, that the perceived world of change, multiplicity and differentiation is incommensurate with changeless non-composite *brahman* because, once again, all change, multiplicity and differentiation are originated and therefore unreal or, at least, mere appearance. Due to the workings of *māyā* (illusion) the differentiated world appears but is a wrong interpretation (*vikalpa*) of reality. Self (*ātman*), along with all phenomena, is mistakenly experienced as being originated, differentiated and composite, when in fact, ultimately, there is no differentiation between any entities or categories.

Gauḍapāda first applies this analysis to the unreality of dream states and then extends it to include the objects of our waking states. In the light of *brahman*'s absolute non-origination, the objects and experiences of our waking states are also originated, and since all that is originated is ultimately unreal, it necessarily follows that both dream and waking states are unreal. To be real they would have to change their (unreal) nature and this, according to Gauḍapāda, is impossible since a thing cannot lose or change its nature.[11]

Hence, the distinction that we commonly make between the veracity of waking states and the unreality of dreams is, according to Gauḍapāda, ultimately illusory; the waking state being as insubstantial or illusory as the dream state.

> The wise declare the unreality [or insubstantiality][12] of all the objects seen in the dream, they all being located within (the body) and on account of their being in a confined space. (*GK* II, 1)

> Different objects cognized in dream (are illusory) on account of their being perceived to exist. For the same reason, the objects seen in the waking state are illusory. The nature of objects is the same in the waking state and dream. The only difference is the limitation of space (associated with dream objects). (*GK* II, 4; Nikhilananda, 1987, pp. 86, 90)

Internal illusion (the dream state) and external illusion (the waking state) therefore share a common identity in their essential insubstantial natures.[13] *Brahman* is the only real existent, thus our waking experience is no more real than dream experience.

Within the text, this startling thesis prompts an obvious experiential objection: '(Objector's question). If the objects cognized in both the conditions (of dream and of waking) be illusory, who cognizes all these illusory objects) and who again imagines them?' (*GK* II, 11; Nikhilananda, 1987, p. 98). From Gauḍapāda's standpoint, the objector's question reflects a confusion of self (*ātman*) with the empirical self (*jīva*). Embedded in the question is a differentiated subject–object notion. Restated from the seeker's point of view the question becomes: 'If all that I commonly experience lacks substance and is ultimately not real, what about the "I" that is taken as the cognizer, as the imaginer, as the experiencer? What about the "I" that I know as *me*?'

This question highlights the radical challenge to personal identity that these teachings provoke, and can be seen as a precursor to the fundamental Advaita deconstructive question 'Who am I?' 'Who is it that is doing this cognizing?' 'Who is it that is doing this imagining?' When confronted with the negation of common empirical experience in both the dream and waking states, the questioner retreats to operating from the dualistic differentiated standpoint of self and other – a standpoint, along with all dualisms, that Gauḍapāda rejects.

Such a question cannot be asked by the self, for it would imply a subject–object distinction; that is, a subject that cognizes, that imagines, that experiences, and an object that is cognized, imagined and experienced, which would mean a cognizer, an imaginer, an experiencer; and these are all false conceptions based on equally false dualistic relationships. From the standpoint of *ātman-brahman*-identity, all questions concerning this 'imagined' empirical, dualistic, self (*jīva*) have no basis in reality and, in effect, never even arise, for from the perspective of the absolute non-dual, which is realized *ātman-brahman*-identity, differentiation is not possible and questions as to the apparent and the real no longer hold any meaning.

The self that we commonly identify with (the *jīva*) is the subject in a world of 'real' objects, while the *ātman-brahman*-identity 'self' is, by definition, beyond the subject–object dualism. From this we can infer that correct identification with the self (*ātman*) would either stop us 'doing it' (i.e., mistaking the non-originated *ātman-brahman* for the originated *jīva*) or simply make the whole process of misidentification irrelevant; a type of 'play' (*līlā*) not to be taken seriously. The world does appear just as dreams do appear, but what is important is understanding that the appearance is the result of 'imagining' or, in Potter's translation, 'construction' (*vikalpa*) (Potter, 1981, p. 68).

Potter notes the difficulty of interpreting the Indian philosophical term *vikalpa* and questions whether Gauḍapāda sees *vikalpa* as a positive activity, an actual 'constructing' or a more negative state, a failure of interpretation on our part, a 'wrong interpretation' (Potter, 1981, p. 68). Based on Gauḍapāda's own example of a 'wrong interpretation' (mistaking a rope in the dusk to be a snake, *GK* II, 17; Nikhilananda, 1987, p. 108) Potter tends towards the latter as being closer to Gauḍapāda's general usage of *vikalpa*. The rope-snake mistake, presented by Gauḍapāda is, according to Potter, 'an analogy to the relation between the Self (*ātman*) and its states (*bhāva*) such as living [and so on]'. And, as such, it is an example of a wrong interpretation of what is presented to the senses. Potter also notes that 'the person who is aware of difference (*bheda*) is termed a *vikalpaka*, one who wrongly interprets' (Potter, 1981, p. 68).

Taking *vikalpa* as wrong interpretation is consistent with the emphasis found in later Advaita dialogues[14] wherein masters insist that all our problems stem from wrong identification. That is, we wrongly interpret the beginningless, boundaryless self (*ātman*) as the finite, conditioned self (*jīva*) and then proceed to treat the insubstantial, ultimately illusory workings of *māyā* as being solid and real.[15] Moreover, according to Potter, Gauḍapāda for the most part seems to use *māyā* synonymously with *vikalpa*, which also indicates that we regularly misinterpret the oneness of reality and find differences where none exist (Potter, 1981, p. 68).

To suggest that a construction can be produced would be contrary to Gauḍapāda's core theory of *ajātivāda*, which clearly posits that all notions and perceptions of production (and by extension, all notions and perceptions of destruction) are unreal; we just wrongly interpret the apparent productions (and, in spiritual practice, posit the apparent beginning and falsely projected end) of *māyā* as being real.

For Gauḍapāda, all wrong interpretations including dualistic subject–object relationships belong to the realm of illusion and are perceived only from the state of ignorance (*avidyā*):

> This perceived world of duality, characterized by the subject–object relationship, is verily an act of the mind. The mind, again (from the standpoint of Reality) is without touch with any object (as it is of the nature of Ātman). (*GK* IV, 72; Nikhilananda, 1987, p. 281)

From Gauḍapāda's standpoint, 'mind is without touch with any object', hence, from this standpoint, all subject–object cognitions are false. Since Gauḍapāda primarily speaks from the standpoint of *brahman* in which there are no divisions, no relationships and ultimately no standpoints, he resorts to dualistic analogies 'for the sake of instruction' (such as real rope and apparent snake, born or originated *jīva* and unborn non-originated *ātman*, and so on). 'When the Highest Truth is known' then the mind is, really, free from all ideas of the subject–object relationship. The idea of the object is superimposed (*adhyāsa*) upon the mind and misinterpreted (*vikalpa*) through ignorance (*avidyā*). These objects have no existence apart from the mind.

From the student's point of view, Gauḍapāda's key instruction is not to adhere to *any* notion about *any* thing including notions of the absoluteness of *brahman*:

> Through adhering to notions about things (such as: it is, it is not, both is and is not or neither is nor is not) happiness is obscured and frustration becomes manifest. One who realizes that the Lord (*bhagavān*) is not touched by these four alternatives (*koṭi*) is all-seeing (*sarvadṛk*) and desires nothing more. (Potter, 1981, p. 113 – summary of *GK* IV, 82–86; Nikhilananda, 1987, pp. 290–295)

To be untouched by the four alternatives is to be free from questions as to the ontological status of things, including the primary spiritual notions of bondage and liberation. Because, according to Gauḍapāda's radical non-dualism, all constructed dualisms, all origination, including the production of an awakened, liberated self through spiritual practice, and the cessation of an ignorant, bound self, are, by definition, apparent, imagined and therefore not real.

This conclusion leads us to the heart of the Advaita deconstruction of duality and goal-orientated spiritual practice (that is, practice that begins in ignorance and ends in liberation), and, for the practitioner, to Gauḍapāda's most radical non-dual proposal: 'There is no dissolution and no creation, no one in bondage and no one who is striving for or who is desirous of liberation, and there is no one who is liberated. This is the absolute truth' (*GK* II, 32; Nikhilananda, 1987, p. 119).

Gauḍapāda's 'answer' to the seeker's 'what about the "I" that I know as me?' is that this dualistic 'I' and all its accompanying projects, projections and plans simply is not real, the whole idea of 'me' (*jīva*) is a wrong interpretation (*vikalpa*) of 'I' (*ātman*). It is mistaking appearance for reality.

Philosophically, Gauḍapāda's statement of 'no bondage, no liberation as the absolute truth' in *GK* II, 32 is the logical and necessary conclusion of his teaching of non-origination (*ajātivāda*); a formal articulation of pure Advaita. For the spiritual aspirant, and in the hands of later Advaita masters,[16] it is a powerful deconstructive negation that demolishes objectifications of a 'self in bondage that is seeking liberation' and any dualistic projections of spiritual attainment that the seeker may entertain.[17]

Śaṅkara (c. 7th–8th century): 'there is no apprehender different from this apprehension to apprehend it'

According to tradition, Śaṅkara met his *guru* Govinda at the 'tender age' of eight and under the following circumstances:

> As the child knocked at the door of the great master [the reply from inside was], 'Who art thou?'
> Little Shankar replied, 'Thou!'
> The teacher recognized the disciple and opened the door.
>
> (Behari, 1991, p. 192)

This traditional story is illustrative of the main thrust of Śaṅkara's Advaita: non-difference (*avaitavāda*), or stated in the positive, identity. To the question 'Who are you?' Śaṅkara's answer is the simple but devastating, 'I am you'. Here, the aspirant's question once again must be 'How can that be?' The non-dual statement of identity proclaimed by the young Śaṅkara is consistent with the Upaniṣadic insistence on the unity of reality (*brahman*) and the identity of self (*ātman*) with reality. In the mature Śaṅkara's teaching this powerful identification becomes absolute and serves to form the cornerstone of his non-dualist Vedānta. Although Gauḍapāda is said to be the first Advaitin and his *GK* the first Advaita commentary, it is Śaṅkara who is traditionally held as the founder and great systematizer of the school of Advaita Vedānta.[18]

In the course of this section, Śaṅkara's core teaching of the identity of *ātman* with *nirguṇa brahman* (*brahman* without qualities, *brahman* as the distinctionless, sole reality) will be analysed by examining the philosophical categories and spiritual methods that he employs to support this teaching. The discussion will begin by delineating the numerous philosophical distinctions that Śaṅkara posits to support his substance-view of reality. Following on from this, Śaṅkara's key concepts of *adhyāsa* (superimposition), and *avidyā* (ignorance) and their relationship to *brahman* will be outlined, primarily from his masterwork, the *Brahmasūtrabhāṣya* (*BSB*), a commentary on the *Brahmasūtras* attributed to Bādarāyaṇa.[19]

Examples of teacher–student interaction will be taken from the dialogues between the *guru* and his imaginary pupil in the prose section of Śaṅkara's *Upadeśasāhasrī* (A Thousand Teachings)[20] entitled 'How to Enlighten the Pupil'. As Śaṅkara's best known non-commentarial work the *Upadeśasāhasrī* offers an interesting insight into Śaṅkara's teaching methods and gives a clear statement of his understanding of the path of *jñāna-yoga*.

The teacher–student dialogues in the *Upadeśasāhasrī* (*Upad.*) are examined by identifying Śaṅkara's teaching techniques as deconstructive moves that serve to prise the pupil away from misidentification with the empirical contingent self (*jīva*) to full understanding of, and identification with, the non-differentiated self (*ātman-brahman*).

Primarily, Śaṅkara insists on the absolute identification of self with *nirguṇa brahman*. *Nirguṇa brahman* is *brahman* without qualities – *brahman* as undifferentiated being, an infinite, self-luminous (*svaprakāśa*) consciousness that transcends all dualities. In this status of pure being no attribution can be made with respect to *brahman*, and the real self (*ātman*), which is also self-luminous, unqualified consciousness, is one with *brahman*. 'This *brahman* is without an earlier and without a later, without an inside, without an outside. This *brahman* is the self, the all perceiving' (*Bṛ. Up.* II:5.19).

In Śaṅkara's thought, questions as to the existence of the self are a non-issue, for to doubt one's own existence is logically impossible, that is, self-contradictory, 'for everyone is conscious of the existence of (his) self and never thinks, "I am not"' (*BSB* I.1.1; Deutsch and Van Buitenen, 1971, p. 155). Here, it is important to note that if the denial of 'I exist' results in self-contradiction then 'I exist' in the Śaṅkaric sense represents a deeper ontological assertion than an entity with mere existential status. The 'I exist' or the 'I am' of Advaita is not relational in the sense of a Cartesian-style subject that predicates its existence as an object of thought (I think, therefore I am); indeed, this 'I' is not an object of knowledge distinct from the knowing subject, rather it is pure consciousness in which the subject–object distinction has been overcome. In other words, the 'I' is not a cognitive assertion indicating psychological continuity but an ontological assertion that presumes a non-dualistic, non-differentiated experience of the self. This is an important point to remember when we see later Advaitins giving the instruction to 'hold the I', as the emphasis is ontological; it is an invitation into pure being as Advaita understands it, not a prop for the cognitive wheels of psychological reification as practitioners often (mistakenly) assume.[21]

For Śaṅkara, it therefore follows that the 'ordinary' experience of the self as the subject in a world of objects is a misidentification of the true self for it indicates a subject–object duality which, by definition, cannot be synonymous with *brahman*. Empirical experience is part of this false identification, because, in reality, it is categorically distinct from and lacking parity with the real nature of the self.

The empirical question now comes as to the relationship between a world that is defined as contingent and changeable and the eternal, changeless nature of *brahman*. Philosophically, Śaṅkara attempts to resolve such problems inherent in substance-views of reality by proposing two definitions of *brahman*, a primary and a secondary. 'The primary definition ... (*svarūpalakṣaṇa*), is given in terms of the essential description. The secondary definition ... (*taṭasthalakṣaṇa*) is given in terms of the modal or "conventional" (accidental) description' (Bilimoria, 1989, p. 164). What is important, according to Śaṅkara, is that the essential definition is one that does not predicate any properties of the thing being defined. So, when later Advaitins define *brahman* in the positive, as undifferentiated, pure consciousness or Being-Consciousness-Bliss (*sat-cit-ānanda*)[22] they are following Śaṅkara's essential description of *brahman* in not taking *sat-cit-ānanda* 'to be three different descriptions or three properties predicated of *brahman*, but rather as the unitary essence of the undifferentiated absolute' (Bilimoria, 1989, p. 166).

Along with Śaṅkara's two definitions of *brahman*, it is important to note 'a crucial distinction that underlies the entire Advaita system of thought: the distinction between the absolutely real (*pāramārthika*) and the empirically real (*vyāvahārika*) points of view' (Fost, 1998, p. 387). Further to this, according to Śaṅkara, *brahman* is understood or 'apprehended' in two ways: from the perspective of *avidyā*, in which *brahman* is qualified by different types of name and form (*nāma rūpa*) or adjuncts (*upādhi*)[23] and from the opposite perspective, that of *vidyā*, that is, free from all limiting conditions or adjuncts (*BSB* I.1.10).

In a similar way to Nāgārjuna's pivotal teaching of the 'two truths', wherein the distinction is made between the 'realms of the empirical "relative" truth (*saṃvṛti-satya*) and non-empirical "supreme" truth (*paramārtha-satya*)' (Inada, 1970, p. 19)[24] Śaṅkara's philosophical distinction of the two 'apprehensions' of *brahman* pervades the entire Advaita system of thought, and an appreciation of the fact that 'what is true from one point of view is not so from another' is central to understanding Advaitic claims as to the nature of reality' (Grimes, 1991, p. 291).

Building on the two perspectives from which *brahman* can be understood, that of *avidyā* and that of *vidyā*, Śaṅkara states that the perspective of *avidyā* is empirically real (*vyāvahārika*) in which *brahman* is understood as being 'qualified by limiting conditions' and that of *vidyā* which is absolutely real (*pāramārthika*) and in which *brahman* is understood as being 'free from all limiting conditions whatever'. In *BSB* I.1.17, it is the former apprehension of *brahman* that Śaṅkara equates with 'ordinary life', stating in *BSB* I.1.18 that once these 'limiting adjuncts' are overcome, identity with the 'highest Self' (*brahman*) is realized.

Of course, it must be remembered that all of the student's questions come from the empirically real (*vyāvahārika*) point of view, and are relevant and urgent as long as this view is in operation. The inquiry into *brahman* begins from the empirically real standpoint and is dissolved with the realization of the absolutely real (*pāramārthika*) standpoint, in which the differentiation of 'standpoints' or 'views' also dissolves. Although ultimately illusory, the student's 'everyday' empirically real view is the mistaken empirical view of reality that the teacher works with and aims to undo. The difficulties and the confusion that the pupil encounters are thus 'grist for the deconstructive mill', as they are representative of a dualistic apprehension of self and world that the teacher needs to push the student to overcome. According to Śaṅkara, the world as we empirically experience it, the world of duality, multiplicity, and change (*vyāvahārika*) thus has some kind of status beyond that of pure illusion, as it is experienced (and lived by most of us) and the all-important inquiry into *brahman* begins there.

In a weakening of Gauḍapāda's strong thesis of the unreality of all phenomena, Śaṅkara posits that empirical experience, experienced as the world of duality, multiplicity and change, is less than 'real'; however it is not utterly unreal 'like the son of a barren woman' because it is experienced and has a practical reality. Potter notes that Gauḍapāda 'seems to only speak of real and unreal', while Śaṅkara indicates 'a three-level view with the empirical world occupying a position midway between brahman and pure nonexistence' (Potter, 1981, p. 79). To the question of 'exactly *how* real are the things experienced in the empirical world' Grimes offers this reading of Śaṅkara's division of real and unreal:

> ... the Real is that which is changeless, eternal, suffers no contradictions and is unsublatable (*pāramārthika*). Things of the world may be said to be real until they suffer sublation. Thus, they are called 'what is other than the real or unreal' (*sadasatvilakṣaṇa*), indescribable as either real or unreal (*sadasadbhyamanirvacanīya*), illusory (*mithyā*). Since they are *cognized*, they are not unreal (*asat*). Since they are sublated,[25] they are not real (*sat*). By this criterion, Brahman alone is absolutely real; Brahman alone is never subject to contradiction. All else is considered real by *courtesy* only. (Grimes, 1991, p. 292, his italics)

Śaṅkara's 'three-level view' can thus be outlined as:

- 'real' (*sat*; *pāramārthika*);
- 'other than real or unreal' (*sadasatvilakṣaṇa*) or 'illusory' (*mithyā*); and
- 'utterly unreal' (*asat*).

As Śaṅkara consistently emphasizes, only *brahman* is *sat* or real, but things of the world are not *asat*, utterly unreal, because they are cognized and, in some sense, can be said to exist. What is utterly unreal, in the sense that they cannot exist, are such logical impossibilities as the 'son of a barren woman' or a 'hare's horn'. Through this distinction, Śaṅkara acknowledges that mistaken or wrong interpretation of reality has a certain empirical reality for the cognizer; indeed, until *brahman* is realized, the world of name and form and the notion of there being a cognizer that cognizes are taken to be real but they lack real substantiality. They are illusory, products of and constituted by *māyā*, which Śaṅkara holds to be an overarching epistemic notion that is 'beginningless (*anādi*) and indescribable (*anirvacanīya*) in terms of being and non-being' (Deutsch and Van Buitenen, 1971, p. 308). From the viewpoint of the student, *māyā* is ignorance (*avidyā*). 'It not only has the power to conceal reality (*āvaraṇa-śakti*), but also to mis-represent or distort it (*vikṣepa-śakti*)' (Deutsch and Van Buitenen, 1971, p. 308). Through ignorance the attributes of one thing are superimposed or alogically identified (*adhyāsa*) onto another, and taken to be reality (*sat*, *paramārtha*); thus, the real nature of the self and the world are mistaken or obscured.

Śaṅkara introduces his masterwork, the commentary on the *Brahmasūtras* (*BSB*) with a detailed description and explanation of the workings of superimposition. He begins by positing that the self (subject) and the superimposed non-self (object) are radically different and cannot be granted any sense of identity:

> [They are] opposed to each other as much as darkness and light [and] cannot be identified. All the less can their respective attributes be identified … In spite of this it is on the part of man a natural procedure – which has its cause in wrong knowledge [*avidyā*] – not to distinguish the two entities (object and subject) and their respective attributes, although they are absolutely distinct, but to superimpose upon each the characteristic nature and the attributes of the other, and thus, coupling the Real and the Unreal, to make use of expressions such as 'That am I,' 'That is mine.' (*BSB adhyāsa bhaṣya*; Deutsch and Van Buitenen, 1971, pp. 151–152)

Despite the clear and definite distinction between self and non-self their natures are nevertheless confused by mutually superimposing the attributes of one onto the other; i.e., we erroneously couple 'the Real with the Unreal'. To Śaṅkara the cause of this confusion is due to a lack of discrimination or 'right knowledge' (*avidyā*) which is removed by knowledge (*vidyā*). Superimposition, says Śaṅkara, is *avidyā*; understanding the true nature of reality by discrimination is *vidyā*. Superimposition, in Śaṅkara's use, can thus be seen as a further analysis of how Gauḍapāda's wrong interpretation (*vikalpa*) takes place and provides us with the necessary condition on which all distinctions of empirical or practical reality (*vyavahāra*) are based.

With Śaṅkara's distinctions and clarifications in mind, the questioning student in search of *brahmajñāna* (liberating knowledge) must now ask Śaṅkara how to proceed. How is knowledge of *brahman* obtained? 'What is the knowledge by which I may find my own nature?' Śaṅkara's answer is clear; following the *Chāndogya Upaniṣad* IV:9.3, he states: 'knowledge of Brahman is not obtained in any other way than through a teacher: "A teacher is a boatman; his [right] knowledge is called a boat here"' (*Upad.* 3; Deutsch and Van Buitenen, 1971, p. 125).

How does the teacher impart 'right knowledge' of *brahman* to a seeker who wants liberation? Given Śaṅkara's insistence on *brahman* as undifferentiated being – an infinite, self-luminous consciousness that transcends all dualities (*nirguṇa brahman*) – the question now arises as to how this non-dual *brahman* can be the subject of an inquiry or an object of knowledge. In other words, how can the teacher access the non-injunctive *jñānakāṇḍa*[26] as a source of knowledge and guide the pupil to liberative 'right' knowledge of *brahman* if *nirguṇa brahman* is, by definition, beyond all definitions and unknowable in the 'usual' sense? The question we must ask Śaṅkara now is: 'what is the knowledge by which I may find my own nature and exactly how will I "know" it?'

In general, Advaita recognizes six means of valid knowledge (*pramāṇas*)[27] which are: perception (*pratyakṣa*); inference (*anumāna*); comparison (*upamāna*); negation (*abhāva*); presumption (*arthāpatti*) and verbal testimony (*śabda*).[28] In Advaita, *śabda* (word or verbal testimony) refers to scripture and is, according to Potter, 'clearly given priority' (Potter, 1981, p. 97). Importantly, 'all knowledge acquired through the *pramāṇas* is valid in its own proper sphere, but insofar as it is subject to contradiction by another qualitatively different kind of experience it is necessarily "relative" knowledge'. Brahman-knowledge is alone incapable of contradiction and 'no *pramāṇa* contradicts *śruti*[29] when the latter is dealing with the nature of Brahman or the Self' (Deutsch and Van Buitenen, 1971, p. 311).

The Advaita view of the (ultimately) 'relative' status of the *pramāṇas* raises an important objection concerning the methods used to impart liberating knowledge (*brahmajñāna*), focused on in *BSB* II.1.14. As stated above, the problem revolves around Śaṅkara's insistence on *brahman* as *nirguṇa*. In other words, as pure undifferentiated subject that cannot, in any sense, be posited as an object of awareness or knowledge. As he says: 'Brahman is not an object of the senses, it has no connection with … other means of knowledge. For the senses have, according to their nature, only external things for their objects, not Brahman' (*BSB* I.1.2; Deutsch and Van Buitenen, 1971, p. 156). Thus, if the knowledge which is provided by the 'instruments of valid knowledge' (*pramāṇa*) is, in the final analysis, relative or sublatable then it cannot be synonymous with *brahman*-knowledge which admits no sublations or contradictions.

Following on from this, in *BSB* II.1.14 an objector questions the use and validity of the *pramāṇas* in the quest for *brahman*-knowledge if the objects that they are granting knowledge of are not real and the necessary distinction between teacher and pupil is also not real. Simply put, the questioner asks: 'If all distinctions are not real, then how is *brahman*-knowledge known?' Śaṅkara insists on the necessity of a teacher; on the importance of a student receiving instruction, but if the teacher has no means of offering veridical proofs of what he is attempting to convey then how can he convincingly instruct a student in the art of discriminating the apparent from the real? If the *pramāṇas* only give us 'knowledge' of 'objects' which, according to Advaita, cannot have any relationship to *brahman* and are at best 'provisionally' real (*sadasatvilakṣaṇa*) then knowledge derived from the *pramāṇas* cannot lead to release (*mokṣa*). On this account even scripture is ultimately false, as, like the other *pramāṇas*, it presupposes the workings of *avidyā*.

Śaṅkara counters this charge by arguing that the *pramāṇas*, although ultimately unreal, can assist in 'producing' liberation which is real, 'because as a matter of fact we do see real effects to result from unreal causes, for we observe that death sometimes takes place from imaginary venom' and [the] 'effects of what is seen in a dream [can be real]' and so on … (*BSB* II.1.14; Deutsch and Van Buitenen, 1971, p. 181). But in any case in *BSB* II.1.14, Śaṅkara reminds the objector that the point to remember is the fact that, according to Advaita, liberation cannot be an effect – as effect, it is unreal.

The 'fact' that liberation cannot be an effect well illustrates the dualistic dilemmas of cause and effect (or ends and means) that confront the student in the practice situation and points to the corresponding deconstructive teaching strategies required to 'undo' them. To expand on this, and anticipate the discussion of Śaṅkara's teaching strategies in the *Upadeśasāhasrī* below, let us unfold the point further.

To restate the problem: instruction is required, but receiving instruction involves a dualistic process that implies activity, agent, instrument and result; in other words, a process that acknowledges difference and distinctions, which, in Advaitic terms, are actually impediments to self-knowledge or *mokṣa*. According to Śaṅkara, self-knowledge cannot be the effect of any *pramāṇa* but is a direct realization, in which *ātman-brahman*-identity is realized in immediate intuition (*anubhava*). At first glance, direct realization could easily be identified with the *pramāṇa* of perception (*pratyakṣa*) but Śaṅkara counters that 'perception involves instruments and objects and distinctions whereas self-knowledge does not' (Potter, 1981, p. 98). For this reason, knowledge of *brahman* is not derived perceptually or inferentially but, once again, by way of immediate intuition (*anubhava*) which is an awareness that Śaṅkara holds to be *nirvikalpaka* (construction-free) and not *savikalpaka* (construction-filled) (Potter, 1981, p. 98).

The two types of awareness, construction-filled and construction-free, represent 'a basic distinction in Indian epistemology', which, according to Potter, Śaṅkara elevates 'to new heights by identifying *nirvikalpaka* (construction-free) awareness with *brahman*' (Potter, 1981, p. 92). Śaṅkara's equation of *nirvikalpaka* awareness with *brahman* suggests that self-knowledge is not an awareness *of brahman* but rather an awareness that *is brahman*.

Self-knowledge cannot be an effect or a 'result' of a *pramāṇa* (or any other means of knowledge) because *nirguṇa brahman* in identity with *nirvikalpaka* awareness is pure undifferentiated subject and as such can only be realized in an immediate intuition (*anubhava*) that admits of no subject–object distinction. In other words, for Śaṅkara self-knowledge is beyond any and all dualisms and dichotomies that are necessary cognates to the subject–object distinction and outside of the threefold distinction of knower (*pramātṛ*), the object known (*viṣaya*), and the means of knowledge (*pramāṇa*): self-knowledge *just is*.

However, Śaṅkara does not use the experience of immediate intuition (*anubhava*) as a critical proof for the Advaita view of self-knowledge. For verification of his conclusions, Śaṅkara turns to scripture, to the word (*śabda*).[30] The reason for this is that when self-knowledge is realized there are no doubts to be cleared by proof, and if proofs are needed then self-knowledge is not realized, as the need for proof indicates the workings of ignorance.[31]

Here, Śaṅkara is appealing, once again, to the two 'levels of reality' for, as long as we are not liberated, all distinctions are accepted as real and the *pramāṇas* and injunctions operate in the way we ordinarily suppose; however, once awakened, all the 'dream distinctions' are seen to be as they 'really' are, that is, unreal. *Brahman*-knowledge is not knowledge that originates as an idea in the mind and is then perfected; rather *brahman*-knowledge is ignited by direct understanding (*anubhava*) of the liberative portion of *śruti* that Śaṅkara identifies as *jñānakāṇḍa*.

Thus, for Śaṅkara, it is through a direct intuition (*anubhava*) of the word (*śabda*) that *brahman*-knowledge is conveyed. But given *brahman*'s quality-less ineffable nature and its status of 'absolute subject-that-takes-no-object', the *jñānakāṇḍa* portions of *śruti* must be accessed by the teacher and conveyed to the seeker in a way that bypasses the pitfalls of the finite, differential nature of language.

The problem of *brahman*'s inexpressibility through words, which are unavoidably finite in their reference, presents yet another teaching dilemma. To bring the student to the threshold of *brahmajñāna*, the teacher cannot avoid using words, but since *brahman* possesses none of the characteristics through which words are normally able to describe or denote a subject – 'genus, quality, relation and activity' – (Rambachan, 1991, p. 67) language as it is conventionally employed cannot help the student. To undo the various misidentifications that are superimposed upon *brahman* without creating yet more misidentifications to be overcome, words must be manipulated by the teacher in certain ways and a unique method of instruction must be employed.

Rambachan (1991) identifies three methods of word manipulation used as a mode of instruction in Advaita and notes that 'the feasibility of *śabda-pramāṇa* as a vehicle for *brahmajñāna* becomes credible only when some method can be demonstrated for overcoming the natural limitations of language' (Rambachan, 1991, p. 55). Furthermore, it is this need for skilful manipulation of words in spiritual instruction that explains Advaita's insistence on a teacher 'who has thoroughly mastered the *śruti* (*śrotriyam*) and who abides in *brahmajñāna* (*brahmaniṣṭham*)' (Rambachan, 1991, p. 68).

Here, the three methods are considered separately for purposes of convenience, but in *śruti* and in actual teaching they are employed together and presuppose each other. The three methods of word manipulation can be seen as deconstructive strategies employed by the teacher to undermine the student's finite, predicative grasp of language by wielding words in such a way as to directly reveal their limitations. In other words, Śaṅkara's methods of word manipulation are a deconstructive teaching strategy that employs the techniques of juxtaposition, pure and contradictory negation (bi-negation) and implication, to ignite a deconstructive process in the actual experience of the practitioner that serves to undo mistaken ontological ascriptions as represented in language. These deconstructive strategies are found throughout modern and contemporary Advaita and, in Śaṅkara's teaching are seen in prototypical form.

Following Rambachan (1991), the three methods are: (1) *adhyāropa-apavāda* (superimposition-desuperimposition); (2) *neti, neti* (negation); and (3) *lakṣaṇā* (implication).

(1) *Adhyāropa-Apavāda* (superimposition-desuperimposition). According to Rambachan, 'the *adhyāropa-apavāda* procedure is a unique method of indicating the immanent and transcendent aspects of *brahman*. *Adhyāropa* definitions are possible because the entire universe is dependent on *brahman*, and nothing is apart from it.' In the actual process of instruction, 'initial attention must necessarily be drawn to *brahman* through its association with the world and the individual' (Rambachan, 1991, pp. 69–70).

Apavāda (desuperimposition) is referred to by Deutsch as the 'sword that cuts away false identifications' in the process of 'the reducing of effects back into their causes [and] the discriminating away of all lower levels of experience' (Deutsch, 1969, p. 110). As a deconstructive tool *apavāda* works to undo the fundamental Advaita problem of superimposition (*adhyāsa*) by paradoxical means; first *brahman* is indicated and then that indication is immediately 'removed' or negated. This juxtaposition works to momentarily suspend any ideas that the student may have of *brahman* and experientially illustrate that, as the non-dual nature of all phenomena, *brahman* cannot be located in dualistic descriptive categories. *Brahman* is at once everything (immanent) and everywhere (transcendent) and once false attributions (*upādhis*) have served to indicate *brahman* to the student, i.e., to focus the student's attention on *brahman*, then they must be removed or negated to prevent the pupil from falsely identifying them as *brahman*. *Apavāda* (desuperimposition) is closely connected to the procedure of negation and works in similar ways to detach words from their primary, limited denotations.

(2) Negation (*neti, neti*). This method of indicating *brahman* is found throughout the Upaniṣads and such negative indicators of *brahman* are employed by Śaṅkara in *Upad.* 7, when he reminds his pupil that *brahman* is: 'Not Thus! Not so!'[32] and, 'This Ātman is [described as] "not, not"'[33] (Deutsch and Van Buitenen, 1971, pp. 125–126). These purely negative definitions of *brahman* are 'intended to distinguish it from the known and limited referents of all words', hence 'the essential aim of the negative method is to deny all specifications which are the result of superimposition' (Rambachan, 1991, p. 70).

Very often the negation employed by *śruti* is twofold. Contrary attributes are side by side negated in order that the negation of one attribute does not lead to the supposition that *brahman* is characterized by its opposite. In his interaction with the seeker of *brahmajñāna* in *Upad.* 7 Śaṅkara indicates *brahman* as: '[It is] not coarse, not fine',[34] and 'This Brahman is without an inside and without an outside'[35] (Deutsch and Van Buitenen, 1971, pp. 125–126). Working with juxtaposing negations in this way serves to remove or lessen the inherent finite implications of words. For Śaṅkara, no single word can directly signify *brahman* but by moving the student's attention from one negation to its opposite Śaṅkara indicates the singular status of *brahman*.

In his commentary (*Bhāṣya*) on the *Bṛhad-āraṇyaka Upaniṣad*, Śaṅkara posits the negative method as the only option of describing *brahman* free from all known and finite specifications:

> By elimination of all differences due to limiting adjuncts, the words [*neti, neti*] refer to something that has no distinguishing marks such as name, or form, or action, or heterogeneity, or species, or qualities. Words denote things through one or the other of these. But *Brahman* has none of these distinguishing marks. Hence it cannot be described as 'It is such and such.' ... Brahman is described by means of name and form and action superimposed on It, in such terms as 'Knowledge, Bliss, Brahman [*vinjñānam, ānandam, brahman*]' (Bṛ. Up. 3:9.28) and 'Pure Intelligence [*vijñānaghana*]' (Bṛ. Up. 2:4.12), 'Brahman,' and 'Ātman.' When, however, we wish to describe Its true nature, free from all differences due to limiting adjuncts, then it is an utter impossibility. Then there is only one way left, viz., to describe It as 'Not this, Not this,' by eliminating all possible specifications of It that have been known. (*Bṛ. UB*. 2.3.6; Rambachan, 1991, p. 71)

The methods of superimposition and desuperimposition highlight the problems of language in relation to *brahman* and point to the nature of *brahman* as being beyond the ordinary signification of any words. Indeed, according to the above commentary, for Śaṅkara, even the designations of 'Brahman' and 'Ātman' on the Real are ultimately superimpositions and therefore false. These methods alert us to the difficulties involved in speaking about *brahman*. According to Rambachan, 'they prepare us for and are made complete by the positive method of definition through *lakṣaṇā*' (Rambachan, 1991, p. 72).

(3) *Lakṣaṇā* (implication). According to Śaṅkara, any single term drawn from general usage can be misleading if applied directly to *brahman*. When, however, carefully chosen expressions are skilfully juxtaposed, they mutually qualify and eliminate from each other their finite associations. Such terms are capable of defining *brahman* by implication. According to Rambachan, 'Śaṅkara proposes *lakṣaṇā* as the method of surmounting *brahman*'s inexpressibility ... [and] ... informing us about *brahman*'s essential nature' (Rambachan, 1991, p. 67).

Lakṣaṇā (implication) is thus informed by Śaṅkara's two definitions of *brahman*: the primary (*svarūpalakṣaṇa*), which is thought of as the essential description, and the secondary definition (*taṭasthalakṣaṇa*), that is, given in terms of the modal or conventional description. As noted above, what is important, according to Śaṅkara, is that the essential definition is one that does not predicate any properties of the thing being defined. So when the *Taittirīya Upaniṣad* II:1.1 gives the positive definition of *brahman* as '*Brahman* is reality, knowledge, and infinite',[36] the three categories of reality, knowledge, and infinite are not taken 'to be three different descriptions or three properties predicated of *brahman*, but rather as the unitary essence of the undifferentiated absolute' (Bilimoria, 1989, p. 166). Thus, in instructing the 'aspirant for real knowledge', i.e., *brahmajñāna*, Śaṅkara is concerned to point his student towards experientially understanding the 'undifferentiated absolute', i.e., *brahman*, in its essential definition that admits none of the ordinary limitations of words.

Following the above outline of Advaita's three methods of word manipulation our question now is 'how to overcome the finite, dualistic signification of words and experientially realize the "undifferentiated absolute"?' Śaṅkara advances the mental-spiritual discipline of *jñāna-yoga*.[37] For the purposes of instruction, the process of *jñāna-yoga*, described by Deutsch as 'a living process of knowing and being' (Deutsch, 1969, p. 105), was traditionally divided into a set of four general qualifications or disciplines (*sādhana catuṣṭaya*) and three general stages. The quest for *brahmajñāna* demanded the utmost from the student and could not be engaged without the aspirant exhibiting the four qualifications of *viveka* (the ability to discriminate between the spiritual and the superficial); *vairāgya* (renunciation); *śamādisādhanasampatti* (mental tranquillity, endurance, control, dispassion, intentness of mind, faith) and thereby satisfying the teacher that he has the fourth qualification; *mumukṣutvam* – a desire for freedom (*mokṣa*) and freedom alone (Deutsch, 1969, p. 105).

Once the seeker's capacity and will to attain *mokṣa* have been established, he embarks upon the three general stages of *jñāna-yoga* proper which are: hearing or listening (*śravaṇa*) to the sacred texts; thinking or reflection (*manana*); and meditation or contemplation (*nididhyāsana*) in which 'the aspirant discriminates all [dualities] that stand in the way of the self. Here, the seeker moves beyond all differentiation: 'You' and 'me' are not different and so on. The concepts of 'my', 'me', 'mine', come to signify nothing (Deutsch, 1969, pp. 109–110).[38]

Given Śaṅkara's insistence on the immediacy or simultaneous nature of knowing *brahman* and being *brahman*, and the 'fact' that liberation cannot be an 'effect', that is, the result of any process or *pramāṇa,* the three stages of *jñāna-yoga* cannot be said to either produce liberation or to culminate in a special act of meditation that leads to a direct experience of *brahman*. The point to emphasize here is that in the reading of this research, for Śaṅkara, a direct experience (*anubhava*) is not a direct experience *of brahman* (or anything else), but rather, it is a direct identity experience that *is brahman*. Śaṅkara's key teaching of identity is in evidence here, as since there is only 'really' *nirguṇa brahman* in absolute identity with *ātman*, then there is nothing or 'no-thing' to have any experience of, but this 'no-thing' or 'nothing' is not a nihilistic void (the status which Advaitins allocate to the Buddhist *śūnyatā*). As non-dual reality, it is, at the same time, 'everything' in the sense of 'all'. 'The highest Ātman … is identical to all' (*Upad.* 8; Deutsch and Van Buitenen, 1971, p. 126).

In his discussion of the three stages, Rambachan refutes the sharp distinctions made between the stages and argues that they do not necessarily follow each other in sequence (Rambachan, 1991, p. 115).[39] For example, Śaṅkara held that the self who has gained *apavarga* (completely free from difference) is liberated upon hearing (*śravaṇa*) the 'great sentences' such as 'that art thou' (Potter, 1981, p. 51), which indicates that, for the properly qualified seeker, the 'listening' stage would suffice. However if the aspirant lacks any of the prescribed qualities of the *sādhana catuṣṭaya* then 'reflection' (*manana*) may be necessary and even then, if the habitual tendency of identifying *ātman* with the body and so on, reasserts itself, contemplation (*nididhyāsana*) in the form of radical discrimination between the real and the apparent may be necessary. The point seems to hinge on the state of mind, or better, the state of *being* of the aspirant; that is, on how much previous spiritual 'work' he has 'put into' undoing the dualistic superimpositions that obscure or distort non-dual *brahman*. Hence, it is the teacher's task to disclose these superimpositions to the student and push him to undo or deconstruct these false identifications so that *ātman-brahman*-identity is experientially revealed. This teaching strategy is illustrated in the student–teacher interaction of the *Upadeśasāhasrī* wherein the student is guided by the teacher through the three stages of *jñāna-yoga* in a series of deconstructive 'moves' designed to bring him to the threshold of liberating knowledge.

Śaṅkara begins the prose section of the *Upadeśasāhasrī*, with the section entitled 'How to enlighten the pupil' in which he outlines the 'method of teaching the means to liberation'. After an introductory section in which Śaṅkara evaluates the aspirant's desire and readiness to 'get out of the ocean of transmigratory existence', Śaṅkara's teaching shifts from instructional mode to a more dialectical and dialogical approach. After impressing the oneness of *ātman-brahman* on the student and reiterating the indicative non-dual marks of *brahman* found in *śruti*,[40] in *Upad.* 9, Śaṅkara then asks the question that points to 'the way out of the ocean of transmigratory existence: "Who are you?"' (Deutsch and Van Buitenen, 1971, p. 126).

With the question 'Who are you?' comes a deconstructive challenge to personal identity as is commonly, empirically, understood, and a testing of the pupil's capacity to move beyond dualistic conceptions of 'my', 'me', 'mine'. Here, Śaṅkara is testing his student's experiential understanding of 'moving beyond all differentiation' and probing how successful his pupil's practices of 'discriminating the real from the apparent' have been.

In *Upad.* 10, the pupil answers: 'I am a Brahmin's son, belonging to such and such a family, I was a student … [but now] I wish to get out of the ocean of transmigratory existence …' (Deutsch and Van Buitenen, 1971, pp. 126–127). With this answer, he is exhibiting the fact that non-eternal attributes (Brahmin's son, student and so on) are being superimposed on the eternal self (*ātman*). Hence, Śaṅkara is ready to counter the workings of superimposition (*adhyāsa*) and wrong identification with name and form, with a further deconstructive question posed in *Upad.* 11:

> My dear, when you are dead your body will be eaten by birds or will turn into earth right here. How then do you wish to get out of the ocean of transmigratory existence? (Deutsch and Van Buitenen, 1971, p. 127)

Śaṅkara moves to undo his pupil's empirical identification with name and form by pointing out that the bodily form that the student is identifying with will eventually perish. In effect, Śaṅkara then asks, 'But are you this body?' and if you are, 'What happens when this body perishes? Does the "I" (*ātman*) perish with it?'

Well versed in the oneness of *ātman-brahman* and the indicative marks of *brahman*, in *Upad.* 12, the seeker responds:

> I am different from the body. The body is born, dies, is eaten by birds, turns into earth, is destroyed by weapons … I have entered this body as a bird enters a nest … Again and again by force of merit and demerit, when this body perishes, I shall enter another body as a bird enters another nest when its previous one is destroyed. Thus I am beginningless transmigratory existence … (Deutsch and Van Buitenen, 1971, p. 127)

Yes. According to Śaṅkara, this is correct, but if the questioner 'knows' this, why then did he incorrectly identify this eternal Self with 'a Brahmin's son, a student', and so on. The fact that 'I am eternal and different from the body' is *known* but the previous answer shows that it is not *realized*. Śaṅkara's position on the necessity of the 'correct understanding' of scripture is in evidence here. It is not enough merely to parrot *śruti*, for without the direct intuitive understanding (*anubhava*) of the self who is completely free from difference (*apavarga*) the liberating genius of scripture (*jñānakāṇḍa*) will not be experienced. Even the *mahāvākyas* can become objectified knowledge if they are understood dualistically.[41] If 'I am eternal' or 'That art thou' are misunderstood as being descriptive or directly indicative of *brahman* according to the 'usual' predications of language, then the student will not experience *brahmajñāna*. That is, if the misunderstanding that *brahman* can actually be denoted by such phrases, in the sense of Śaṅkara's secondary 'conventional' definition of *brahman* (*taṭasthalakṣaṇa*), is not corrected, then liberation (*mokṣa*) will not result. As noted in the discussion above, *brahmajñāna* is not knowledge in the usual subject–object sense, it is a construction-free awareness (*nirvikalpaka*) that *is brahman*, not an awareness *of brahman*.[42]

For Śaṅkara, liberating knowledge is 'knowing-*nirguṇa brahman*-in-identity'. Hence, if this *brahman* admits no qualities, distinctions or relations then all of the possessive, indicative and predicative elements of grammar are not really appropriate and this is why conventional language, with its relational structures and subject–object predicates, is also ultimately a product of the ignorance (*avidyā*) that breeds mental constructions that distort reality.

The difficulty that the student is experiencing here is due to his dualistic appropriation of language, and the accompanying ascription of the possessives 'me, my, mine' onto the self. To undo these misidentifications without creating yet more misidentifications, Śaṅkara begins to use the pupil's mounting confusion against him by pointing out the inconsistencies in his ascription of dualistic, relational, categories of language to *brahman*.

In *Upad*. 13, Śaṅkara's response to his student's 'correct' description of the eternal, undifferentiated self is a further deconstructive challenge that highlights the contradiction from which the pupil is operating. He throws the dualistic answer back to his pupil: '[Yes, says Śaṅkara:] ... You are right. Your view is correct. [Then] why did you say incorrectly, "I am a Brahmin's son ..." [and so on]' (Deutsch and Van Buitenen, 1971, p. 127, square brackets in text). Śaṅkara has pointed out to his pupil that his two previous answers are contradictory. How can one be 'beginningless' and 'eternal' and yet limited to such transitory and changing identifications as 'I am a Brahmin's son ... I was a student' and so on. The discursive, discriminatory, objectifying mind of the student is stumped – he has a certain knowledge of what he is, of what scripture says, but he has not yet experientially understood the full significance of the teachings that he has intellectually mastered. He cannot be both eternal and transitory. Śaṅkara's question is greeted with incomprehension; identification with the empirical, constructed 'I-as-me-which-is-different-from-you' is still in operation; in *Upad*. 14, the seeker expresses his bewilderment: 'Your Holiness, how have I spoken wrongly?' (Deutsch and Van Buitenen, 1971, p. 127).

The conceptual mastery of *śruti* is there: the seeker can correctly articulate the nature and marks of *ātman-brahman*, but the answer to Śaṅkara's counter-question still shows that the idea of an 'I' that is identified as something else has not yet been overcome. Śaṅkara is challenging his pupil to deconstruct the epistemic frame and the accompanying ontological construction that holds the identification of 'I' as a 'brahmin's son' and so on, and move to a direct and intuitive (*anubhava*) experiential knowing of undifferentiated oneness that is the direct import of the scriptures. However, there is not yet an experiential dimension to the seeker's knowledge, highlighted by his inability to 'see through' the epistemic frame that locks his sense of identity to a 'brahmin's son' and so forth. The crucial non-dual intuitive experiential identification of *ātman-brahman* is not yet realized, hence the aspirant's incomprehension.

In the next section of the *Upadeśasāhasrī* entitled 'Apprehension', Śaṅkara delineates how an eligible pupil is spurred on to a more in-depth form of radical discrimination. In the triple process of the path of *jñāna-yoga*, Śaṅkara's ideal pupil has listened (*śravaṇa*) to the *guru* and investigated the import of the *mahāvākyas* and attempted, with the help of his *guru*, to internalize the philosophical principles of Advaita by the process of reflection (*manana*). In combination with this, he has contemplated (*nididhyāsana*) the ultimate falsity of such dualistic distinctions as 'you and me' and 'my', 'me' and 'mine'. In short, the seeker is prepared and eligible for the inquiry into *brahmajñāna* and displays this to Śaṅkara by requesting the highest knowledge. In *Upad.* 49, the seeker asks: 'What is that nescience? And what is its object? And what is knowledge, remover of nescience, by which I can realize my own nature?' (Deutsch and Van Buitenen, 1971, p. 137). To which Śaṅkara answers:

> Though you are the highest Ātman and not a transmigrator, you hold the inverted view, 'I am a transmigrator.' Though you are neither an agent nor an experiencer, and exist [eternally], [you hold the inverted view, 'I am] an agent, an experiencer, and do not exist [eternally]' – this is nescience. (*Upad.* 50; Deutsch and Van Buitenen, 1971, pp. 137–138, square brackets in text)

This unequivocal statement describes the key superimpositions of *avidyā*. The non-self is erroneously superimposed on the highest non-dual self (*ātman*) from which follows the mistaken superimpositions of agent, experiencer, and finite, limited being. The method of removing *avidyā* is simply to cease holding such 'inverted views' and then *ātman-brahman* is seen for what it is: the undifferentiated all. This is *vidyā*. The statement is pure Advaita, although the student is not yet ready for such a succinct non-dual teaching and Śaṅkara's answer provokes a volley of empirically based questions.

In the teachings of *Upad.* 45–111,[43] Śaṅkara guides his imaginary pupil through all of the empirical, dualistic objections to the above statement. Many of the pupil's questions revolve around the counter-intuitive nature of the Advaitic claim that self is not an agent or an experiencer. According to the seeker, the 'I' that is experienced as 'me' does act and experience and 'know' objects 'out there' by sense perception and other means of knowledge so the 'I' cannot be the 'highest Ātman':

> Even though I exist [eternally], still I am not the highest Ātman. My nature is transmigratory existence which is characterized by agency and experienceship, since it is known by sense perception and other means of knowledge. [Transmigratory existence] has not nescience as its cause, since nescience cannot have one's own Ātman as its object. (*Upad.* 51; Deutsch and Van Buitenen, 1971, p. 138)

This objection is representative of all that follow; the seeker is confusing his nature (which is the 'highest Ātman') with transmigratory existence and thereby separating it from *brahman*. This primary 'inverted view' leads to the undifferentiated *ātman* being construed as the 'doer' and 'haver' of all the (ultimately) illusory actions and experiences that follow.

Śaṅkara counters with arguments and questions aimed to undo this erroneous superimposition and, in the first 'breakthrough' in *Upad.* 64, Śaṅkara brings the seeker to a point where he 'admits that "false superimposition is the seed of [every] calamity"'. To which Śaṅkara responds: 'If you know that the false superimposition is the seed of [every] calamity, then do not make it!' (Deutsch and Van Buitenen, 1971, p. 140). The student's confusion centres on not understanding that by nature, i.e., in essence, *ātman* is identical with *brahman* and, in essence, the pupil's own nature is identical to *ātman-brahman*. There is neither a difference nor a distinction. According to Advaita teachings, a thing cannot change its nature, hence all the student has to do is stop making these false superimpositions which are the 'seed of every calamity'. In short he has to cease mistaking 'what he is' for 'what he is not'.

The crux of Śaṅkara's teaching here is that only *ātman-brahman* is not composite and exists for its own sake; everything else is composite and exists for another. In other words, there is only *brahman*. In *Upad.* 93, Śaṅkara reinforces this absolute non-composite status of *brahman* by framing the issue in terms of the seeker's original question 'How can I know Brahman?' *Brahman*, says Śaṅkara, cannot be the object of any means of knowledge since *brahman* is by nature, the knower, the knowledge and the means of knowledge.

> The eternal discernment does not require any means of knowledge in order to be itself the means of knowledge or the knower since the eternal discernment is by nature the means of knowledge or the knower. (Deutsch and Van Buitenen, 1971, p. 144)

This serves to frame the seeker's problem directly in the arena of knowledge – 'how can he know this all-knowing knower when there are no means to know it?'[44] – and brings us to the pivotal question of *Upad.* 102 in which the seeker asks:

'If the knower is not the subject of empirical knowledge, how is it a knower?' (Deutsch and Van Buitenen, 1971, p. 146). And in *Upad.* 103, the seeker is told:

> Because there is no distinction in the nature of empirical knowledge, since empirical knowledge is apprehension. There is no distinction in the nature of this [empirical knowledge] whether it be non-eternal, preceded by remembrance, desire and the like, or transcendently changeless and eternal ... although the knower is nature of eternal apprehension, it is not contradictory to designate [It] as 'knower', since the result is the same. (Deutsch and Van Buitenen, 1971, p. 146, square brackets in the text).

From the standpoint of the highest truth (*pāramārthika*) there are simply no distinctions. Knower, known and means of knowledge cannot be separated. To the pupil, still operating from the empirical standpoint (*vyāvahārika*) this statement is contradictory. In *Upad.* 108, the pupil objects to this apparent contradiction by asking 'How can that which is eternal be a result of the means of knowledge if its nature is transcendentally changeless and the eternal light of Ātman [i.e., self-knowledge]?' Replying to this, in *Upad.* 108 Śaṅkara says, 'It is not contradictory.' 'How then' asks the pupil 'is it not contradictory?'

> Although [apprehension] is transcendentally changeless and eternal, [it] appears at the end of the notion [-forming process] due to sense-perception and other [means of knowledge] since [the notion-forming process] aims at it. If the notion due to sense-perception and other [means of knowledge] is non-eternal, [apprehension, though eternal,] appears as if it were non-eternal. Therefore, [apprehension] is figuratively called the result of the means of knowledge. (Deutsch and Van Buitenen, 1971, p. 147)

Śaṅkara is pushing the boundaries of his pupil's subject–object structures of knowing. From the empirically real point of view in which the construction-forming process holds sway, apprehension (*brahman*-knowledge) is figuratively said to be the result of a means of knowledge, but in reality, *brahman*-knowledge cannot be a result or an effect of any process or means of knowledge since *brahman is* knower, known, and means of knowledge. So there is no contradiction, it is merely a matter of correct view; from the standpoint of the highest truth the question cannot even arise.

Śaṅkara's dismissal of the above apparent contradiction undoes the student's dualistic identification with knower and known and frees him to radically discern the nature of non-dual self. In *Upad.* 109, he answers:

> If so, Your Holiness, apprehension is transcendentally changeless, eternal, indeed of the nature of the light of Ātman, and self-established, since it does not depend on any means of knowledge with regard to itself; everything other than this is non-conscious and exists for another's sake, since it acts together [with others]. (Deutsch and Van Buitenen, 1971, p. 147)

The pupil begins by recognizing of nature of apprehension. Apprehension is seen as being identical with *ātman-brahman* without contradiction. The 'light of Ātman' is by nature self-established and continuous, independent of all means of knowledge. As non-dual knowledge, the 'transcendentally changeless' and the *ātman*'s apprehension of this transcendentally changeless nature are the same. The pupil now recognizes Self-knowledge in its status as pure non-dual knowledge, and as such, does not depend on any other means of knowledge. The knowing subject and known object contradiction is no longer valid.

The student then moves on to the nature of duality. The notion of duality only exists as a misapprehension, it is the rope mistaken for the snake which is discounted when seen for what it really is. From the standpoint of the highest truth, non-*ātman* does not exist; however, as we have seen, Śaṅkara grants it a practical 'reality'. The pupil now recognizes that dualistic understandings in the waking and dreaming states are a 'useful fiction' that only exist as long as there is belief in the 'notion-forming process' as being real. Duality is experienced but from the standpoint of the highest truth it is not real.[45]

Śaṅkara's student concludes by confirming his understanding of the 'highest Ātman' by stating:

> In this manner, Your Holiness, apprehension, i.e., the light of Ātman, is uninterrupted; so it is transcendentally changeless, eternal and non-dual, since it is never absent from any of the various notions. But various notions are absent from apprehension. Just as in the dreaming state the notions in different forms such as blue and yellow, which are absent from that apprehension, are said to be non-existent from the standpoint of the highest truth, so in the waking state also, the various notions such as blue and yellow, which are absent from this very apprehension, must by nature be untrue ... (Deutsch and Van Buitenen, 1971, pp. 147–148)

The pupil recognizes that as the distinctionless, changeless substratum to all knowing and being, 'the light of Ātman is uninterrupted, eternal and non-dual'. According to Advaita teachings, this is *ātman-brahman*-identity realization that cannot be sublated. The pivotal non-dual understanding is expressed in the pupil's culminating assertion in *Upad.* 109: 'And there is no apprehender different from this apprehension to apprehend it; therefore it can itself neither be accepted nor rejected by its own nature, since there is nothing else' (Deutsch and Van Buitenen, 1971, p. 148). In other words, the pupil has come to an understanding of the absolute, singular status of self-knowledge. Self-knowledge is beyond any and all dualisms and dichotomies that are necessary cognates to the subject–object distinction and outside of the threefold distinction of apprehender (*pramātṛ*), the apprehension (*viṣaya*), and the means of apprehension (*pramāṇa*): self-knowledge is neither to be accepted nor rejected by any sense perception or means of knowledge; it just is – since there is nothing else.

Recognizing that the pupil has discerned his self-nature and 'knows' that there is nothing else, in *Upad.* 110, Śaṅkara declares:

> Exactly so it is. It is nescience [*avidyā*] that is the cause of transmigratory existence which is characterized by the waking and dreaming states. The remover of nescience is knowledge. And so you have reached fearlessness. From now on you will not perceive any pain in the waking and dreaming states. You are released from the sufferings of transmigratory existence. (Deutsch and Van Buitenen, 1971, p. 148)

Nescience (*avidyā*) is thus removed by non-dual knowledge (*vidyā*). The entire process has been a dialectic between the highest understanding of the *guru* (*pāramārthika*) and the relative, empirical understanding of the student (*vyāvahārika*) in which Śaṅkara has moved his pupil from mistaking that which is superimposed upon his self-nature to realizing non-dual understanding of self-nature (*brahman*) as all.

Grimes' point that Śaṅkara's philosophical distinction of the two 'apprehensions' of *brahman* pervades the entire Advaita system of thought, and that an appreciation of the fact that 'what is true from one point of view is not so from another' is central to understanding Advaitic claims as to the nature of reality (Grimes, 1991, p. 291), is very well taken in terms of the above analysis. In the above interactions between Śaṅkara and his ideal student, we see how a teacher deconstructively works with his student's relative understanding by constantly undermining the source of all empirically based questions. In doing this he pushes his student to question and 'undo' the false superimpositions that are binding him to limited understandings of reality. Once non-dual *brahman* is revealed in the student's understanding, all ideas of distinctions and 'standpoints' are seen to be un-real, and are for 'instructional use only'.

The philosophical distinctions and categories that Śaṅkara employs to support the Advaita substance view of reality can be seen in action in Advaita instructional discourse and practice instructions. In this way they serve to inform and form some of the basic instructional methods in modern and contemporary expressions of Advaita, even though many of the traditional requirements placed on an aspirant are no longer followed.

Śaṅkara's Advaita is a foundational source for modern Advaita and contemporary Western expressions of Advaita. This in-depth discussion of Śaṅkara's teachings on non-dual realization and the workings of the teacher–student dialogues in the practice situation lay the foundations for the exploration of modern and contemporary Advaita that follows where points of continuance and divergence from traditional teaching in modern and contemporary Advaita practice situations will be highlighted.

Modern and Contemporary Masters

The Advaitin that we know as 'Gauḍapāda' strove to reveal the ultimate falsity of all dualistic experience. According to Gauḍapāda, only the non-originated, non-dual *brahman* is *really* real and the entire world of duality is merely an appearance: nothing ever really comes into being, for nothing other than *brahman* really exists. By exposing the workings of *māyā* and deconstructing the dualistic constructs (*vikalpa*) that support incorrect interpretation(s) of reality, Gauḍapāda's emphasis rests on the real and true reality of *brahman* and *brahman* alone. According to Gauḍapāda there is a non-relationship between that which is originated (phenomenal experience) and that which is non-originated (*brahman*) and there is no possibility of that which is originated being real or existent. In declaring the nonexistence of all phenomena he works from the ultimate standpoint in which only the reality of *brahman* counts.

In contrast, Śaṅkara views the phenomenal from the standpoint of *māyā*, granting it a provisionary reality because it is cognized and experienced. This 'in-between' reality (*vyāvahārika*), considered real by 'courtesy only', operates until *brahman* is realized as the only 'real' reality (*pāramārthika*). Simply put, from the instructional point of view, Gauḍapāda emphasizes the non-relationship between empirical reality and *ātman-brahman* as a focus for the student, while Śaṅkara emphasizes the identity of *ātman-brahman* as the focal point of his teachings. In their efforts to undo habitual 'wrong interpretation' of reality Gauḍapāda emphasizes that the world is false while Śaṅkara emphasizes that *brahman* is real. These two modes of approach are utilized in the teachings and practice instructions of the modern Advaitins Sri Ramana Maharshi and H. W. L. Poonja. Ramana Maharshi, like Śaṅkara, seems to operate primarily from the standpoint of the absolute reality of the self, while in the teachings of Ramana's disciple H. W. L. Poonja we see an echo of Gauḍapāda in his instructional emphasis on the non-reality of the world. However, whether they emphasize 'the world is false' or '*brahman* is real' these modern masters (and contemporary Western Advaita teachers that claim their lineage) work with exposing the ultimate unreality of the phenomenal standpoint of the questioning student in a different way. Rather than presenting philosophical scripture-based argumentation for their spiritual teachings and instructions, both modern masters emphasize the experience of self-realization as the 'aim' of their teachings and strive to ignite this realization in the immediate experience of their students.

This shift away from traditional emphasis on knowledge of the Vedas and renunciation as necessary preparation for the path of *jñāna-yoga* is accompanied by a change of instructional emphasis. Unlike traditional Advaita teachers, neither Ramana Maharshi nor H. W. L. Poonja cite suitable interpretations of scripture as the authentication of their teachings but rather invite or challenge the student to authenticate Advaita teachings in his or her own experience. Ramana and Poonja make occasional references to scripture and, when asked, generally confirm that their teachings tally with scripture, but their instructional modes are not focused on conveying the liberating intent of scripture through study and interpretation of spiritual categories or structures. The primary concern of both masters is to bring the student to the point of recognizing the self that he or she already is. To this end, neither Ramana nor Poonja invites or encourages philosophical speculation but rather focuses the inquiry on the self of the student in front of them with the aim of igniting self-realization in the actual experience of the seeker. It is this shift in emphasis that prompts Fort to classify Ramana Maharshi and other modern Advaitins[46] as 'neo-Vedantins' and to suggest:

> … both that they are part of a tradition based on the Upaniṣads and Śaṅkara's non-dualist interpretation thereof, and that these figures are participating in and contributing to a new understanding of this Vedanta tradition, one influenced by Western premises and categories (imposed *and* chosen), which include humanistic globalism, the importance of egalitarian social ethics, and a focus on psychological experience. (Fort, 1998, pp. 129–130)

The shift away from traditional scriptural sources and commentaries raises questions as to what we regard as source material for these masters and teachings. Ramana Maharshi wrote very little,[47] hence most of his teachings come filtered through the understandings of his devotees and must be approached with caution. Also, all of Ramana's published interactions with students are based on transcriptions of oral dialogues recorded by devotees (usually in Tamil) and translated into English. There are no audio recordings of Ramana's interactions with seekers.[48] Thus, the literature by and on Ramana presents a variety of hermeneutical problems. After a survey of the literature, and a comparison of chosen dialogues from different translations and compilations, the most suitable sources of Ramana's interactions with students were found to be the early compilation of *Talks with Sri Ramana Maharshi* (1984) – collected from the transcriptions of Sri Munagala S. Venkataramiah[49] – which cover the period from 1935–1939 and the volume edited by David Godman, *Be As You Are: The Teachings of Sri Ramana Maharshi* (1992), which gives a general overview of Ramana's teachings through interactions with seekers.

Thus, to an extent, we will be reading Ramana through these two 'filters', although our examination will be informed by other understandings, such as Godman's interviews and biographies of disciples of Ramana,[50] and my two visits to Sri Ramanasramam in 1995 and 2000. In 1995 I had *satsang* with one of Ramana's oldest disciples, Sri Annamalai Swami (now deceased), and was able to ask for his interpretations of Ramana's teachings, which were consistent with the emphasis found in the above-mentioned sources.

In terms of source material, H. W. L Poonja is less problematic, as he taught in English and enjoyed a long teaching career. Hence, there is a wealth of material available that documents his interactions with seekers in the form of books, audio recordings and video recordings.[51]

Ramana Maharshi (1879–1950): 'Who am I?'

According to traditional biographies,[52] in 1896, a 16-year-old south Indian schoolboy named Venkataraman was sitting alone in a room on the first floor of his uncle's house in Madurai when he was suddenly seized by an intense fear of death. In the following few minutes he underwent a transformative experience in which he realized that the 'I' is not the body and although the body dies, this 'I' does not. Venkataraman described this realization as total 'absorption in the Self'.

According to his biographers, in the weeks that followed this experience, Venkataraman found that his total 'absorption in the Self' meant that he could no longer sustain the pretence of living life as expected of a boy his age and that he was increasingly drawn to the holy mountain Arunachala in the town of Tiruvannamalai. Unable to ignore this calling, he left his parent's home and made his way to Tiruvannamalai, spending the rest of his life at the base of the sacred hill Arunachala, first in the great temple, then in caves on the hill, and finally at the foot of the hill itself where eventually an ashram grew up around him and he became known as the *jñāni* or *jīvanmukta* (liberated being) Sri Ramana Maharshi.

The traditional account of Ramana Maharshi's transformative 'death experience' and his purported spontaneous inquiry into the real nature of the self by asking the existential question 'Is the body I?' is paradigmatic for the practice of deconstructive spiritual inquiry in later Advaita teachings. Ramana's process of radically questioning bodily identification with the questions 'What is it that dies?' and 'Is the body I?' developed into his core practice instruction of 'Who are you?' and is the key source of the contemporary Advaita deconstructive practice of self-inquiry in the West. Furthermore, this traditional account displays some similarities to Śaṅkara's teaching strategies in the teacher–student exchange of *Upadeśasāhasrī* which are, for our purposes, useful to note. To this end, although already well known, the account of Ramana Maharshi's 1896 experience is worth examining here.

> I seldom had any sickness, and on that day there was nothing wrong with my health, but a sudden violent fear of death overtook me. There was nothing in my state of health to account for it, and I did not try to account for it or to find that there was any reason for the fear. I just felt 'I am going to die' and began thinking what to do about it. It did not occur to me to consult a doctor or my elders or friends; I felt that I had to solve the problem myself, there and then.
>
> The shock of the fear of death drove my mind inwards and I said to myself mentally, without actually framing the words: 'Now death has come; what does it mean? What is it that is dying? This body dies.' And I at once dramatized the occurrence of death. I lay with my limbs stretched out stiff, as though rigor mortis had set in, and imitated a corpse to give greater reality to the enquiry. I held my breath and kept my lips tightly closed so that no sound could escape, so that neither the word 'I' nor any other word could be uttered. 'Well then,' I said to myself, 'this body is dead. It will be carried stiff to the burning ground and there burnt and reduced to ashes. But with the death of this body am I dead? Is the body I?' (Osborne, 1970, pp. 7–8)

The question 'But with the death of this body am I dead?' carries the same deconstructive intent as the challenge to bodily identification posited by Śaṅkara to his student in *Upad.* 11: 'My dear, when you are dead your body will be eaten by birds or will turn into earth right here. How then do you wish to get out of the ocean of transmigratory existence?' (Deutsch and Van Buitenen, 1971, p. 127).

In the above, Śaṅkara asks the question in an attempt to undo empirical identification with the body by pointing out that the bodily form that the student is identifying with will eventually perish. As we have seen, Śaṅkara is asking, 'But are you this body?' and if you are, 'What happens when this body perishes? Does the "I" (*ātman*) perish with it?' Interestingly, Ramana's purported spontaneous inquiry proceeds with similar deconstructive questions. Spontaneously he asks, 'But with the death of this body, am I dead?' Following this, Ramana's inquiry continues by acknowledging that the body is indeed dead, reduced to ashes, but is that all? 'What happens when this body perishes?' 'Am I dead?' Then, breaking with the bodily identification that initiated the inquiry, the pivotal deconstructive question 'Is the body I?' is asked, with the 'answer' being the existential recognition that there is a 'force' that is not body-dependent. For the body is now

> ... silent and inert but I feel the full force of my personality and even the voice of the 'I' within me, apart from it. So I am Spirit transcending the body. The body dies but the Spirit transcending it cannot be touched by death. That means I am the deathless Spirit. (Osborne, 1970, p. 8)

The similar insight that 'I am the deathless Spirit' that Śaṅkara's ideal pupil first gleaned from scripture and experientially completed with his *guru*'s deconstructive assistance, Ramana is claimed to have directly, intuitively apprehended (*anubhava*). Even without identification with the body, the full potency of the 'I' is felt. From this, it is concluded that this 'I' cannot be touched by death. The body ages and perishes but the 'I' that is not identified with the body does not. This 'I' is not the 'I-notion' (*jīva*) that is subject to change and fragmentation, but rather, the 'I-force' (*ātman*) that is identical to the changeless substratum to being. This 'I' is realized as 'Spirit transcending the body'; it is deathless, and that 'deathless Spirit' is experientially understood to be 'what "I" am'. Here, according to Advaita teachings, Ramana has broken through the veil of ignorance (*avidyā*) with true experiential non-dual knowledge (*vidyā*) of what 'I' is. Importantly, this realization was 'very real' (*sat*) and was not a process of thought:

> All this was not dull thought; it flashed through me vividly as living truth which I perceived directly, almost without thought-process. 'I' was something very real, the only real thing about my present state, and all the conscious activity connected with my body was centered on that 'I'. (Osborne, 1970, p. 8)

In this description, the undeniable fact of bodily death led Ramana Maharshi to radically ask 'What is it that dies?' By questioning exactly 'who or what he was' (*ātman vichara*), identification with the form of the body (and all its implications) was realized to be an erroneous identification and 'who "I" really am' is realized to be the non-dual self (*ātman*): permanent, unchanging and not subject to birth and death.

The teaching that one's self cannot ultimately be identified with the body, or any other object, is emphasized in Hinduism and Vedānta in general, and the question 'Who am I?' did not originate in Advaita with Ramana Maharshi. Questioning the veracity of 'what one is' is articulated in the Upaniṣadic dialogues[53] and is a traditional way of spiritual practice in Hinduism. 'The self is to be meditated upon for in it all these become one' (*Bṛ. Up.* I:4.7).

In a common form of traditional Upaniṣadic *sādhana* (spiritual practice) the seeker either affirms his or her identity with *brahman*[54] or negates all identifications with the bodily form and all their implications.[55] As Godman notes, questioners often assumed that Ramana's teaching also followed this traditional path.[56] However, Ramana's emphasis is somewhat different. According to Ramana Maharshi, the method of inquiring into 'who one is', is not to impress the positive 'I am *brahman*' onto the mind nor to mentally reject all objects of identification with name and form in the traditional '*neti, neti*' (not this, not this) approach. Hence, when asked, 'Shall I meditate on "I am Brahman?"', Ramana responds:

> The text is not meant for thinking 'I am *Brahman*'. *Aham* ['I'] is known to everyone. *Brahman* abides as *aham* in every one. Find the 'I'. The 'I' is already *Brahman*. You need not think so. Simply find out the 'I'. (Godman, 1992, p. 70)

And when asked, 'Shall I meditate on "neti-neti?"', Ramana also responds:

> No – that is not meditation. Find the source. You must reach the source without fail. The false 'I' will disappear and the real 'I' will be realised. The former cannot exist apart from the latter. (Godman, 1992, p. 70)

Ramana's instruction in both cases is for the practitioner to focus his inquiry on the 'source', without following any thoughts, whether they pertain to *brahman* or not. Whether the seeker affirms his or her identification with *brahman* or denies what self is not, for Ramana the seeker is still working with objects located in the mind. In Ramana's teaching, affirmation of self or denial of not-self still locks the seeker into an 'I'-thought that is either affirming or denying: To say that 'I am not this' or 'I am that' there must be the 'I'. This 'I' is only the ego or the 'I'-thought. After the rising up of this 'I'-thought, all other thoughts arise (Godman, 1992, p. 69). This potential objectification of *brahman* is what Śaṅkara is pointing his students to in his commentary on the *Bṛhad-āraṇyaka Upaniṣad* (*Bṛ. UB.*

2.3.6) in which he talks of the mistake of describing or indicating *brahman* by imposing any descriptions that superimpose 'name and form and action' on *brahman*. For, ultimately, *brahman* is even beyond the very designations of '*ātman*' and '*brahman*' (Rambachan, 1991, p. 71). Śaṅkara, however, follows this with acknowledging that, despite *brahman* being beyond all limiting adjuncts and objectifications, it is possible to use the *neti, neti* description to eliminate all specifications superimposed on *brahman*: 'Then there is only one way left, viz., to describe It as "Not this, Not this," by eliminating all possible specifications of It that have been known' (*Bṛ.UB*. 2.3.6). In this sense, Ramana's approach is more radical in that he does not want the seeker to recognize superimposition as a problem and cut away at the 'false' 'I'-thought with the support of scripture, but wants rather for the practitioner to experientially narrow the inquiry down to the 'I' and to 'hold' it there. 'Think "I", "I" and hold onto that one thought to the exclusion of all others' (Godman, 1992, p. 71).

Hence, in Ramana's view, the seeker does not need to identify (provisionally or otherwise) with 'I am this', for even to repeat *aham Brahmasmi* or to focus thought on it, the idea of a doer is necessary. Furthermore, in Ramana's instructions, 'You are not to think of other thoughts such as "I am not this body" but to utilize the "I"-thought to realize the "I"-source.' In other words, according to Ramana, if the practitioner 'trace[s] back the source of the "I"-thought, the Self alone will remain' (Godman, 1992, pp. 70–71). In sum, Ramana's instructions to the practitioner are to trace the idea of 'I' to the reality of 'I' and to fully experientially recognize being as in 'I am' and nothing else.

In dialogues Ramana consistently admonishes his questioners to 'Be that 'I'' (Godman, 1992, p. 71) and not to identify with the objectified 'I am some *thing*'. There is, however, a paradox here that a seeker points out:

> [*S*]: If 'I' also is an illusion, who then casts off the illusion?
> [*R*]: The 'I' casts off the illusion of 'I' and yet remains as 'I'. Such is the paradox of Self-realisation. The realised do not see any contradiction in it.
> (Godman, 1992, p. 87)

Here Ramana, like Śaṅkara, appeals to the two truths or the two 'apprehensions' of *brahman*. For as long as questions arise, the empirically real (*vyāvahārika*) point of view is in operation. Self-realization[57] admits of no paradoxes because from the absolutely real (*pāramārthika*) point of view there is no duality, there is no separation of not-'I' for the self to cast off. The paradox only operates as long as the seeker 'seeks'. In Ramana's words, 'As long as you seek to know how to realise, this advice is given to find your Self. Your seeking the method denotes your separateness' (Godman, 1992, p. 71).

Part of the radical nature of Ramana's approach lies in locating the 'investigation into the self' in the experiencing of the practitioner without grounding the inquiry in scriptural knowledge or study under the guidance of a *guru*. Ramana claimed that his reading of scripture came after his experience of the 'self' and that he found this reading to tally with his experience. When asked by a French scholar, 'Is Maharshi's teaching the same as Sankara's?', Ramana is reported to have replied:

> [*R*]: Maharshi's teaching is only an expression of his own experience and realisation. Others find that it tallies with Sri Sankara's.
> [*S*]: Quite so. Can it be put in other ways to express the same realisation?
> [*R*]: A realised person will use his own language ... SILENCE is the best language.
>
> (Maharshi, 1984, p. 155, his emphasis)

In this statement, Ramana emphasizes his preference for the 'silent teaching'[58] and makes no claim to continuity with the Advaita lineage, nor does he dismiss the non-dual similarities.[59] In his teachings, Ramana does refer to scripture and when scripture is quoted to him affirms that the inquiry that he speaks of tallies with scripture, but he affords no precedence to the study of or meditation on scripture. 'No learning or knowledge of scriptures is necessary to know the Self, as no man requires a mirror to see himself' (Godman, 1992, p. 122). Advaita Vedānta also emphasizes direct experience but the aspirant must be prepared for the path of *jñāna-yoga* by service to and study of the Vedas with a *guru*. Ramana's emphasis on experience is a radical departure from tradition and represents the beginning of the move away from orthodox Advaita as seen in Ramana's disciple H. W. L. Poonja and the subsequent teaching of Advaita in the West.

In keeping with the impetus to his own purported realization, the main thrust of Ramana Maharshi's teaching was on undoing his students' mistaken identification with the body (and all subsequent misidentifications) and experientially focusing them on the source of all superimpositions, the 'I'-thought. According to Ramana, objectified superimpositions of ideas of body, mind, thoughts, and so on onto the self could be undone by inquiring into the 'I'-thought with the deconstructive question 'Who am I?'

> [*Student*]: How should a beginner start this practice?
> [*Ramana*]: The mind will subside only by the enquiry 'Who am I?' The thought 'Who am I?', destroying all other thoughts, will itself finally be destroyed like the stick used for stirring the funeral pyre.

> If other thoughts rise one should, without attempting to complete them, enquire 'To whom did they rise?' What does it matter how many thoughts rise? At the very moment that each thought rises, if one vigilantly enquires 'To whom did this rise?', it will be known 'To me'. If one then enquires 'Who am I?', the mind will turn back to its source [the Self] and the thought which had risen will also subside.
>
> (Godman, 1992, p. 56)

Thus the question 'Who am I?' is a radical examination of the subject–object nature of all thoughts and identifications. If the subjective 'ownership' of each thought is questioned with a 'Who is having this thought?' and answered with 'I am', and then back to 'Who am I?' and 'Who is asking who am I?' and on and on, then, according to Ramana, the mind will eventually 'corner itself' and will subside into its source, i.e., the self (*ātman-brahman*-identity or the 'I'-force) and the question 'who am I' itself will dissolve 'like the stick used for stirring the funeral pyre'.

According to Ramana, the self is always realized and within everyone's experience, therefore directions, i.e., instructions, are not 'really' possible. It is a matter of looking within. However, misidentifications and false superimpositions mistaken for self can be undone or deconstructed by questioning. In the following dialogue, Ramana indicates the absolute non-dual nature of self and points the student towards removing ideas of 'one and two' 'higher and lower' and identifying with pure non-dual self:

> [*Ramana*]: If the way is external, directions are possible, but it lies within. Seek within. The self is always realised. Something not already realised might be sought afresh. But the self is within your experience.
> [*Student*]: Yes. I realise myself.
> [*R*]: *Myself.* Are there two – *my* and *self*?
> [*S*]: I do not mean it.
> [*R*]: Who is it that has or has not realised?
> [*S*]: There is only one self.
> [*R*]: The question can arise only if there be two. Abandon the wrong identification of the Self with the non-self.
> [*S*]: I mean the higher stage of consciousness.
> [*R*]: There are no stages.
>
> (Maharshi, 1984, pp. 139–140)

After pointing out that the self is always realized and does not need to be 'sought afresh', Ramana instructs his student to 'seek within'. The student agrees but superimposes a possessive onto the self that Ramana immediately challenges: '*Myself.* Are there two – *my* and *self*?' Acknowledging his mistake, the student moves to correct it. Ramana responds by challenging his student to locate the 'I' that has or has not realized: 'Who is it that has or has not realised?' Still operating with an objectified idea of self, the student answers: 'There is only one self.' Yes. According to Advaita teachings, *ātman-brahman* is one, quality-less and without differentiation, but here the student is objectifying the idea of 'one' as opposed to 'two'. The seeker is superimposing the idea of the quality one onto self, in other words he is reifying 'self as one' not realizing the oneness of self. To this, Ramana gives the uncompromising non-dual 'answer': 'The question [of one] can arise only if there be two' and the pure Advaita instruction: 'Abandon the wrong identification of the Self with the non-self.' His confusion mounting, the pupil appeals to the 'higher stage of consciousness' but is still objectifying self as a higher 'thing'. Ramana immediately negates any progressive ideas of stages: 'There are no stages.'

In the following instruction Ramana elaborates further on the absolute non-dual nature of self which, in reality, is beyond the duality of duality and non-duality:

> The Self is free from all qualities. Qualities pertain to the mind only. It is beyond quality. If there is unity there will also be duality. The numeral one gives rise to other numbers. The truth is neither one nor two. IT is as it is.
>
> (Maharshi, 1984, p. 129)

In Ramana's terms, self-knowledge 'is as it is'. Many of the problems that seekers encounter hinge on superimposing such qualities or objects on self and then mistaking these objects as self.

> [*S*]: The thought 'I am a man' is so natural.
> [*R*]: Not so. On the other hand 'I am' is natural. Why do you qualify it with man?
>
> (Maharshi, 1984, p. 555)

According to Ramana, there is no need to qualify being. The student disagrees: '"I am a man" is so obvious whereas "I am That" is not understood by us.' Once again the student's answer shows that superimposition is at work. The student is focusing on being some *thing*. Whether it be 'man' or a *mahāvākya* ('That art thou') according to Advaita, no objectifications can be placed on self (*ātman*). According to Ramana, the student is focusing on trying to grasp a reification of self that is projected as not directly experienced (That) and overlooking what is directly experienced (I am). Ramana counters by moving the student beyond the duality of this *or* that:

> [*R*]: You are neither *That* nor *This*. The truth is 'I am'. 'I AM that I AM' according to the Bible also. Mere *Being* is alone natural. To limit it to 'being a man' is uncalled for.
>
> (Maharshi, 1984, pp. 555–556)

The student points out that this 'limitation' appears to be what most people feel:

> [*S*]: (Humorously) If votes be taken the majority will be on my side. (Laughter).
>
> [*R*]: I cast my vote also on your side (Laughter). I say also 'I am a man'; but I am not limited to the body. It is in ME. That is the difference.
>
> (Maharshi, 1984, pp. 555–556)

Ramana agrees but immediately undermines any objectification of 'man' by pointing out the limitless nature of self: self (*ātman*) is not limited to any of the superimpositions of name, form and action. The body is a limitation whereas self is all.

Ramana's status as a *jīvanmukta* and his simple life attracted many pilgrims and devotees to seek audience with him in the form of *darshan*, that is, to gain the traditional 'blessing' or 'merit' from merely being in the presence or the 'sight' of a great saint. In addition to this, seekers also came to Ramana for *satsang* or *sat-sanga* (literally association or meeting with truth or reality), which is the traditional way of engaging with a sage either by offering worship (performing *pūjas*, singing devotional songs), reading or reciting scripture, or discussing spiritual topics.[60] Ramana gave daily audiences with seekers and devotees but gave no formal or informal lectures or spontaneous discourses. He would sit in silence unless questioned and then he would directly respond to the questioner.[61] Ramana's approach to *satsang* is well illustrated in response to this seeker's question:

> [*S*]: All I want to know is whether *sat-sanga* is necessary and whether my coming here will help me or not.
>
> [*R*]: First you must decide what is *sat-sanga*. It means association with *sat* or reality. One who knows or has realized *sat* is also regarded as *sat*. Such association with *sat* or with one who knows *sat* is absolutely necessary for all …

> *Sat-sanga* means *sanga* [association] with *sat*. *Sat* is only the Self. Since the Self is not now understood to be *sat*, the company of the sage who has understood it is sought. That is *sat-sanga*. Introversion results. Then *sat* is revealed.
>
> (Godman, 1992, p. 107)

Association with *sat*, according to Ramana, is absolutely necessary for all. But *sat* is only the self. According to this definition one is always in association with *sat* but just does not know it. Association with one who knows and is *sat* can be helpful. But, on the other hand, that does not mean that *sat* and self can be separated, because, in reality, they are non-dual: 'Can anyone remain without the Self. No. So no one is away from *sat-sanga*' (Godman, 1992, p. 107).

Many seekers were content to sit in Ramana's silent presence but Ramana's openness to questions led to dialogues and exchanges with seekers. As he attracted more and more followers and visitors,[62] including many Westerners, the exchanges and dialogues were increasingly reported and transcribed.[63]

The contemporary use of *satsang* in the West as a vehicle of Advaita teachings is indebted to these early exchanges of seekers with Ramana Maharshi. Ramana's emphasis on experience, his view that self-realization is available to all, and the uncompromising non-dual orientation that informs Ramana's interactions with seekers are hallmarks of contemporary Western presentations of Advaita. However, it is in the teachings of Ramana's disciple H. W. L Poonja that the emphasis on direct experience and the use of *satsang* was fully developed and employed as the vehicle for Advaita teachings in the West.

H. W. L. Poonja (1910–1997): 'You have to do nothing to be who you are!'

After an inexplicable 'awakening' experience at six years of age, interpreted by his mother as an experience of the Hindu God *Kṛṣṇa*,[64] Hariwansh Lal Poonja (later known as Poonjaji or Papaji) dedicated his life to the quest for an external God in the form of devotion (*bhakti*). After over a quarter of a century of visiting teachers, going on pilgrimages and an arduous daily regime of devotional practices and *pūjās* (ritual worship) he went to Sri Ramana Maharshi in the 1940s with this question:

> Have you seen God? I asked. And if you have, can you enable me to see him? I am willing to pay any price, even my life, but your part of the bargain is that you must show me God.
>
> No, [the Maharshi] answered, I cannot show you God or enable you to see God because God is not an object that can be seen. God is the subject. He is the

> seer. Don't concern yourself with objects that can be seen. Find out who the seer is. He also added, You alone are God. (Godman, 1998a, pp. 105–106)

Ramana Maharshi goes right to the Advaitic heart of the matter with a deconstruction of any ideas of an objectified God that is separate from self. Denying the importance of objects that are seen (and therefore perceived as separate and distinct from the self) he directs Poonjaji to inquire, not into that which is seen, but into the seer itself, that is, to focus attention on finding out who the seer is, to uncover the subject, the seer, rather than objects which are perceived to be seen.

Although he received a clear, uncompromising instruction for self-inquiry from Sri Ramana, Poonjaji was unable to discontinue his cherished devotional practices immediately and continued until one day he found that he could no longer perform them.[65] After questioning several *gurus* and sages, he returned to Ramana Maharshi and explained that the desire to practice had fallen away. What had happened? After explaining that practice was like a vehicle, when one has arrived, one gets off the train and leaves it behind, Ramana said: 'You yourself did not give up your practices; they left you of their own accord because they had served their purpose. You have arrived' (Godman, 1998a, pp. 120–121). Ramana then looked intently at Poonjaji who reported that:

> ... [S]uddenly, I understood. I knew that this man who had spoken to me was, in reality, what I already was, what I had always been. There was a sudden impact of recognition as I became aware of the Self. I use the word 'recognition' deliberately because as soon as the experience was revealed to me, I knew, unerringly, that this was the same state of peace and happiness that I had been immersed in as a six-year-old boy ... The silent gaze of the Maharshi[66] re-established me in that primal state. (Godman, 1998a, p. 122)

This 'sudden awareness of the Self' was to become a driving force in Poonjaji's later teachings wherein he geared his teaching strategies to jolt the questioning student into the 'sudden impact' of all-encompassing self-recognition. As the transcripts and recordings of his many *satsangs* show, Poonjaji employed vigorous, often humorous, deconstructive 'attacks' on conceptual barriers and objectifications that students superimposed on their 'selves' – conceptual barriers disclosed by the dualistic nature of their questions.

In the following dialogue with an Indian devotee, Poonjaji undoes the idea of 'working on' or 'working out' the deconstructive question 'Who am I?' by moving the questioner into direct confrontation with the self that, according to Advaita teachings, is already and always there. In this dialogue, Poonjaji is challenging the questioner to experientially recognize the 'I' that he already is:

> [*Poonjaji*]: Who are you? I'll give you five minutes because you are Indian. These others may think I treat you better because you are an Indian and they are all foreigners. So I will. I will give you five minutes for this question.
> [*Student*]: Five minutes! I've been working on this question for 2½ years!
> [*P*]: You are right. Five minutes is too long, but you are a guest. I want to treat you well. Look, how far is it from Kanpur, where you came from, to here?
> [*S*]: About 90 kilometers, about three hours.
> [*P*]: Three hours. Now why does it take three hours?
> [*S*]: Because of the distance.
> [*P*]: Very good, very good. So where is the 'I' that is asking the question? And where is the 'I' in 'Who am I?' I gave you five minutes to be polite. But if there is no space – no distance – your answer should take no time.
> (Poonja, 1992b, pp. 11–12)

Here, Poonjaji attempts to deconstruct the seeker's projections that the 'I' can be found as a result of inquiry over time. 'I've been working on this question for 2½ years!' protests the seeker. 'How can I possibly answer in five minutes?' This is correct, counters Poonjaji, you cannot answer in 2½ years or in five minutes for the 'answer' is now. What distance can there be between being and knowing 'I'? Where is the space that separates knowing and being 'I'? Here, Poonjaji is attempting to directly ignite the key Advaita tenet of the absolute immediacy of self-realization; knowing *ātman-brahman*-identity is being *ātman-brahman*-identity. 'He, verily, who knows the Supreme *Brahman* becomes *Brahman* himself' (*Mu. Up*. III:2.9).

In this encounter, Poonjaji's implicit deconstructive instruction is 'find it!' Find this 'I' that you say is not already fully present! In keeping with the Advaita insistence on the immediacy of *ātman-brahman*-identity, when confronted with questions that posit self-realization as a problem or as a question that can be solved or 'worked on' Poonjaji immediately counters by undoing such reified notions of cause and effect in the questioner's immediate experience.

Over twenty years after his decisive meeting with Ramana Maharshi, speaking of the impact of Sri Ramana's instruction and its implications for his own teaching, Poonjaji remarked:

> I knew that all my lifetimes in *samsara* were unreal, and that the Maharshi had woken me up from this wholly imaginary nightmare by showing me the Self that I really am. Now, freed from that ridiculous *samsara*, and speaking

> from the standpoint of the Self, the only reality, I can say, 'Nothing has ever come into existence; nothing has ever happened; the unchanging, formless Self alone exists.' That is my experience, and that is the experience of everyone who has realised the Self. (Godman, 1998b, pp. 7–8)

Poonjaji's reported experiential realization of the unchanging and formless self as the only reality, with its attendant knowledge of the nonexistence of phenomena and the non-production of entities, is a contemporary echo of Gauḍapāda's core teaching of non-origination (*ajātivāda*). Poonjaji emphasizes 'you have to do nothing to be who you are' because nothing needs to be produced for realization, i.e., how one 'really' is, is non-originated, unconditioned, infinite and so on, hence no originated, conditioned, finite, practice can have any meaningful relation to this pure, non-originated nature. In this sense, Poonjaji's emphasis on this 'nothing to do' can be said to be an attempt to experientially ignite Gauḍapāda's theory of *ajātivāda* as an existential reality in the awareness of his students. The self ever-is, *ātman-brahman*-identity is not born, created or caused but although this identity is ever-present it is obscured and does need to be *realized*. In Poonjaji's own case this realization was said to be obscured by superimposing devotion to the Hindu God *Kṛṣṇa* onto his direct experience of *ātman-brahman*-identity thereby creating a separation or a dualism consisting of a devotee and the object of his devotions.[67]

According to Advaita teachings, as articulated by Gauḍapāda and reiterated by Poonjaji, nothing has ever been created, no one has ever striven to attain liberation, and no one has attained it, so what meaning could the concepts of bondage and liberation possibly have? Once the bondage–liberation dualism is experientially undone or deconstructed all questions about liberation and bondage dissolve:

> How did this concept [of creation] take form and manifest? Because that's all it is – a concept. In reality nothing has ever been created. No one has ever striven to attain liberation and no one has ever attained it. What about these concepts of bondage and liberation? What meaning do they have when no one has ever been bound or made free? (Godman, 1998c, p. 215)

Like Gauḍapāda before him, Poonjaji orientates his teachings and practice instructions from the liberated view and insists again and again on the 'fact' that his students have to do 'nothing' to be who they are. To this end, he tirelessly deconstructed any projections of goal-orientated spiritual practice and static dualisms that his students may have harboured; the dualistic conceptualizations of subject and object, cause and effect, and linear ideas of space and time were all 'targeted' with what Poonjaji referred to as his 'No Way' method (Godman, 1998c, p. 15), in which his most direct instructions are given thus:

> [*Student*] Please tell me how to realise the Truth.
> [*Poonjaji*] You don't have to do any practice. You don't have to chant any mantras. You don't have to do any yogic *asanas*, and you don't have to go on any pilgrimages. You simply have to look within at your own Self. In no time at all you will see that you have always been free, but you didn't realise it before because you were always looking outwards.
>
> (Godman, 1998b, p. 62)

This reiteration of the core Advaita teaching that the self is inherently complete and that self-knowledge cannot be the 'result' of any ritual or practice is direct and simple although certainly difficult for the practitioner to understand if there is not an immediate experience of the 'sudden impact of self-recognition'. A further, deconstructive move is needed to undo objectifications and reifications of stubborn dichotomies such as cause and effects. To this end, Poonjaji moves from an instructional discourse mode to a more dialectic, dynamic presentation of self-realization:

> [*Student*]: What advice would you give to someone who wants to start on the spiritual path?
> [*Poonjaji*]: You only need start if you have a goal to attain. To start a journey, you must know where your destination is. What is the place you want to reach?
> [*S*]: The Self.
> [*P*]: In that case the destination is also the starting point. Why do you need to move or do anything to reach it?
>
> The mind has a tendency to make the Self an object that it wants to reach or attain after a process that takes place in time. The Self is out of time, out of space. No journey through time or space can ever take you there.
> [*S*]: How to get and keep this awakening of the Self?
> [*P*]: By not letting any concept take hold of you.
> [*S*]: Do you sit every morning and meditate in this way?
> [*P*]: Here we are learning how not to sit on anything.
> [*S*]: How does that happen?
> [*P*]: If I told you, I would start sitting on it.
>
> (Godman, 1998c, pp. 38–39)

Again, the pure Advaita dictum of the inherent completeness of self; no journey or practice through space and time can take you where you already are. There is no 'way' or 'method' to 'get' to where one already is. However, the questioner persists in dualizing – how does that happen? There must be a process. How do I 'get it' (self-realization) and 'keep it'. Poonjaji's deconstructive response humorously cuts such conceptualizations at their source. Explanation is not experience, and would merely proliferate conceptual grasping; the questioner must realize for himself.[68]

Again, this devastatingly simple negation of the dualized path is a difficult teaching. In the following dialogue, a long-time Indian student of Poonjaji's confronts him with the obvious objection:

> You say that no effort is necessary to realise the Self, but for any accomplishment some effort is necessary. If I am on the banks of the Ganga and I want a pot of water to drink, I have to dip my pot in the river, lift it to my lips and then swallow it. The water will not jump into my mouth by itself. Similarly, I cannot expect enlightenment to descend on me suddenly, without any preparation on my behalf. If I don't make some effort, it will not come to me.
>
> [Poonjaji responds:] For the Ganga to be the Ganga, it must be enclosed by two banks. Now, if you throw away the banks where is the Ganga?
>
> (Godman, 1998a, pp. 209–210)

Reacting to Poonjaji's insistence that the spiritual path requires no effort,[69] the questioner is once again asking how that can be. Nothing in his previous experience has come to him without effort and preparation so how can it be that this great thing that he seeks can be found without effort? 'The water will not jump into my mouth by itself' nor will spiritual awakening descend on his being without some kind of action or effort on his part. Implicit in the question is the commonsense notion that I am doing this and that 'it' will 'happen' to 'me' and the reification that liberation is an accomplishment, a state that can be achieved. From the Advaitic point of view, as taught by Poonjaji, these two inherent misidentifications need to be deconstructed or undone to enable the seeker to shift from a constricted cause-and-effect view to an experiential understanding of the Advaitin greater self (*ātman*). Poonjaji's 'answer' challenges the notion of a separate, isolated self by pointing to the boundaries that name and form (*nāma-rūpa*) necessarily imply. The 'effort' that Poonjaji is negating is the dualistic goal-orientated effort towards a projected objectified result. In Poonjaji's teaching, realization of self (*ātman*) cannot be compartmentalized into dualized patterns of cause and effect; *brahmajñāna* (liberating knowledge) admits of no definitions and is limitless. How is the Ganga defined? By its banks, by that which limits it. Throw away that limitation and who is dipping from what?[70]

Where Ramana Maharshi emphasized bringing the inquiry back to the primary question of 'Who am I?' thereby challenging the questioner to locate the 'I' that is so readily assumed, Poonjaji's challenge often centred around deconstructing the fixation that there is some 'gap' between what the seeker is now and what he or she will be once 'enlightened', and that there is some kind of necessary practice, something to be done, to close this 'gap'.

> [*Student*]: Does it [realization] go quickly or slowly, slowly?
> [*Poonjaji*]: Slowly is only the mind that fools you. To be right now, what understanding is needed? To be right now, what you already are, you don't need any understanding or misunderstanding.
> [*S*]: Why did I come here then?
> [*P*]: You came *here* because you thought you were *there*!
>
> (Poonja, 1992b, p. 17)

Throwing a seeker's dualistic spiritual aims and intentions into question is a strikingly effective deconstructive technique. 'Why did I come here then?'/'What am I doing here?' is probably the most difficult question that a spiritual aspirant can ask him or herself. In the same way that Ramana Maharshi deconstructed his questioner's projections on the teacher–student relationship with a disavowal of any possibility of the teacher acting with intention, provoking the student to ask 'What is the use of people like me coming to see you?' (Godman, 1998c, p. 334), Poonjaji collapses his student's projections of attaining any sort of understanding or even misunderstanding from being in the *guru*'s presence 'Why did I come here, then?' In one pivotal deconstructive move Poonjaji undoes any conceptualizations of being here or being there and by extension being in bondage or being liberated. According to Advaita, there is only Being. 'To be right now' is not dependent on here or there. The student's objectifications of attaining are exposed as mistaken: 'You came *here* because you thought you were *there*!' To another student Poonjaji reiterates this 'there is neither coming nor going [in liberation]. One does not go there and stay there. Coming and going are ideas of the mind' (Godman, 1998c, p. 45).

According to Poonjaji, even being in the *guru*'s presence in *satsang* is really 'an idea of the mind'. For in *satsang*: 'There is no one to be seen, felt, or spoken to. This is satsang. Not even oneness, let alone twoness. Not even oneness. Then satsang takes place' (Poonja, 1993, p. 15). Although he stressed the importance of meeting and questioning a realized teacher in *satsang*, Poonjaji's definition of *satsang* serves to undermine any dualistic projections that students may have of 'coming to' *satsang* and 'attaining liberation'. In this statement, Poonjaji is exposing the contradictory nature of the idea of *satsang* being a 'vehicle' for Advaita teachings. Self-inquiry is not a subject–object inquiry. It is an inquiry of the 'Self with Self'[71] hence the very notion of an exchange or a dialogue between a 'teacher' and a 'student' is an *avidyā*-fuelled superimposition. If 'meeting' with a teacher in *satsang* is to be identified in any way with self-realization or self-knowledge (*brahmajñāna*) then this 'meeting' must be beyond any and all dualistic projections that are necessary adjuncts to the subject–object distinction and outside of knowledge conceived as knower (*pramātṛ*), the known (*viṣaya*) and the means of knowing (*pramāṇa*): self-knowledge or self-realization is neither one nor two: self-knowledge – since there is nothing else – just is.

For Poonjaji, the same dualistic problem arises with the idea of a teaching, a teacher, and one who is taught. To undo these projections, Poonjaji claims that there is no trace, i.e., there is nothing to be committed to memory or 'transmitted' from a teacher to a student. According to Poonjaji, this teaching 'never was, never will be and never is'.

> Just as a bird leaves no trail in the sky as it flies, the true teaching leaves no trace in memory. The teaching must have no teacher and no student. If the teaching comes from the past or memory or concept, it is *preaching* not teaching. This teaching never was (*he smiles and looks around the room*). It never will be (*he pauses and then laughs*). And it never is. (Poonja, 1992b, p. 145; italics in text)

In keeping with the Advaita insistence that self-realization is undifferentiated, objectless, non-dual knowing, Poonjaji's insistence on 'you are that which you seek' reflects Śaṅkara's insistence that liberation cannot be an effect; as effect it is unreal.[72] That is, *ātman-brahman*-identity or self-realization cannot be the product or the object of any process of investigation or knowledge, but rather is an immediate intuition (*anubhava*), or in Poonjaji's term a 'sudden awareness' of 'what one is'.

In *satsang*, that is, in the Advaita practice situation, all Poonjaji's deconstructive 'efforts' are geared to undo the mistaken superimpositions of dualities and ignite *advaitavāda*, the absolute non-difference of subject and object in the actual experience of the seeker. To this end, Poonjaji's teachings attempt to experientially demonstrate to the student that bifurcation between categories such as self and other, coming and going, here and there, liberation and bondage, is the dualistic 'problem' that the student must undo. In this way, his deconstructive strategies attack the 'problem' at the roots, that is, he works to undo the dualistic thought processes and structures that create oppositional categories, which, according to Advaita, lock the student into the contracted, ultimately un-real, empirical (*vyāvahārika*) point of view.

Gangaji (b. 1942): 'You are That!'

Gangaji, (born Antoinette Roberson), is a contemporary Western disciple of Poonjaji.[73] After many years of seeking, Gangaji reports that her spiritual search ended on the banks of the Ganges with Poonjaji's direct admonishment not to seek freedom or truth outside the self: 'You are freedom. You are truth' (Gangaji, 1995). In her words, at this instruction she 'caught fire and burned on the banks of the Ganga' (Gangaji, 1995).[74] Charged with the responsibility to teach in the West, Gangaji, who has been teaching since 1990, now has a large international following and holds *satsang* worldwide. She is perhaps the best known of Poonjaji's direct disciples.[75]

In keeping with the affirmation of *ātman-brahman*-identity that was the impetus to her own purported realization, Gangaji emphasizes the teaching 'You are That!' and as such she represents a return to fundamental non-dualistic Upaniṣadic teachings as found in the *mahāvākyas*, 'That art thou' (*Ch. Up.* VI:13.1) and 'This *brahman* is the self' (*Bṛ. Up.* II:5.19). In the following interaction with a student, Gangaji reiterates the key Advaita spiritual method of discriminating between reality and appearance and the core tenet of the 'ever-attained nature of self'. Interestingly, in this dialogue, she also employs Buddhist terminology and utilizes deconstructive strategies from the Mahāyāna Heart of Perfect Wisdom Sūtra (*Prajñāpāramitā Hridaya Sūtra*) to illustrate Advaitic non-dual tenets.

Gangaji begins by inviting the student to test the veracity of 'anything that stands between her and her true Self'. She says, 'If you imagine that there is anything that stands between you and your true Self, please, let us expose it and see what is the reality of it. Is it imaginary, or is it real?' (Gangaji, 1995, p. 54). The student locates the obstacle in her mind, 'It's in my mind.' Immediately Gangaji challenges her to locate this mind and to determine its status: is it real or imagined?

> [*G*]: Where is your mind? Find it right now. If mind is the obstacle to knowing yourself, then we must see if mind is real or imagined.
> [*S*]: Where did it go?
> [*G*]: Yes, where did it go? Where does the mind go in the moment of investigation?
> [*S*]: It didn't exist.

[*G*]: Where is this mind? Find it.
[*S*]: In substance I can't.

(Gangaji, 1995, p. 54)

In the moment of investigation mind cannot be found. Gangaji continues by instructing the seeker 'to turn awareness towards thought' and locate what she is calling 'my' thoughts:

[*G*]: When you look at this thought, *It's my thoughts*, what is there? What is there when you actually turn awareness directly towards thought?
[*S*]: Nothing.

(Gangaji, 1995, p. 55)

The self-reflexive attempt to 'turn awareness to its source' discloses to the student that there is 'nothing' that she can actually identify or grasp as 'her thoughts'. Pre-empting the misconception that this 'nothing' is some sort of dead or blank void, Gangaji asks her student to be more precise:

[*G*]: And this nothing? ... I want to know, is this nothing some kind of blankness or deadness, or is it conscious, alive intelligence?
[*S*]: Sometimes it's intelligence.
[*G*]: If it is intelligence only sometimes, it is not reliable intelligence.
[*S*]: Yes, because lots of times it's clouded.

(Gangaji, 1995, p. 55)

The student cannot yet discern a reliable, steady source of awareness; intelligence is described as 'clouded'. Gangaji points her beyond the dualisms of clarity and 'clouds' to that which is aware of both:

[*G*]: This that is aware of clouds, and aware of some kind of intelligence that comes and goes, what is this?
[*S*]: That is who I am.
[*G*]: Yes! What you are telling me is that who you are is that which is aware when there are clouds, and that which is aware when there is clarity. Am I understanding you correctly?

(Gangaji, 1995, p. 56)

The student has discriminated the real which cannot be sublated as 'who I am'. Superimpositions in the form of 'clouds' and intelligence are seen to be objects that 'come and go' and therefore not reliable or permanent. What she 'is' is that which does not come and go *in* awareness but that which *is* awareness (*ātman-brahman*-identity). Gangaji reiterates this point to test her student's understanding:

> [*G*]: If I have heard you correctly, you have said that who you are is what is always present; the awareness of judgment, the awareness of mind, the awareness of cloud, *awareness* period.
> [*S*]: Yes.
> [*G*]: Awareness is always present. Everything else comes and goes *in* awareness.
> [*S*]: Yes, I see the trance more and more. I see the hypnotism.
> (Gangaji, 1995, p. 56)

The student has acknowledged the real. In an echo of the Yājñavalkya's deconstructive instruction of the *Bṛhad-āraṇyaka Upaniṣad* III:4.2, 'You cannot see the seer of seeing', Gangaji offers a further deconstructive probe with the paradoxical instruction to 'Now see the seer.'

The student answers by identifying the 'seer' as 'she', thereby superimposing an object on objectless awareness. Identification with objects that arise in awareness is still in place. To cut this identification, Gangaji deconstructively counters with the radical negations of the Buddhist Heart Sūtra. The exchange goes thus:

> [*G*]: Does awareness have gender?
> [*S*]: No.
> [*G*]: Correct! No gender. Does awareness have eyes?
> [*S*]: Not really.
> [*G*]: Does awareness have ears?
> [*S*]: No.
> [*G*]: Does awareness have form?
> [*S*]: No.
> [*G*]: The living Heart Sutra is revealed when you see what is truly here. Nothing! Nobody! Is there ever a moment when this that has no eyes, no ears, no form, no gender, is not totally present?
> [*S*]: No. It is always present!
> [*G*]: What is always present is who you truly are. Correctly identify yourself as eternally present awareness and take refuge in That.
> (Gangaji, 1995, p. 57)

By guiding her student through the radical negations of the Heart Sūtra, Gangaji attempts to prise her away from any objectified identification with the attributes of bodily form, and then away from the idea of form itself. In doing this she moves her teaching very close to Buddhist ontology with the capping statement that these negations reveal 'Nothing' and 'Nobody'. However, Gangaji immediately negates this 'no-self' by positing awareness as being that which is always present and identifying 'who the student truly is' with that which is 'ever-present'. She thus uses Buddhist deconstructive negations for primarily Advaitin ontological ends. This merging of teachings and terminology well illustrates the point that, experientially speaking, the crucial focus of deconstructive teaching strategies in both Advaita and Zen is on the undoing of dualistic conceptual structures and bifurcated oppositional ways of thinking which, according to both traditions, obscure direct non-dual insight.

Advaita Vedānta Summary: 'Nothing Ever Happens'

The final position of the Advaitin is well stated in Poonjaji's summary of Advaita teaching: 'This teaching never was. It never will be. And it never is' (Poonja, 1992b, p. 145). Thus, for the Advaitin, nothing is happening, ever has happened, or ever will happen. *Brahman/ātman* alone is, was, and will be. The 'idea' that reality is impermanent, changing and differentiated is only a superimposition (*adhyāsa*) placed on immutable *brahman* by the *māyā*-fuelled workings of *avidyā* (ignorance). Since ignorance is not permanent, at the level of empirical or practical reality (*vyavahāra*), it can be removed, but, in absolutely 'real' reality (*pāramārthika*), even the removal of *avidyā* through *brahmajñāna* does not 'really' happen in the usual sense of the verb 'to happen', as the idea that *brahman* is obscured or distorted by *avidyā* is in itself only appearance, for in reality, *brahman-ātman* identity is ever-present and ever-realized.

Thus, the core 'problem' that an Advaita practitioner faces is mistaking empirical reality (*vyavahāra*) for absolute reality (*pāramārthika*). In other words, taking the perspective of *avidyā* to be real when in fact it is mere appearance. Spiritual practice in Advaita is thus geared to disclose the superimpositions that are mistaken for the real and bring the practitioner to the threshold of non-dual knowledge (*vidyā*) of self (*ātman*).

Taken as an evolving continuum, Advaita teachings display a deconstructive emphasis in that, in the practice situation, they are employed by teachers to experientially undo erroneous dualistic superimpositions that have been placed on non-dual reality. In keeping with the Advaita tenet of the twofold nature of reality, Advaita teacher/student exchanges can be seen as a dialectic between the two levels of reality: the absolute non-dual standpoint (*pāramārthika*) of the teacher and the relative dualistic standpoint of the pupil (*vyavahāra*) in which the student is pushed to higher levels of understanding until finally the idea of levels or understandings dissolves. Ramana Maharshi well illustrates this point when he describes the deconstructive question 'Who am I?' as the thought that will destroy 'all other thoughts, [and] will itself finally be destroyed like the stick used for stirring the funeral pyre' (Godman, 1992, p. 56).

As we have seen, in contemporary expressions of Advaita, structural adherence to orthodox interpretations of doctrine and traditional modes of teaching have lessened in importance with the emphasis being placed on the practitioner experiencing *ātman-brahman*-identity with or without the authentication of scripture. The move away from scriptural authority and the appropriation of spiritual categories from other religious traditions technically places contemporary Advaitins outside of the classical tradition of Advaita Vedānta and makes them neo-Vedantin in orientation. However, links and points of affinity remain: Gauḍapāda's core non-dual doctrine of non-origination (*ajātivāda*) and Śaṅkara's insistence on the identity of self (*ātman*) with *nirguṇa brahman* (*brahman* without qualities, *brahman* as the distinctionless, sole reality) are echoed in the teachings and practice instructions of Ramana Maharshi and H. W. L. Poonja . The difference being that these modern masters challenge their questioners to directly ignite these abstract key Advaita tenets in their actual experience. Also, as we have seen in the idealized teacher/pupil exchanges of the *Upadeśasāhasrī*, Śaṅkara's teaching strategies exhibit the use of the primary deconstructive techniques of negation and unfindability analysis that are cornerstones of contemporary Advaita deconstructive spiritual inquiry.

In Advaita Vedānta, liberating knowledge is non-dual knowledge. Hence, traditional, modern and contemporary expressions of Advaita all work towards the undoing or deconstruction of the grip of dualistic ways of thinking and being in the actual experience of the practitioner. The techniques employed and the dynamics of this experiential undoing is the subject of part two. In this chapter we have been concerned to delineate the philosophical underpinnings to spiritual practices in Advaita Vedānta and to highlight their deconstructive orientation.

Chapter 3

Zen Buddhism: Philosophical Foundations and Deconstructive Strategies

According to tradition, in his first teaching after enlightenment the Buddha 'set the wheel of the Dharma in motion' by identifying 'Four Noble Truths', a teaching that characterized human existence as being bound by suffering (*duḥkha*) and which revealed a way of overcoming this problem. In the standard formulation, the Four Noble Truths are: (1) there is suffering; (2) suffering is caused by craving; (3) suffering can be extinguished by eliminating its causes; and (4) the way to extinguish the causes of suffering is to follow the middle way (*madhyamā pratipad*).

Based on this insight, in this first discourse the Buddha advised five questioning mendicants neither to pursue a path of austerities nor to hedonistically indulge the senses but to practice a 'middle way' that is not dependent on the two extremes: 'I have given up both these extremes, and have found another path, a middle way. It leads to the appeasing of all ill, and yet it is free from happiness and joy' (Conze, 1977, p. 56).

In keeping with the Buddha's instruction, negotiating a 'middle way' that is not dependent on the 'two extremes' is a defining characteristic of Buddhist thought and practice. In the light of this, the Four Noble Truths do not invoke a notion of reality that stands above or outside of human presence and action, for, according to the Buddha, *duḥkha* arises from an identifiable cause and steps can be taken to eliminate it. The Four Noble Truths thus present the dilemma of existence and offer a way to its resolution. In this sense, they are a call to action to which the practitioner's questions must be 'How is *duḥkha* extinguished?' and, more to the point, 'What must I do to overcome it?'

The main philosophical implications of Buddhist teachings are contained in the doctrines of the non-substantiality of things or impermanence (*anitya*), and the non-substantiality of self or 'no-self' (*anatta*), which are in turn underwritten by the doctrine of dependent co-origination (*pratītyasamutpāda*), the teaching that all things are interdependent and in constant flux. The central Buddhist doctrines of impermanence and no-self are pointers to reality as a series of ongoing processes of mutually dependent factors. If reality is of the nature of process then it follows that adequate or stable definitions are not possible, for whatever may be defined would belong to past stages of the process and never to the present reality of the process.

No-self is not only the denial of a substantial, fixed entity we call the self but also a recognition of the self and reality as processes in immanent relationship with one another in their dynamic unfolding. The 'great chain of being' is dynamically linked in a stream of creative processes in which nothing persists or endures. Since both impermanence and no-self rely on a conception of reality as a non-directional flux as opposed to a static, linear phenomenon, the doctrine of dependent co-origination is their necessary presupposition. Buddhist spiritual inquiries into the nature of 'selves and things' are thus undertaken to uproot and undo static, linear, conceptions of reality and experientially disclose to the practitioner 'things as they are' (*yathābhūtam*).

The fact that suffering is caused opens up the question of the relations between things and the world, and between the world and the self, while the claim that suffering can be extinguished necessitates the formulation of a method. As Buddhism developed, the practitioner's question 'What must I do?' was answered with differing philosophical interpretations of the interrelated nature of all things and variations on meditative spiritual methods drawing from the Buddha's fundamental insights as encapsulated in the Four Noble Truths.

With the advent of the Mahāyāna, early doctrinal formulations of the Buddha's practical philosophy were expanded and extended by Buddhist adepts to encompass the developing non-dual philosophical and spiritual issues that the Mahāyāna scriptures were generating. In discussing the overall spiritual focus of the Mahāyāna, Conze notes that 'the metaphysics of the Mahāyāna expresses a state of intoxication with the Unconditioned, and at the same time attempts to cope with it, to sober it down' (Conze, 1983, p. 202). 'Sobering down' the Unconditioned is an apt description of the deontologizing emphasis of the Mahāyāna *sūtras* where the focus is on the non-substantial nature of all things and not on directing energy to an ontologized 'absolute'.

In this chapter I will examine the non-dual deconstructive orientation of the Mahāyāna with emphasis on the philosophical underpinnings and practice developments that are of importance to Sōtō Zen. The focus here is on identifying practice instructions and teachings that serve to shift the questioner away from dualistic perceptions of the world and dichotomous ways of thinking. In other words, practice instructions and teachings that serve to deconstruct practitioners' 'erroneous' fixed perception of reality and experientially disclose reality to the seeker as Zen claims it to be: void of specific nature or own-being (*svabhāva*), without ontological substance, hence empty (*śūnya*), and in essence, not different from one's original nature or Buddha-nature (*buddhatā*).

The Mahāyāna, of course, did not come out of a vacuum, so in the course of the discussion links to early Buddhism will be noted and contrasts and comparisons to the discussion of Advaita Vedānta in the previous chapter will be made where appropriate.

Sources of the Tradition

The *Laṇkāvatāra Sūtra* and the *Vajracchedikā Prajñāpāramitā Sūtra*: 'All things ... are not independent of each other and not two'[1]

Traditionally, the *Laṇkāvatāra Sūtra* (*Laṇkā*), is held to be one of the key texts of early Chan Buddhism, purported to have been introduced into China by the first patriarch of the Chan tradition, Bodhidharma.[2] The *Laṇkā* was compiled in India during the fourth century CE and is part of the Mahāyāna Vaipulya-sūtras (Kalupahana, 1992, p. 176).

The *Prajñāpāramitā* literature consists of 38 different books that were composed in India between 100 BCE and CE 600 (Conze, 1958, p. 10) and is traditionally considered to be the originating text of the Mahāyāna. Given the Mahāyāna tenet that the fundamental characteristic of all reality is non-dual, detaching the seeker from dualistic thinking is a central concern of Mahāyāna Buddhist practice and is one of the overriding themes of the instructional dialogues and philosophical teachings of the *Prajñāpāramitā* literature. Along with the *Laṇkā*, the *Vajracchedikā Prajñāpāramitā Sūtra*[3] (hereafter *Vajra*) is also a traditional Zen reference point, associated with the enlightenment of the Sixth Patriarch and the supposed 'shift' in early Chan from the Northern school's emphasis on 'gradual' enlightenment to the Southern school's 'sudden' approach to enlightenment.[4]

To illustrate the deconstructive strategies of the above-mentioned *sūtras*, the discussion will focus on the *Laṇkā*'s negation of dualistic conceptual thinking and its distrust of words to convey 'reality-as-it-is', and the *Vajra*'s desubstantializing 'formulas' of affirmation and negation. In the course of this discussion we shall outline how both *sūtras* work to undo the reifying tendencies of language and resulting ontological commitments to such reified concepts. A strategy that is important to the development of deconstructive spiritual inquiry in Zen.[5]

Both the *Laṇkā* and the *Vajra* consist of dialogues between the Buddha and questioning *bodhisattva(s)* and both are presented in an unsystematic, fragmentary, and repetitive manner, causing pioneer English translators such as D. T. Suzuki (*Laṇkā*) and Edward Conze (*Vajra*) to label the texts as 'highly chaotic' or to conjecture an original cohesiveness that has been lost or corrupted.[6]

However, the unsystematic, fragmentary structure of the *sūtras* and the repetitive, sometimes chaotic nature of the dialogues are akin to the structures and contents of classical Chan encounter dialogues that employ similar non-linear avenues of expression to undermine the dualistic presuppositions of a seeker's question. In terms of Zen (C. Chan) deconstructive strategies, the structures and formats of the *sūtras* can be read as being rhetorical devices that serve to undermine any ontologically static meanings that could be imposed on the text and as spiritual templates for Chan/Zen patterns of discourse.

According to the Mahāyāna, all phenomena are empty, unborn, non-dual and possess no self-nature. In the second chapter of the *Laṇkā*, the Bodhisattva Mahāmati asks the Buddha to elaborate on these four fundamental Mahāyāna tenets:

> Tell me, Blessed One, how all things are empty, unborn, non-dual, and have no self-nature, so that I and other Bodhisattva-Mahāsattvas might be awakened in the teaching of emptiness, no-birth, non-duality and the absence of self-nature, and quitting the discrimination of being and non-being, quickly realise the highest enlightenment. (Suzuki, 1999, p. 65)

The Buddha responds by instructing Mahāmati to 'listen well and reflect upon what I tell you'.

> Emptiness, emptiness, indeed! Mahāmati, it is a term whose self-nature is false imagination. Because of one's attachment to false imagination, Mahāmati, we have to talk of emptiness, no-birth, non-duality, and absence of self-nature. (Suzuki, 1999, p. 65)

The Buddha begins by refusing to grant the term 'emptiness' any ontological substance. The term 'emptiness' is a concept, with a 'falsely imagined' self-nature, and it is because of attachment to these falsely imagined constructions that we have to talk about emptiness, no-birth, non-duality and absence of self-nature. Here, the Buddha warns Mahāmati of the provisional nature of all concepts and the inherent discriminating that is involved in any act of naming. The terms themselves possess no inherent substance and should not be granted any. In short, in a deconstructive move reminiscent of one of the central premises of Nāgārjuna's *MMK*, the Buddha is saying that emptiness as a term is 'empty'.

According to the Buddha, the teaching that 'all things are unborn' does not mean 'that things are not born but that they are not born of themselves', that is, that they have no intrinsic self-nature that ontologically substantializes them:

> To have no self-nature is, according to the deeper sense, to be unborn, Mahāmati. That all things are devoid of self-nature means that there is a constant and uninterrupted becoming, a momentary change from one state of existence to another; seeing this, Mahāmati, all things are destitute of self-nature. So one speaks of all things having no self-nature. (Suzuki, 1999, p. 67)

To be devoid of self-nature, i.e., to possess no enduring, changeless, substance, is to be in constant, uninterrupted becoming, in momentary change from one state of existence to another. Here the Buddha is describing reality as process and pointing to the basic Buddhist doctrines of *anitya* (impermanence) and *pratītyasamutpāda* (dependent co-origination) in which all phenomena rise and fall in a process of constant change yet in themselves possess no qualities of constancy or essence.

Thus, for the Buddha, emptiness, the unborn, and no self-nature are indicators pointing the student to the flux of reality-in-process that, properly understood, cannot be objectified into solid ontological entities. Mahāmati has asked the Buddha to explain *how* all things are 'empty, unborn, non-dual and have no self-nature so that he can stop the discrimination of being and non-being and quickly realize the highest enlightenment'. His question indicates that he has understood that discriminating between being and non-being is what is 'stopping' him from 'realizing the highest enlightenment' and that a 'correct' understanding of the 'true' nature of things (i.e., empty, unborn, non-dual, with no self-nature) would dissolve all such obstructive discrimination. There is, however, a subtle objectification of the concepts of emptiness, unborn, and so on, that the Buddha immediately moves to undermine by emphasizing the empty and provisional nature of concepts and the impermanence and constant change of all reality. The 'highest enlightenment' is not a 'thing' to be 'grasped' nor is it to be conceived in a dualistic relationship to some kind of unenlightened state. In his articulation of non-duality the Buddha makes this point clear:

> [W]hat is meant by non-duality? It means that light and shade, long and short, black and white, are relative terms, Mahāmati, and not independent of each other; as Nirvana and Samsara are, all things are not two. There is no Nirvana except where is Samsara; there is no Samsara except where is Nirvana; for the condition of existence is not of mutually-exclusive character. Therefore, it is said that all things are non-dual as are Nirvana and Samsara. (Suzuki, 1999, pp. 67–68)

'All things', says the Buddha, 'are not two.' Here the Buddha details the interdependent nature of all conceptual dualisms *including* the dualism of *nirvāṇa* and *saṃsāra*; enlightened and unenlightened. That is, reality objectified into polarized dualistic pairings is not 'reality-as-it-is', 'for the condition of existence is not of mutually-exclusive character'. Thus, like all discriminated dichotomies, the concept *nirvāṇa* cannot exist apart from its counterpart *saṃsāra*. The Buddha has 'answered' Mahāmati's question by deconstructing any objectifications he may harbour about liberation itself: liberated knowledge is knowledge free of conceptual distinctions. The undermining of *nirvāṇa* and *saṃsāra* as static dualistic entities to be attained or rejected is a pivotal Mahāyāna Buddhist deconstructive strategy that serves as the cornerstone of the logical demolition of dichotomous views in Nāgārjuna's *MMK* and the deconstructive dynamic behind much of Dōgen's phenomenological non-dual expressions.

Continuing in this deconstructive vein, the Buddha closes his answer to Mahāmati with a warning to avoid granting ontological substance to any words, even the *sūtras* themselves:

> Mahāmati, it is like unto the mirage which entices the deer with its treacherous springs, the springs are not there but the deer is attached, imagining them to be real. So with the teachings disclosed in all the sutras, they are for all beings for the gratification of their own discriminating minds. They are not truth-preserving statements meant for noble wisdom to grasp. For this reason, Mahāmati, be in conformity with the sense and be not engrossed in the word-teaching. (Suzuki, 1999, p. 68)

Even the teachings disclosed in all the *sūtras* are not 'truth-preserving statements meant for noble wisdom to grasp' and must not be taken to be 'real' in any objective sense. The Buddha's instruction to 'be in conformity with the sense and … not … the word-teaching' echoes throughout Chan and Zen teachings where there is a constant undermining of the ability of words, even the words of the *sūtras*, to convey reality-as-it-is.[7]

The Mahāyāna's concern with negating the objective status of concepts is emphasized and well illustrated in the *Vajra*'s various applications of a deconstructive affirmation–negation–affirmation 'formula' employed to highlight the provisional nature of concepts and to eliminate ontological commitment to language.

A clear example of the formula is found in the following dialogue between the Buddha and the Bodhisattva Subhuti:

> The Lord asked: What do you think, Subhuti, does it then occur to the Arhat, 'by me has Arhatship been attained'?
> Subhuti: No indeed, O Lord. And why? Because no dharma [thing] is called

> 'Arhat'. That is why he is called an Arhat. If, O Lord, it would occur to an Arhat, 'by me has Arhatship been attained', then it would be in him a seizing on a self, seizing on a being, seizing on a soul, seizing on a person. – And why? I am, O Lord, the one whom the Tathagata, the Arhat, the Fully Enlightened One has pointed out as the foremost of those who dwell in Peace. I am, O Lord, an Arhat free from greed. And yet, O Lord, it does not occur to me, 'an Arhat am I and free from greed'. If, O Lord, it could occur to me that I have attained Arhatship, then the Tathagata would not have declared of me that 'Subhuti, this son of good family, who is the foremost of those who dwell in Peace, does not dwell anywhere: that is why he is called "a dweller in Peace, a dweller in Peace"'.
>
> (Conze, 1958, p. 44)

For the purposes of this discussion, the two most significant aspects of the above passage are the Buddha's emphasis on the utilization of language without grasping (seizing), i.e., without ontological commitment, and the affirmation–negation–affirmation process in which Subhuti is affirmed to be one 'who dwells in peace', negated as one who 'dwells not anywhere', and once again affirmed 'therefore he is called a dweller in peace, a dweller in peace'.

First, Subhuti would not be a 'dweller in peace' if he were to entertain the idea that he has reached or attained some thing designated by the concept of Arhatship. If this were so, Arhatship would be seen as an absolute entity, as an attainable goal that can be reached and consolidated. Moreover, realization would then entail a way of being which would require an ontological commitment to the entity called Arhatship. If Subhuti were to conceptualize himself as an Arhat, the grasping of a self, a being, a soul, a person, would necessarily follow and this grasping would grant substance or self-nature to concepts which the Buddha has declared to be 'empty'.

Secondly, as Kalupahana points out, the affirmation–negation–affirmation process or 'formula' serves to desubstantialize concepts while retaining their pragmatic use (Kalupahana, 1992, p. 156). Here, the raft simile used in the early discourses of the Buddha and reiterated in the *Vajra* can also be invoked: concepts and therefore language are to be used as one would use a raft, to 'cross over' the 'ocean of suffering', but not to be held as absolute truths (Conze, 1958, p. 34).

In contrast to the attempt to be as comprehensive as possible, as found in the vast *Abhidharma* texts which utilized enumeration, classification and synthesis to bring out the pragmatic meaning of concepts, the *Vajra* advances the more succinct, concentrated method of applying the above-mentioned desubstantializing formula to selected concepts with the aim of cutting off all arbitrary conceptions and thereby breaking down all forms of absolutist metaphysics.

To move beyond the 'static' standpoints of affirmation and negation the *Vajra* presents us with variations on a threefold dynamic process: this is A; this is no-A; 'therefore it is called A'. Here, thesis and antithesis are held in tension rather than working toward resolution, and then restated in quotation marks indicating a 'new energized' status.[8] This last 'restatement' has at least two functions; first, it dissolves any idea of substance or absolute meaning by showing the pragmatic and non-substantial nature of concepts, and secondly, it indicates a moving away from dualities and dichotomies by placing concepts and entities in dynamic restatement, thereby affirming process rather than solid ideas of substance.

In the application of this desubstantializing formula, the student is required to hold two apparently contradictory views simultaneously in mind. The statement of a thesis immediately followed by its antithesis produces a tension wherein suddenly the concept in question cannot be epistemologically 'grasped' or ontologically 'labelled', and, if one cannot 'get it' through knowing or naming, then the process by which meaning is constructed is brought into question. The seemingly solid semantic structures of language are undermined and 'undone'; in other words, 'universal propositions are [therefore] denied meaning by subverting the basic paradigms through which meaning in language is generated' (Doherty, 1983, p. 123).

The interplay of affirmation and negation to deontologize concepts is reiterated throughout the *Vajra*. This abstract point becomes clearer, and more relevant to a spiritual aspirant, when we look at the application of the desubstantializing formula to the concept of the Buddha's teaching or '*dharma*':

> The Lord asked: What do you think Subhuti, does it occur to the Tathagata, 'by me has Dharma been demonstrated'? Whosoever, Subhuti, would say, 'the Tathagata has demonstrated Dharma', he would speak falsely, he would misrepresent me by seizing on what is not there. And why, 'Demonstration of dharma, demonstration of dharma', Subhuti, there is not any Dharma which could be got at as a demonstration of Dharma. (Conze, 1958, p. 61)

Thus, whoever claims that the Buddha has demonstrated the *dharma* is misrepresenting the Buddha's teaching by 'seizing on what is not there', i.e., attaching ontological substance to the teaching which is by nature free of such objectifications. Here, the Buddha is reiterating that, in itself, the *dharma*, like the Arhat, is not a 'thing' that can be reified and consolidated. Hence affirmation ('demonstration of dharma'), reaffirmation ('demonstration of dharma'), and negation ('there is not any Dharma which could be got at as a demonstration of Dharma') lead to an emptying of the concept '*dharma*'. In this instance, the Buddha is undoing the reification of *dharma* as a thing that can be 'got at', i.e., attained or grasped by the student or bestowed by the teacher.

In the *Prajñāpāramitā* literature, the Bodhisattva path is communicated by negating all metaphysical absolutes that could be misconstrued or 'fixed' as being substantial entities. Central Buddhist notions are affirmed then negated and then restated in various patterns of affirmation and negation to empty them of all substantial ontology: 'the path itself is said to be a no-path, or a non-coursing; the Buddha's position is described as having no place to stand, his teaching as no-words and the attainment of enlightenment is actually a no-attainment' (Streng, 1987, p. 154). From the practitioner's point of view 'yes' becomes 'no' and then becomes 'yes' again in a constantly shifting configuration of meanings and structures, leaving the seeker with no ontological certainty or support.

In the light of this, the Buddha encapsulates the unsupported 'thought of perfect enlightenment' in the *Vajra* by the following teaching:

> Bodhi-being the great being, after he has got rid of all perceptions, should raise his thought to the utmost, right and perfect enlightenment. He should produce a thought which is unsupported by forms, sounds, smells, tastes, touchables, or mind-objects, unsupported by dharma, unsupported by no-dharma, unsupported by anything and why? All supports have actually no support. (Conze, 1958, p. 54)

According to the Buddha, 'all supports have actually no support' and this is the deconstructive rationale of the *Prajñāpāramitā*'s 'attack' on all possible objectifications and reifications of *dharma* in which no 'support' is spared. (There is also a paradox of expressibility here – 'all supports have actually no support' hence no support is their support – that Nāgārjuna and later Dōgen will exploit to deconstructive ends.)

As we have seen, the deconstructive processes of these *sūtras* not only target substantialized elements of Buddhist thought but also focus on deconstructing reifications of the Buddhist path itself. The *Laṇkā*'s distrust of words to represent reality is extended to the words of the *sūtras* themselves, and the *Vajra*'s deconstruction of reified concepts includes Buddhist teachings or *dharma*. The deconstructive strategies of the *Laṇkā* and the *Vajra* thus 'spare no ontological support' that a practitioner may attempt to uphold.

In doing this, the *sūtras* point to the radical deconstruction of reified conceptions of Buddhist teaching that is at the heart of the Zen 'outside of words and letters' maxim and provide the 'authority' for Dōgen's reinterpretations and sometimes radical rewritings of standard Buddhist doctrine in the *Shōbōgenzō*. This deontologizing strategy is also one of the underpinnings of Nāgārjuna's critical analysis of substantialized conceptions of the Buddhist path in the *MMK* in which the Buddha's non-dual insights are dialectically stripped of all reifying and objectifying tendencies that practitioners may foster.

Nāgārjuna (c. 113–213): '*Saṃsāra* is nothing essentially different from *nirvāṇa*. *Nirvāṇa* is nothing essentially different from *saṃsāra*'[9]

In the *Sagāthakam* section of the *Laṇkāvatāra Sūtra*, the Buddha foretells of Nāgārjuna's life and teachings by announcing that a 'Bihikshu most illustrious and distinguished' by the name Nāgāhvaya will be born. He will be the 'destroyer of the one-sided views based on being and non-being' and 'he will declare My Vehicle, the unsurpassed Mahāyāna to the world' (Suzuki, 1999, pp. 239–240).

This traditional story exemplifies the spiritual and philosophical thrust of Nāgārjuna's master work the *Mūlamadhyamakakārikās* (*Fundamental Verses of the Middle Way*, *MMK*): to refute one-sided views based on dichotomous conceptualizations. Following the Buddha, Nāgārjuna did not accept 'the two views of the world in terms of being and non-being and the bifurcation of entities into existence and non-existence' (*MMK* XV:7). For the Mādhyamika, reality is a dynamic 'not-two' (*advaya*) in which 'neither being nor non-being is to be taken hold of'.[10] Hence, the philosophical and liberative project of the *MMK* is to expose the inconsistencies and contradictions of dualistic one-sided views that are subject to the extremes of being and non-being. Like the Vedāntic exponents, Nāgārjuna makes no claim to establish or argue for an independent philosophical position. Rather, his undertaking is to recover the 'middle way' of the Buddha's teachings from the philosophical abstractions of substantialism and absolutism.

Lindtner notes that Nāgārjuna's philosophical works were 'planned as textbooks for monks who had completed their courses in traditional Buddhist dogmatics (*Abhidharma*)' (Lindtner, 1997, p. 356). Writing for practitioners some seven centuries after the death of the Buddha, Nāgārjuna's texts presuppose a knowledge of foundational Buddhist tenets and the systematizations and classifications of the voluminous *Abhidharma* corpus. In the *MMK*, described by Lindtner (1997, p. 364) as a 'revolutionary manual of meditation', Nāgārjuna confronted the dangers of reification that practitioner misconceptions of the *Abhidharma* systems may have fostered.

The chapters of the *MMK* are generally constructed as a critical investigation (*parīkṣā*) of one or more views (*ḍṛṣi*) put forward by various Buddhist schools. According to Nāgārjuna, the dualistic trap of ontologically substantializing one side of a dichotomy at the expense of the other is inherent in all understandings of reality framed in terms of existence and nonexistence. To this end, by means of a process of refutation that works on the dynamic of identity and difference and a critical dialectic in the form of a *reductio ad absurdum* (*prasaṅga*), Nāgārjuna employs his non-dual analytical method to show conceptual dichotomies (*vikalpa*) to be an extreme view 'deriving from discursive development (*prapañca*) and related to either eternalism or nihilism, the twin extreme positions that the Middle Way eschews by its very definition' (Ruegg, 1977, p. 9).

Working with the presupposition of the core Buddhist doctrine of dependent co-origination (*pratītyasamutpāda*), Nāgārjuna applies this means of analysis to opponents' views on concepts such as causality, time, and self (*ātman*) and abstractions of key Buddhist categories such as the fully enlightened one (*tathāgata*), the Four Noble Truths, and *Nirvāṇa* (among others). In this way, Nāgārjuna follows the *Prajñāpāramitā Sūtras*' deontologizing orientation by attempting to undo any forms of 'subtle self-seeking' that practitioners may attach to Buddhist doctrine. In their traditional settings, 'the verses [of the *MMK*] were learned by heart, discussed, and the content acquired by solitary meditation' (Lindtner, 1997, p. 356). Hence, from the practitioner's point of view, the *MMK* is a text to be engaged with in discussion and internalized in practice.[11]

Nāgārjuna opens the *MMK* by paying homage to the Buddha and saluting the teaching of dependent co-origination (*pratītyasamutpāda*)[12] as 'the blissful cessation of all phenomenal thought constructions' wherein 'every event is marked by':

> non-origination, non-extinction,
> non-destruction, non-permanence,
> non-identity, non-differentiation,
> non-coming (into being), non-going (out of being).
>
> (Inada, 1970, p. 39)

These dedicatory verses set the tone and intent of the *MMK*. First, Nāgārjuna identifies the key doctrine of dependent co-origination. Second, by introducing the text from the standpoint of the Buddha, the ultimate standpoint, Nāgārjuna presupposes the doctrine of the 'two truths': conventional (*saṃvṛti-satya*) and ultimate (*paramārtha-satya*), which are central to understanding the Mādhyamika. Third, the four negative oppositional pairings or the 'eight negations' that open the *MMK* alert us to the importance of the Mādhyamika tenet that everything lacks independent existence (*niḥsvabhāvatā*) and illustrate Nāgārjuna's understanding of the pivotal doctrine of emptiness (*śūnyatā*), which 'epitomizes the teaching for subsequent generations of Buddhist thinkers' (Streng, 1987, p. 155). In Nāgārjuna's analysis, these key tenets are interrelated and a correct understanding of their non-dual, non-substantialized nature constitutes the middle way of liberative insight.

Nāgārjuna's emphasis on 'right understanding' of Buddhist doctrines echoes throughout the *MMK*. As one of the principles of the Noble Eightfold Path, 'right view' or right understanding is essential for practising the Buddha's middle way. Like the classical Advaita emphasis on correct understanding and interpretation of foundational texts, Nāgārjuna was also concerned to interpret the Buddha's teaching correctly. Aside from the introductory and concluding salutations to the Buddha, one of the clearest indications of Nāgārjuna's concern to demonstrate that he is true to the Buddha's teachings comes in *MMK* XV where he defines the concept of self-nature and argues against the dualistic bifurcation of entities. In doing this he aligns his exposition with the *Kaccāyanagotta-sutta* (*Discourse to Kātyāyana*)[13] in which the Buddha argues that to assert the self-nature of things is to fall into reification while to assert their nonexistence is to fall into nihilism. In this context, Bugault notes that 'very often, Nāgārjuna is only actualizing the practical teaching of the ancient texts, but in the face of a new situation, Buddhist scholasticism' (Bugault, 1983, p. 51).

Nāgārjuna defines self-nature (*svabhāva*)[14] as 'something which cannot be made and has no mutual correspondence with something else' and which has no 'varying character' (XV:2, XV:8). *Svabhāva* is thus uncaused, unchanging, and has no dependence on another.[15] Hence, for the Mādhyamika, no entity has intrinsic self-nature for that would mean that it is substantial, non-relational and fixed, when, according to the doctrine of dependent co-origination, all entities are non-substantial, relative and in constant flux. To adhere to the notion of inherent self-nature is to reify reality and it is reified views of reality that Nāgārjuna is refuting in the *MMK*.

In the course of the *MMK*, Nāgārjuna issues several 'warnings' to alert practitioners to the substantializing trap of reifying pivotal Buddhist insights by 'falling to the extreme' of 'is-ing' them, i.e., granting them ontological status. In the first of these warnings that we will consider, Nāgārjuna cautions against reifying *nirvāṇa*, the goal of Buddhist practice, by conceptualizing it as a self-substantialized entity. In his *Examination of Bondage and Release* (*MMK* XVI:9), Nāgārjuna states: 'Those who delight in maintaining, "Without the grasping, I will realize nirvana; Nirvana is in me;" are the very ones with the greatest grasping.'

Here, Nāgārjuna is pointing out two potential reifications: the conceptualization of a substantial self that will continue as a subject from *saṃsāra* into *nirvāṇa*, and the grasping of *nirvāṇa* as an attainable goal that is inherently distinct from *saṃsāra*.[16] Most importantly, Nāgārjuna is also warning that the grasping after *nirvāṇa* is 'the greatest grasping'[17] and one of the biggest obstacles to realizing emptiness. In this verse, Nāgārjuna is both steering practitioners away from substantialized ontologies and pointing out that attempting to 'grasp' *nirvāṇa* is to grant it a self-nature, i.e., to reify it as an 'entity' that can be 'attained'. The practitioner is thus adhering to a notion of inherent self-nature which Nāgārjuna 'corrects' in this warning. According to Nāgārjuna, no entity, *nirvāṇa* included, possesses a substantial, non-relational, self-nature and to grant such substance is to fall into ignorance (*avidyā*).

But the situation is more complex: to state that no entity has intrinsic self-nature is to fall into the extreme of 'is not'. In *MMK* XV:6, Nāgārjuna issues a warning against such dualistic thinking by stating that if phenomena are viewed in the structures of binary concepts as 'self-nature' and 'other-nature' (*parabhāva*)[18] or 'existence' and 'nonexistence' then the 'real truth in the Buddha's teaching cannot be perceived'. In other words, if one thinks in absolutized polarized dichotomies such as 'existence' versus 'nonexistence' then core Buddhist doctrines such as dependent co-origination, impermanence, emptiness, and liberation itself would be unintelligible.

Nāgārjuna's equation of emptiness (*śūnyatā*) and dependent co-origination or relational origination (*pratītyasamutpāda*) in *MMK* XXIV:18, serves to illustrate the interrelated nature of these key tenets and underwrite the necessary understandings that the text is pointing the practitioner to. According to Nāgārjuna, all that is dependently co-originated is empty and understanding this constitutes the 'middle path':

> We declare that whatever is relational origination is *śūnyatā*. It is a provisional name (i.e., thought construction) for the mutuality (of being) and, indeed, it is the middle path. [Furthermore:] Any factor of experience which does not participate in relational origination cannot exist. Therefore, any factor of experience not in the nature of *śūnya* cannot exist. (*MMK* XXIV:19)

For Nāgārjuna, to be dependently co-arisen, as all things are, is to be empty and to be empty, as all things are, is to have no self-nature (*svabhāva*). However, the terms themselves are not to be mistaken for the processes that they are pointing to. According to Nāgārjuna, 'dependent co-origination' and 'emptiness' as terms are provisional. That is, like all linguistic conceptualizations they have a pragmatic use but are themselves empty and should not be granted any substantializing ontology. In short, as terms, they are conventional truth (*saṃvṛti-satya*). Conventional truth is, however, a 'truth' (*satya*) and, as we shall see, does not have a trivial function in Nāgārjuna's thought.

The provisional status and pragmatic function of discourse brings us to Nāgārjuna's exposition of the 'two truths': conventional (*saṃvṛti-satya*) and ultimate (*paramārtha-satya*). In Chapter XXIV, one of the pivotal sections of the *MMK*, Nāgārjuna explains the relationship between emptiness, dependent co-origination, and the middle way in the light of the two truths. In verses 1–6, Nāgārjuna responds to a hypothetical opponent who protests that if everything is *śūnya*, as Nāgārjuna asserts, then not only would the everyday world be nonexistent but the Four Noble Truths (*āryasatya*), the Three Treasures (*buddha*, *dharma* and *saṅgha*), and the possibility of liberation itself would not exist.

Nāgārjuna retorts that his opponent does not understand the 'real purpose of *śūnyatā*, [and] its nature and meaning' and is therefore condemned to 'frustration and hindrance of understanding' (verse 7). According to Nāgārjuna, the root problem is that, first, his opponent does not understand that 'whatever is dependently co-originated is empty' (verse 18) and second, that experiential events can *only* take place by participating in the empty nature of dependent co-origination (verse 19). In short, the doctrines of emptiness and dependent co-origination do not destroy the Four Noble Truths but provide the very means by which they can be accounted for, i.e., the only way that they can be *practised.*

In verse 24 Nāgārjuna makes this point clear: 'If the way to enlightenment possesses self-nature, then its practice will not be possible. But if the way is practiced, your assertion of a way involving self-nature is inadmissible (i.e., cannot exist).' For Nāgārjuna, the correct understanding of dependent co-origination leads to the correct practice and understanding of the Four Noble Truths themselves: 'One who rightly discerns relational origination will, indeed, rightly discern universal suffering, its origination, its extinction, and the way to enlightenment' (verse 40).

However, 'rightly discerning relational origination' is connected to understanding the relationship between the conventional and the ultimate and emptiness. Nāgārjuna explains the connection in the following verses:

> *XXIV:8.* The teaching of the *Dharma* by the various *Buddhas* is based on the two truths; namely, the relative (worldly) truth and the absolute (supreme) truth.
>
> *9.* Those who do not understand the distinction between the two truths cannot understand the profound nature of the Buddha's teaching.
>
> *10.* Without relying on everyday practices (i.e., relative truths), the absolute truth cannot be expressed. Without approaching the absolute truth *nirvāṇa* cannot be attained.
>
> *11.* A wrongly conceived *śūnyatā* can ruin a slow-witted person. It is like a badly seized snake or a wrongly executed incantation.

In verses 18 and 19 (quoted above), Nāgārjuna both affirmed the basic Buddhist tenet that the world 'is' because of interrelated conditions and stressed that emptiness is not nonexistence but *interdependent* existence. This crucial non-dual distinction, alluded to in verse 9 (above), also applies to his exposition of the two truths. In accordance with the Mādhyamika emphasis on not falling to extremes, in verse 10, Nāgārjuna states that the relative and the absolute should be understood in relationship, that is, the absolute relies on the relative for its expression but without the absolute *nirvāṇa* is not a possibility. The two truths are 'not two' (*advaya*) and the ultimate is not taught apart from the conventional or relative. Thus to realize emptiness as the highest insight into the nature of things is not, as Streng notes, 'to reject conventional, conditioned existence (*saṁskṛta*) as if it were reality qualitatively different from absolute, unconditioned reality (*asaṃskṛta*)' (Streng, 1971, p. 265).

The point hinges on right understanding of emptiness. In verse 11, Nāgārjuna warns against reifying emptiness into a self-substantiated reality by stating that a mistakenly ontologized emptiness can 'backfire' or 'turn around and bite'. Nāgārjuna emphasizes this in verse 14 where he states that emptiness makes all things possible: 'Whatever is in correspondence with *śūnyatā*, all is in correspondence (i.e., possible). Again, whatever is not in correspondence with *śūnyatā*, all is not in correspondence.'

If emptiness 'works', i.e., if it is not hindered by mistaken ontologizing, then the necessary corollary of dependent co-origination is 'working', and, by extension, all things 'work'. In other words, in emptiness all things are possible. 'Emptiness', cautions Nāgārjuna, 'should not be regarded as another viewpoint or some self-substantiated reality opposite to non-emptiness' (Streng, 1967, p. 84) and it is the basic function of the critical dialectic that Nāgārjuna uses throughout the *MMK*, to steer the practitioner away from any attachment to a self-existing reality.

In keeping with the Mādhyamika insistence on the non-substantiality of all views and entities, Nāgārjuna issues his most important caution against the reification of emptiness in *MMK* XIV:8.

> The wise men (i.e., enlightened ones) have said that *śūnyatā* or the nature of thusness is the relinquishing of all false views. Yet it is said that those who adhere to the idea or concept of *śūnyatā* are incorrigible. (Inada, 1970, p. 93)

The significance of recognizing that all things are empty is not that it substitutes one concept for another, which is the basis of the Buddhist critique of Śaṅkara's concept of *brahman*, but to develop an attitude that frees one from attachment to any single idea or experience while not rejecting all ideas and experiences for some projected opposite. In this view, all phenomena participate in the empty dynamic of dependent co-origination. For the practitioner, understanding how experiential factors come to be is thus a key factor in understanding emptiness.

Like Gauḍapāda, Nāgārjuna is concerned with the problem of origination, how an experiential event comes to be. Based on the absolute undifferentiated pure being of *brahman*, the Advaita answer is that nothing really originates, the world that we perceive as contingent and changing is appearance and is seen as such once *brahmajñāna* dawns. From a Mādhyamika point of view, to posit an entity with such an absolute 'self-nature' like *brahman* would render all 'things', including the Buddhist path, as fixed and substantial hence unintelligible and impossible. For the Mādhyamika, absolute, undifferentiated, being would mean that nothing could change and if nothing can change then nothing can exist. For the Advaitin, the fact that nothing can change means that nothing but *brahman* exists and this is the insight to be realized.

These diametrically opposed views of causality, the Advaita non-origination (*ajātivāda*) and the Mādhyamika dependent co-origination (*pratītyasamutpāda*), work on different philosophical templates. Because only *brahman* is really 'real', the Advaitin works to undo practitioners' erroneous views of reality through the categories of reality and appearance. The aim being to disclose empirical reality as appearance and to establish the absolutely 'real' status of *brahman*. However, for Nāgārjuna, to posit (for example) 'emptiness' as reality and empirical reality as appearance would be to substantialize emptiness and fall to one side of the absolute-versus-relative dichotomy. Nāgārjuna's analysis aims to undo ontologized conceptualizations with the aim of disclosing reality as dynamically interdependent. Hence, Nāgārjuna works to undo practitioners' erroneous views of reality through the notions of identity and difference and 'commonsense' procedures of identification.

For Nāgārjuna, the crux of the matter, once again, rests on insight into the 'way things are', i.e., dependently co-originated. All that exists, becomes, and that which becomes is in process; that is, strictly speaking, entities can be identified neither as themselves nor as other. As Nāgārjuna's 'principle of reason, dependent co-origination is directly opposed to the principle of identity' (Bugault, 1983, p. 46). Hence, for Nāgārjuna, 'relational existence admits of neither identity nor difference, therefore it is neither nonexistent in time (interruption) nor permanent (constancy)' (*MMK* XVIII:10). In the light of this, Nāgārjuna challenges his opponents to 'show him' identity and difference and/or to 'prove to him' that such claims about identity and difference are valid.

According to Bugault (1983, p. 23), Nāgārjuna's dialectic seeks to capture his opponents between two arms of a pincer called 'show me (*na vidyate*)/prove to me (*na yujyate*)'. He offers the following table to illustrate this:

Table 3.1

Show me what you're speaking about	Prove your point to me, justify what you say
Alas, you cannot show it to me; it can not be found anywhere (*na vidyate*). An appeal to haecceity.	What you say is not logically coherent (*na yujyate*). It does not 'come out right' (*nopapadyate*)
Extrinsic coherence: a prohibition against speaking against imaginary entities, which are never given in critically analysed experience. Denouncing such pseudo-entities: this does not exist (*nāstī*). The critique of pseudo-identity.	Intrinsic coherence: the obligation to avoid contradiction.
The verdict of experience.	The verdict of reason.

According to this analysis, Nāgārjuna is 'squeezing his adversaries' between the 'twin pincers' of the factual or the experiential (show me) and the rational or logical (prove to me). Bugault offers a philological inventory of the *MMK* which accounts for 88 occurrences of the logical 'prove to me' and 74 occurrences of the experiential 'show me'. Bugault's philological analysis is detailed and outside the scope of this study, but in terms of this discussion the point of interest is his assertion that 'the empirical analysis of the Buddhist discipline does count considerably in Nāgārjuna's dialectic'. In Bugault's view, this is most apparent in Nāgārjuna's analysis of the problems of identity and haecceity (Bugault, 1983, p. 24).

How Nāgārjuna approaches the problem of identity and difference is crucial to his understanding of the interrelated tenets of absence of self-nature, dependent co-origination, and emptiness. In plain terms, according to these interrelated teachings, the attempt to 'pin down' dependent co-originated entities and examine them is impossible, because there is no stable, inherent, self-essence to grasp hold of and examine. For Nāgārjuna, the very act of grasping is reification. Therefore, from the point of view of the inquiring practitioner, the attempt to grasp any entity is to grant it intrinsic self-nature and is incompatible with insight into reality as it is. When the essence, i.e., the very 'thingness', of entities is 'broken down' by analysing how they are identified as 'that' thing and not as another 'thing' then the practitioner discovers that such essences and such entities are experientially 'unfindable'.

Bugault summarizes the challenge that Nāgārjuna issues to his opponents thus: 'If there are essences (*bhāva*), individual natures, or entities in themselves (*svabhāva*), then show them to me. These alleged entities (*bhāva*) of yours, it is up to you to find them. Otherwise they are unfindable' (Bugault, 1983, p. 48).

This challenge to commonsense dualistic empirical assumptions echoes throughout Buddhist discourse and is put into action in Zen teachings. 'Show me this enlightened nature of yours!' and 'What is it?' are common Zen challenges employed to counter practitioners' reifications of the path.[19] Further, by placing the onus on practitioners to 'pin down' this alleged 'self' that they claim is or is not enlightened, fixed ideas of identity and difference (that Nāgārjuna logically 'undid') are juxtaposed in dynamic relationship by Zen masters and phenomenologically deconstructed in the actual experience of the practitioner. Reading Nāgārjuna in this way highlights the experiential challenge that the *MMK* presents without de-emphasizing the logical thrust of the text.

In a commentary on this point, the Dalai Lama expands on this deconstructive reading by explaining the inevitable unfindable endpoint of reductive analysis:

> whenever we examine physical, mental, or abstract entities, we find as a result of reductive analysis nothing but their unfindability. So you can't really speak coherently of identity or of entities. This is the fundamental teaching of Mādhyamika. (Garfield, 1995, p. 252, fn. 97)

Ultimately, all of the commonsense entities that correspond with practical functions and designations such as 'I', 'me', and 'mine' cannot actually be found.[20] In other words, according to Nāgārjuna, they are devoid of inherent substantializing self-nature and empty. Under critical examination, objectified abstractions about reality are seen to be attempts to 'grasp' or reify reality which, ultimately, cannot be grasped. Nāgārjuna strikes at the heart of the matter in XV: 10:

> Existence is the grasping of permanency (i.e., permanent characteristics) and non-existence is the perception of disruption. (As these functions are not strictly possible), the wise should not rely upon (the concepts) of existence and non-existence.

Since we cannot 'rely upon' the concepts of existence or nonexistence or adhere to 'is' or 'is not' without falling into reification, Nāgārjuna employs the classical Indian notion of the four alternative positions (*koṭi*) or tetralemma in the service of exhausting 'all conceptually imaginable positions about the nature of a postulated entity and its predicate'.[21] Ruegg notes that the term tetralemma (*catuṣkoṭi*) 'is not actually employed by Nāgārjuna in the *MMK* but the four positions of the tetralemma frequently appear [in the *MMK* and other early

Mādhyamika literature][22] where they are usually negated either explicitly or implicitly' (Ruegg, 1977, pp. 1, 3). Thus, in Ruegg's reading, the four positions of the tetralemma – positive; negative; a conjunction of positive and negative; and a bi-negation of the positive and negative – are employed in the *MMK* to reject all possible positions that can be adopted about the ontological position of something.

Thus in *MMK* XXII:11, when Nāgārjuna declares 'nothing could be asserted to be *śūnya* [empty], *aśūnya* [non-empty], both *śūnya* and *aśūnya*, and neither *śūnya* nor *aśūnya*. They are asserted only for the purpose of provisional understanding', he is applying the 'basic Mādhyamika method' to establish the 'inapplicability of any imaginable conceptual position ... that might be taken as the subject of an existential proposition and become one of a set of binary doctrinal examples (*antadvaya*)' (Ruegg, 1977, p. 9).

In Garfield's (1995) analysis 'this negative tetralemma is a crucial verse for understanding the relation between discourse on the conventional level and the understanding of emptiness or the ultimate truth'. Here, Nāgārjuna is claiming that nothing can be said of emptiness from the ultimate standpoint, for ultimately there is no substantial entity of which the terms empty, not-empty and their combinations can be predicated. These designations are just 'terms', i.e., they are provisional; perhaps we can say that they are pragmatically useful but that is all. For Garfield, the 'central claim in this verse is that all assertion, is, at best nominally true' and 'discourse about the ultimate character of things is not exempt from this generalization'. Predication always requires an entity of which the predicate can be true and the emptiness of phenomena accounts for no such self-existing entities (Garfield, 1995, p. 280).

According to Nāgārjuna, because things possess no inherent self-nature, they are empty. Hence there are no self-existing entities to predicate any assertion on. The point is not that everything is nonexistent (this would be falling to an extreme) but rather that everything is interdependently coexistent by virtue of lack of self-nature. Thus, the choice between any of Nāgārjuna's paired oppositional 'extremes' (permanent and impermanent and so on) 'is only binding for someone who persists in postulating substances as the subjects of becoming' (Bugault, 1983, p. 41). In short, for the practitioner, substantializing entities and ascribing an ontology to emptiness is the crux of the problem. To convey this insight to practitioners and to undo mistaken views about things, a non-dual dynamic is needed that can function at the interface of dichotomous pairings without falling to one extreme or the other. This is one of the functions of the tetralemma in the *MMK*; in particular, the positions of the positive and negative conjunctions and the bi-negation.

As discussed above, Nāgārjuna uses the tetralemma to negate all conceptually imaginable positions about the nature of a postulated entity and its predicate. Hence one of the functions of the tetralemma is to place us outside of ontologized views of things. However, when viewed through the prism of the non-duality of the two truths, the dynamic of the tetralemma, especially the both/and contradiction and the neither/nor bi-negation, highlights a paradox that deconstructive methods of spiritual inquiry ignites in the experience of the practitioner by undermining 'two valued' lines of either is or is not oppositional thinking. This shift into seemingly contradictory modes of thought is not meant to remove or resolve paradox, but rather to experientially place the practitioner in a cognitive interface wherein 'both/and' and 'neither/nor' configurations can coexist within the practitioner's awareness without contradiction. This contention will be examined and explained in part two of this study; what is important here is to note Garfield and Priest's contention that Nāgārjuna's analysis works at the limits of thought and that 'people are driven to contradictions in charting the limits of thought, precisely because those limits themselves are contradictory. Hence any theory of the limits that is anywhere near adequate will be inconsistent' (Garfield and Priest, 2003, p. 3). In many ways, the interplay between the two truths and the subsequent contradictions and paradox that can be generated from the both/and and neither/nor combinations that Nāgārjuna (and Zen masters after him) highlights is pivotal to understanding the deontologizing strategies of the *MMK* and the deconstructive strategies of Zen teachings.

The 'not two' of the two truths is recognized in Garfield and Priest's understanding of Nāgārjuna's use of positive and negative tetralemmas and their relationship to conventional (*saṃvṛti-satya*) and ultimate truth (*paramārtha-satya*). Garfield notes that 'Nāgārjuna makes use both of positive and negative tetralemmas and uses this distinction in mood to mark the difference between the perspectives of the two truths' (Garfield and Priest, 2003, p. 13). As an example of a positive tetralemma, asserted from the conventional perspective, he gives *MMK* XVIII:6: 'The Buddhas have provisionally employed the term *ātman* and instructed on the true idea of *anātman*. They have also taught that any (abstract) entity as *ātman* or *anātman* does not exist.' Garfield's gloss on this is: provisionally, or conventionally, there is a self that we all recognize. But ultimately, there is no self as the Buddha instructed in the 'true idea of *anātman*'. Selves exist conventionally and are empty. Selves don't exist ultimately. But these are exactly the same thing. According to this reading, this verse 'affirms the two truths and demonstrates that we can talk coherently about both, and about their relationship *from the conventional perspective*' (Garfield and Priest, 2003, pp. 13–14, my italics).

The negative tetralemmas, which Garfield describes as 'distinctly Nāgārjunian' are representative of the contradictory situation that we are in when the ultimate perspective is taken. *MMK* XXII:11, discussed above, is given as an example of a negative tetralemma. Revisiting the discussion above, in the light of Garfield's analysis, when Nāgārjuna states that 'nothing could be asserted to be *śūnya*, *aśūnya*, both *śūnya* and *aśūnya*, and neither *śūnya* nor *aśūnya*. They are asserted only for the purpose of provisional understanding', he is 'discussing what can't be said from the ultimate perspective – from a point of view transcendent of the conventional'. Here, it seems nothing can be said, 'in fact we can't even say that nothing can be said. But we just did. And we have thereby characterized the ultimate perspective, which if we are correct in our characterization, can't be done' (Garfield and Priest, 2003, p. 14). This paradox 'makes sense' if we remember that, for Nāgārjuna, all assertion is at best nominally true, *including* discourse about the ultimate character of things. As such it is as close as we can get to describing the non-dual empty nature of 'things as they are'.

In keeping with this non-dual perspective, according to Garfield and Priest, the positive and negative tetralemmas say the same thing: 'each describes completely (although from different directions) the relationship between the two truths'. The positive tetralemma 'asserts that conventional phenomena exist conventionally and can be characterized from that perspective, and that ultimately nothing exists or satisfies any description'. The negative counterpart 'asserts the same thing: that existence and characterization make sense at, and only at, the conventional level, and that, at the ultimate level, nothing exists or satisfies any description. But in doing so it contradicts itself, it asserts its own non-assertability' (Garfield and Priest, 2003, p. 14). This 'paradox of expressibility' is implicit in the attempt to conventionally describe or characterize anything which is claimed to be beyond description or characterization (an empty ultimate), in that such a descriptive attempt pushes the very limits of the conventional processes that bind it.

From the point of view of the practitioner, to perceive all things as dependently co-originated or empty requires a shift from the conventional mode of perception that binds one to an ontologized, reified view. 'Conventional experience divides the world into likes and dislikes, desires and fears, and "you" and "me" as separate entities. This hides the fact that these perceptions can only exist in interrelationship' (Streng, 1987, p. 155). For the practitioner, Nāgārjuna's most vivid example of the kind of shift that this understanding requires is found in his radical non-dual equation of *saṃsāra* and *nirvāṇa* in *MMK* XXV:19: '*Saṃsāra* (i.e., the empirical life–death cycle) is nothing essentially different from *nirvāṇa*. *Nirvāṇa* is nothing essentially different from *saṃsāra*.' *Saṃsāra* and *nirvāṇa* have the same essential nature – no nature – like all things they share the same empty natures. Furthermore, their 'limits' or spheres of influence also share this empty nature and are not different: 'The limits (i.e., realm) of *nirvāṇa* are the limits of *saṃsāra*. Between the two, also, there is not the slightest difference whatsoever' (*MMK* XXV:20).

Hence, liberation is not overcoming the bondage of *saṃsāra* and achieving freedom in *nirvāṇa*; such a view is a dualistic reification of both the path and the goal of Buddhist practice. *Saṃsāra* and *nirvāṇa* are not-two. *Nirvāṇa* is not a separate realm for the practitioner to aspire to; it is right here in the midst of *saṃsāra*. The conventional is the only means to the ultimate, moreover, properly understood, there is no difference between them. This is a pivotal non-dual insight that, as we shall see, is mobilized in Zen thought and practice.

Nāgārjuna's claim to reject all possible positions and refute all views via the critical dialectic while putting forward no position of his own is referred to by several commentators as a kind of 'philosophical slight of hand'.[23] Stafford Betty calls it 'a word game' (Stafford Betty, 1983, p. 125) and Streng remarks that 'in some instances [Nāgārjuna's] analysis is simply a play on words' (Streng, 1967, pp. 181–182), while Robinson likens Nāgārjuna's method to playing a 'shell game' in the sense that 'its elements are few and its operations are simple though performed with lightning speed and great dexterity. And the very fact that [one] cannot quite follow each move reinforces the observer's conviction that there is a trick somewhere' (Robinson, 1972, p. 325).

In a sense, these critiques are correct. Nāgārjuna does play a deconstructive 'shell game' in the *MMK* with the two truths. Nāgārjuna tells us that 'there are two truths, that they are one; that everything both exists and does not exist; that nothing is existent or non-existent; and that he rejects all philosophical views including his own; that he asserts nothing' (Garfield and Priest, 2003, p. 1). On the conventional level, Nāgārjuna claims to assert nothing because he is merely exposing wrong views and recovering the Buddha's teachings, but on an ultimate level he claims to assert nothing because, in empty reality, ultimately nothing *can* be asserted (or, for that matter, denied). The added twist to this is that, in essence, the conventional and the ultimate are not different. In this sense, not only does Nāgārjuna run up against the limits of what we can express but also he pushes the boundaries of what we can think.

Aside from the paradox of expressibility that Nāgārjuna's analysis generates, Garfield and Priest also identify an ontological paradox that Nāgārjuna's thought reveals and explores 'that is intimately connected to the paradox of expressibility, yet quite distinct', and which 'brings a new insight into ontology and into our cognitive access to the world' (Garfield and Priest, 2003, p. 2).

The ontological paradox centres on Nāgārjuna's fundamental tenet of the absence of self-nature. Based on this, and the 'purely negative character of the property of emptiness', Garfield and Priest argue that, according to Nāgārjuna:

'If all things lack self-nature then it turns out that all things have the same self-nature, that is, emptiness, and hence all things both have and lack that very nature' (Garfield and Priest, 2003, pp. 18–19). This insight functions on a non-dual template of identity and difference that the equation of *saṃsāra* and *nirvāṇa* points to. Entities are not identical nor are they different; they both have and lack self-nature. Here we are reminded of the affirmation/negation strategies of the *Prajñāpāramitā* literature that prompted Conze to remark 'when duality is hunted out of its hiding places the results are bound to be startling' (Conze, 1958, p. 204).

For Nāgārjuna, emptiness is not an accidental property; it is the very nature of all things, including emptiness itself: as we have seen, emptiness is empty. Indeed it is the emptiness of emptiness that prevents Nāgārjuna's two truths from collapsing into the Advaita reality/appearance distinction or a Kantian phenomenal/noumenal distinction. Moreover, the fact that emptiness itself is empty 'permits the "collapse" of the distinction between the two truths revealing the empty to be simply the everyday' (Garfield and Priest, 2003, p. 19). In other words, in emptiness conventional and ultimate are not mutually exclusive but mutually *entailing* and by virtue of dependent co-origination, dynamically related. As such, emptiness is the dynamic behind the deontologizing strategies of the *MMK* and, for the practitioner, the hinge on which experiential undoing turns.

Early Buddhism conceived of *nirvāṇa*, to the extent that it could be conceived or expressed, as some kind of release or liberation from the cycles of birth and death (*saṃsāra*). Nāgārjuna's dialectic, however, shows that even *nirvāṇa* and *saṃsāra* are 'not two' and that the locus of liberation is 'right here' and 'right now'. In short, from the point of view of the practitioner, Nāgārjuna's most radical insight is that the 'way out' of the cycles of birth and death is right in the middle of them (Stambaugh, 1990, p. 2) – an insight that is taken up and extended in Japanese Sōtō Zen with the non-dual phenomenological articulations of Eihei Dōgen's thought and practice.

Eihei Dōgen (1200–1253): 'If I am already enlightened, why must I practice?'

Eihei Dōgen Zenji begins one of his key teachings on the nature and method of *zazen* practice, *Fukanzazengi* (*The Universal Promotion of the Principles of Zazen*),[24] with a restatement of the intensely troubling question that plagued him as a young Tendai Buddhist monk: 'The Way [*bodhi*, original awakening, reality] is basically perfect and all-pervading. How could it be contingent upon practice and realization? The Dharma-vehicle is free and untrammelled. What need is there for man's concentrated effort?' (Waddell and Abe, 1973, p. 121). Well schooled in the Tendai Buddhist doctrine of original awakening (*hongaku*), the doctrine that all sentient beings are originally awakened or enlightened, the young Dōgen pondered the seemingly contradictory relationship between the doctrine of innate enlightenment and Buddhist emphasis on sustained practice.

With his teachers unable to resolve the question, Dōgen found himself enveloped in a great doubt.[25] The intensity of Dōgen's doubt and his failure to find a satisfactory resolution in Japan led him to seek a teacher in China where, in 1225, he met the Caodong (J. Sōtō) master Tiantong Rujing (J. Tendō Nyojō 1163–1228) and experientially dissolved the dualism of his question in 'the casting off of body and mind' (*shinjin-datsuraku*),[26] a spiritual awakening that hinged on the realization that spiritual practice and spiritual awakening are one (*shushō-ittō* or *shushō-ichinyo*).

With this question, Dōgen illuminated one of the pivotal dualisms to be undone in Buddhist practice: the linear causal projection of practice as means and realization as ends. Variants of the young Dōgen's question echo through Zen master–student dialogues and, in modern times, we see this same question asked of the Sanbōkyōdan[27] Master Yasutani-rōshi by the young American Zen student Philip Kapleau. 'Isn't the all-embracing Buddha-nature our common possession, so why strive to acquire what is already ours?' Kapleau's reification of Buddha-nature and objectification of attainment is immediately challenged by his teacher's reply, 'Can you show me this enlightened nature of yours?' (Kapleau, 1989, p. 226). Thus, for the practitioner, Dōgen's question hits directly at the core of one of the thorniest dilemmas in Buddhism: 'If I am already enlightened, why must I practice?'

Dōgen's question not only throws the relationship between practice and enlightenment into relief, but also points to other key dualisms that fuel much of Buddhist debate and which are experienced by seekers as genuine dilemmas to be overcome or resolved in Zen practice. According to Abe, Dōgen's non-duality of practice and realization is a key to understanding crucial relationships in Buddhist thought, such as the relationship between 'illusion and enlightenment, beings and Buddha-nature, temporality and continuity, and life and death' (Abe, 1985, p. 101). Such polarized relationships are animated by Dōgen's question and deconstructively resolved in his experiential non-dual interpretation of Buddhist teachings. At a deeper level, we are once again dealing with the dynamic of polarized dichotomies that animated much of Nāgārjuna's exposition of the two truths. In Dōgen's thought, these dilemmas are also non-dualistically 'resolved' by pointing to the interrelated, interpenetrating, empty nature of all things, practice and realization included. But whereas Nāgārjuna addressed the question logically, Dōgen addresses it in an experiential and phenomenological manner.

In this section, Dōgen's thought will be explored in three ways: first by examining the philosophical and experiential implications of his definition of casting off body and mind (*shinjin-datsuraku*) in the light of the key non-dual tenet that practice and realization are one (*shuhō-ittō*); second, by explicating the central practice instruction of non-thinking (*hishiryō*) as a phenomenological description of the process of *shikantaza*; and third, by analysing Dōgen's pivotal encounter with an elderly monk during his early days in China as an example of the deconstructive/reconstructive dynamic in Zen and as the precursor to two of Dōgen's central non-dual practice strategies (i.e., his emphasis on 'wholehearted practice' and the 'liberation of words and letters'), which lie at the heart of the deconstructive strategies of his masterwork, the *Shōbōgenzō*.[28]

Following Abe, Dōgen's original question can be contrasted with the same question posed from the standpoint of acquired awakening (*shikaku*), which serves to illustrate the complexity of Dōgen's original doubt and the dilemma facing most Buddhist practitioners:

> If our own resolution and practice are indispensable, we cannot legitimately say that we are originally endowed with the Buddha-nature or that all sentient beings are originally enlightened. Why then does Tendai Buddhism expound the primal Buddha-nature and the original awakening of all sentient beings? (Abe, 1985, pp. 99–100)

Phrased in this way, the question is now 'If I need to practice how can it be said that I am innately enlightened?' From this standpoint, Buddha-nature is taken as something to be realized as a result of resolution and practice and is not understood as existing directly without the mediation of practice in time and space. Here, it is not seen as being originally endowed. Once again, we see an idealization and conceptualization of Buddha-nature but from the opposite viewpoint. Buddha-nature is idealized as the goal to be reached and resolution and practice are conceptualized as the means to attain it. By taking resolution and practice in time and space as indispensable, they are misconceived as the indispensable basis for attaining Buddha-nature, or, in Buddhist terms, 'awakening to one's own true nature'.[29]

As Abe points out, the above question 'If I need to practice how can it be said that I am innately enlightened?' and its contrary 'If I am enlightened, why must I practice?' are nothing but the

> idealization, conceptualization and objectification of the Buddha-nature in the Mahāyāna from opposite directions. Both of them abstract equally in

> taking as an object the reality of the Buddha-nature or awakening which is fundamentally unobjectifiable and cannot be idealized. (Abe, 1985, p. 100)

The non-dual understanding that Dōgen realized in his enlightenment experience in China 'overcame all previous idealization, conceptualization and objectification which he had previously projected into the relationship of attainment and practice' (Abe, 1985, p. 102). This is indicated by Dōgen's use of inversion in his 'casting off body-mind' statement. Dōgen's statement 'The practice of Zen is the casting off of body-mind' is the break in the impasse of practice and attainment wherein the innate self is fully realized as the 'body-mind which has been cast off'. The 'casting off of body-mind' is thus simultaneously the 'body-mind which has been cast off'. Dōgen's 'both way' statement is indicative of the mutually entailing, interpenetrating nature of practice and attainment and, by extension, all things. This dynamic is the experiential basis of his extensive use of inversions and reversals in the *Shōbōbenzō* and the underlying thrust of his emphasis on 'just sitting' (*shikantaza*).

According to Dōgen, practice and realization are identical for the following reason:

> To think practice and realization are not one is a heretical view. In the Buddha Dharma, practice and realization are identical. Because one's present practice is practice in realization, one's initial negotiation of the Way in itself is the whole of original realization. Thus, even while one is directed to practice, he is told not to anticipate realization apart from practice, because practice points directly to original realization. As it is already realization in practice, realization is endless; as it is practice in realization, practice is beginningless. (*Shōbōgenzō Bendōwa*; Waddell and Abe, 1971, p. 144)

Here, Dōgen is saying that awakening is not a subordinate to practice, Buddha-nature to becoming a Buddha, or vice versa. Both sides of such contraries are indispensable and dynamically related to each other. 'Unless one becomes a Buddha, the Buddha-nature is not realized as the Buddha-nature, and yet at the same time one can become a Buddha only because one is originally endowed with Buddha-nature' (Abe, 1985, p. 103). It is at this point that the dynamic truth of the simultaneous realization of Buddha-nature and its attainment becomes apparent. Further, this dynamic non-dual relation also applies to time and space in the form of 'continuous practice' (*gyōji*).

> In the Great Way of Buddhas and patriarchs there is always continuous practice which is supreme. It is the way which is circulating ceaselessly. There

is not even the slightest gap between resolution, practice, enlightenment, and nirvana. The way of continuous practice is ever circulating. (*Shōbōgenzō Gyōji*; Abe, 1985, p. 103)

Dōgen's realization of 'continuous practice' goes beyond the irreversible relationship of that which must be a ground (Buddha-nature) and that which must be a condition (resolution-practice) without invalidating it. For the practitioner to arrive at the reality of the issue the realization must be non-dual, that is, that both attainment (awakening the Buddha-nature) and practice (discipline or becoming a Buddha) are indispensable and their relationship is irreversible. In this sense, according to Abe, attainment is more fundamental than practice. But this relationship must be fully realized and must not be conceptualized or abstracted by saying that only attainment has reality whereas practice lacks it (Abe, 1985, p. 105). This is the 'first prong' of Dōgen's 'both way' 'casting off of body-mind' and this is why Dōgen says: 'This Dharma is amply present in every person, but unless one practices, it is not manifested: unless there is realization it is not attained' (*Shōbōgenzō Bendōwa*; Waddell and Abe, 1971, p. 129).[30]

The 'second prong', 'body-mind casting off', is the realization that attainment (Buddha-nature) is not something substantial; 'in itself it is non-substantial and non-objectifiable no-thingness' (Abe, 1985, p. 106). As Dōgen states, 'Because the Buddha-nature is empty it is said to be no-thing' (*Shōbōgenzō Busshō*; Waddell and Abe, 1975, p. 105). Consequently, even though the Buddha-nature is the ground which is realized only through practice as its condition, it is not a 'substantial ground or a ground which is something, but a ground which is no-thing, a non-substantial, unobjectifiable ground' (Abe, 1985, p. 106). Hence, the distinction between ground and condition in the ordinary sense is overcome, and with it the irreversibility between them is also overcome.

For Dōgen 'impermanence is in itself Buddha-nature'. Dōgen's equation of impermanence and Buddha-nature conjoins that which is limited by time and space (impermanence) with that which is beyond time and space (Buddha-nature), and his realization that 'There is not even the slightest gap between resolution, practice, enlightenment, and nirvana' is a statement of the fundamentally non-dualistic status of Buddha-nature. 'The way of continuous practice is ever circulating' in the sense that in complete realization ends and means are not separable, but rather, point at a 'dynamic intersection of irreversibility and reversibility' (Abe, 1985, p. 108).

The 'oneness of practice and attainment, the ever-circulating way of continuous practice', in Dōgen's view, indicates a 'reversible identity, in which an absolute irreversibility between attainment and practice, the Buddha-nature and becoming a Buddha, can be reversed by virtue of the nonsubstantiality of attainment and the emptiness of Buddha-nature' (Abe, 1985, p. 107).

In other words, in a reflection of the desubstantializing strategies of the Mahāyāna *sūtras*, attainment is not a 'thing' that can be 'got at' or grasped, and concurrently, for Dōgen, as for Nāgārjuna, the emptiness of Buddha-nature admits of no ontologized 'self-nature'. The relationship is not that of a linear causality, but rather of the dynamic of dependent co-origination. In short, for Dōgen, practice and Buddha-nature are not dualities positioned in a direct causal relationship. Like all things, they are impermanent and in an interdependent co-conditioned relationship.

Dōgen's dynamic oneness of practice and attainment is an attempt to articulate the non-dual basis of reality as he experienced it. For the purposes of this discussion, the key points are that this realization is beyond the polarities of now and then, before and after, means and end, potentiality and actuality, and reversibility and irreversibility, yet it contains them all. Realization cannot be considered to occur either prior to practice, as an innate potentially from the past awaiting actualization, or at the conclusion of practice, as some kind of teleological goal to be achieved in the future. In Dōgen's thought, the dynamic unity of practice and attainment is realized as a ceaselessly unfolding event fully integrated with all aspects of temporality.

For Dōgen, the thought-constructed dualism that posited practice as means and enlightenment as goal objectified the non-dual self or Buddha-nature into something that, insofar as it is understood to be something separate from us, can never be attained. Mutually exclusive categories can do nothing but objectify reality but in Dōgen's two-way *casting off of body-mind* and *body-mind casting off*, each term of the dichotomy 'overflows' into the other in a dynamic interdependence.

The points to note from the above discussion are that, for Dōgen, like Nāgārjuna, all dichotomies, including that of practice and realization, are not in an appearance-and-reality relationship but rather in a reciprocal dynamic of identity and difference. To grant one side of a dualism 'reality' relegates the other to the status of less than real if not completely unreal. This substantializes one side of a dualism at the expense of the other. As we have seen, in Advaita non-dualism, given *brahman*'s status as absolute, uncaused, undifferentiated, being, Śaṅkara was obliged to extend the notion of 'non difference' (*advaita*) to all phenomena, forcing him to characterize the empirical world as an in-between 'reality' that cannot be described as either real or non-real (*sadasatvilakṣaṇa*). Dōgen, however, is under a different non-dual obligation. In keeping with the core Buddhist doctrines of impermanence and dependent co-origination, Dōgen emphasizes the reciprocal interrelated nature of dichotomies and attempts to address the 'not two' (*advaya*) relationship between *saṃsāra* and *nirvāṇa*, practice and enlightenment, being and non-being, identity and difference –relationships that are at the heart of Buddhist non-dual thought – on liberative and phenomenological grounds.[31]

The dimensions and implications of Dōgen's question and the resulting non-dual resolution of his dilemma are articulated in the *Shōbōgenzō*. The *Shōbōgenzō* is a comprehensive attempt at 'explicating the non-dual nature of Zen experience and showing its relationship to ordinary, unenlightened consciousness' (Kasulis, 1985, p. 70). The relationship of the 'ordinary' and the 'ultimate' animates much of Buddhist thought and debate, for it brings into sharp relief the dangers of two-way reification. It was the genius of Nāgārjuna's logical argumentation to show that neither reification of the ordinary *nor* reification of the ultimate were acceptable for a practitioner of the 'middle way'.

Dōgen also works to uphold the fundamental Buddhist tenet of the middle way, in that the practitioner should avoid falling to the extremes of nihilism (impermanence) and eternalism (permanence) at all costs. In his non-dual articulation of practice and realization, Dōgen reinforces Nāgārjuna's 'warnings' against reification by stating that practice cannot be reified by granting it substance and innate awakening or Buddha-nature cannot be reified by 'making it a thing'. Both of these 'extremes' presuppose some kind of inherent existence or an idea of permanent 'things'. In his efforts to overcome all reification, conceptualization, idealization, and objectification of the 'ultimate' and the 'ordinary' or attainment and practice, Dōgen takes an experientially based phenomenological approach that couples the fundamental doctrine of the impermanence of all things with an experiential understanding of the mutual interpenetration of all things.[32] Nāgārjuna's 'shell game' with the two truths showed that *properly understood saṃsāra* is *nirvāṇa*. By structuring his thought on the non-dual dynamic of practice and realization, Dōgen also focuses on identity and difference to show that *properly understood* (or perhaps, in Dōgen's case we should say properly *practised*) practice is enlightenment.

For Dōgen, the non-duality of practice and realization and the 'two way' dynamic of 'casting off body-mind' are 'actualized' in the practitioner's experience in the dynamics of the practice of 'just sitting' (*shikantaza*), an objectless yet physically precise form of seated meditation (*zazen*). In *Fukanzazengi*, Dōgen gives his fundamental practice instructions for *shikantaza* (just sitting) which have become paradigmatic for the Sōtō school:

> At the site of your regular sitting, spread out thick matting and place a cushion above it. Sit either in the full-lotus or half-lotus position. In the full-lotus position, you first place your right foot on your left thigh and your left foot

on your right thigh. In the half-lotus, you simply press your left foot against your right thigh. You should have your robes and belt loosely bound and in order. Then place your right hand on your left leg and your left palm (facing upwards) on your right palm, thumb-tips touching. Thus sit upright in correct bodily posture, neither inclining to the left nor to the right, neither leaning forward nor backward. Be sure your ears are on a plane with your shoulders and your nose in line with your navel. Place your tongue against the front roof of your mouth, with teeth and lips both shut. Your eyes should always remain open, and you should breathe gently through your nose.

Once you have adjusted your posture, take a deep breath, inhale and exhale, rock your body right and left and settle into a steady, immovable sitting position. (Waddell and Abe, 1973, pp. 122–123)

After establishing the necessary bodily conditions, Dōgen continues: 'Think of not-thinking. How do you think of not-thinking? Non-thinking. This in itself is the essential art of zazen' (*Fukanzazengi*; Waddell and Abe, 1973, p. 123).[33] From a phenomenological perspective, Kasulis offers the following formalization of the relationship between the three distinctions:

(1) 'Thinking (*shiryō*): is a positional noetic attitude (either affirming or negating). Its noematic content is conceptualized objects.'

Hence, in Kasulis' analysis 'thinking includes most of what we typically regard as consciousness – that is, any mental act whereby we explicitly or implicitly take a stance toward some object, whether that stance be emotional, judgmental, believing, remembering or assumptive' (Kasulis, 1985, pp. 73–74).

(2) 'Not-thinking (*fushiryō*): is also a positional noetic attitude (only negating). Its noematic content is thinking (as objectified).'

According to Kasulis, 'not-thinking in its intentional or act aspect, is like certain forms of thinking in that it takes a negating, denying, or rejecting attitude'. It is distinguished 'from thinking only in its noematic aspect, that is, only with regard to the *what* toward which it takes its position. The object of not-thinking's intentionality is thinking (*shiryō*) itself' (Kasulis, 1985, p. 74).

(3) Non-thinking (*hishiryō*)[34] is a nonpositional noetic attitude (neither affirming nor negating). Its noematic content is the pure presence of things as they are.

'Non-thinking is distinct from thinking and not-thinking precisely in its assuming *no* intentional attitude whatsoever: it neither affirms nor denies, accepts nor rejects, believes nor disbelieves.' In fact, 'it does not

> objectify either implicitly or explicitly. In this respect, the noetic (or act aspect) of non-thinking is completely different from that of thinking or not-thinking' (Kasulis, 1985, p. 75).

From an experiential point of view, that is, from the point of view of the sitting practitioner, contemporary Sōtō Zen master Ekai Korematsu offers the following analysis:

> … in making effort to sit like a mountain you are thinking, and also thoughts coming is thinking, making effort is thoughts coming and engaging and thoughts come and go. Thought going is not thinking and non-thinking is not 'this' or 'that', it's both – it's the dynamic of it." (Korematsu, 2000)

According to this view, in following Dōgen's physical instructions for *zazen*, the practitioner is 'thinking'. He or she is either affirming or negating – thinking about the body; sit this way, not that way and so on. 'Making effort' to 'sit like a mountain' is intentional and requires the 'positional noetic attitude' of thinking (*shiryō*).

In this 'effort' thoughts come and go. According to Ekai Korematsu, 'thoughts going is not-thinking' (*fushiryō*): not-thinking is related to thinking because 'thinking' is the object that it negates. In other words, they are mutually entailing. Not-thinking cannot be 'thought' without thinking. Not-thinking is thus negatively positional *vis-à-vis* thinking.[35]

'Non-thinking (*hishiryō*)', according to Ekai Korematsu, 'is not "this" or "that", it's both – it's the dynamic of it.' The dynamic of *zazen* is thus a non-positional neither affirming nor negating attitude that allows the pure presence of things as they are. Non-thinking is, according to Dōgen, the 'essential art of *zazen*', but most importantly, as Ekai Korematsu acknowledges, non-thinking is not so much the transcendence of thinking and not-thinking but the 'dynamic relation of thinking and not-thinking in the ascesis of zazen' (Kim, 1985, p. 77). According to Kim, 'all in all, zazen is authentic thinking – the trinary complex of thinking, not-thinking and non-thinking – which is none other than the most concrete reality of the self and the world' (Kim, 1985, p. 78).

Based on this analysis, from a non-dual phenomenological point of view, the dynamic of thinking and not-thinking 'turns on' the 'empty' ground that is the neither affirming nor negating 'space' of non-thinking. This contention will be fully addressed in part two of this study. What is important to note here is that for Dōgen, in the practice of *zazen*, none of these three aspects are to be suppressed or rejected; in effect they are the dynamic of the '*zazen* mind' which, for Dōgen, is the fundamental mode of consciousness that can be actualized in the realization of 'continuous practice' (*gyōji*) in which 'there is not even the slightest gap between resolution, practice, enlightenment, and nirvana' (*Shōbōgenzō Gyōji*; Abe, 1992, p. 103).

According to Kasulis, 'Dōgen came to believe that the mode of consciousness in *zazen* is fundamental in all modes of consciousness' (Kasulis, 1985, p. 69). This fundamental, non-objectified, non-substantialized '*zazen* mind' is the basis for Dōgen's extension of *zazen* into all aspects of life; when this fundamental consciousness is realized it is simultaneously *actualized* and, for Dōgen, action in the world then becomes non-dual and an embodiment of the Way. The paradigmatic model for this insight comes from an episode in Dōgen's biography that prefigures his awakening experience and is the precursor to two of his central non-dual practice strategies; the emphasis on 'wholehearted practice' and the 'liberation of words and letters'.

Dōgen's awakening experience under Rujing and the spiritual practice of '*zazen*-only' or 'just sitting' (*shikantaza*) that disclosed the non-duality of his question are central to any understanding of his mature Zen teachings, but almost equally important to Dōgen's understanding of the Buddhist Path was a pivotal meeting with a chief cook (*tien-tso* J: *tenzo*) prior to his decisive 'dropping off body and mind' or 'body-mind cast off' (*shinjin-datsuraku*) breakthrough under Rujing.[36] Following in the tradition of the Chan encounters, Dōgen's meeting with the cook (*tenzo*) presented him with an example of a practitioner 'embodying the Way' and orientated him towards the idea of action in the world as 'wholehearted practice'. Moreover, this encounter served as a deconstructive correction to the young Dōgen's intellectually based search and presents us with an excellent example of the deconstructive/reconstructive experiential shifts that Buddhist practice can ignite.

The encounter with the *tenzo* is described in detail by Dōgen in his 'Instructions for the Tenzo' (*Tenzo Kyōkun*), which we will draw from here (Leighton, 1996, pp. 40–42). It was a meeting of great significance for Dōgen that James Kodera identifies as 'one of the most critical moments of Dōgen's study in China and, indeed, his entire life' (Kodera, 1980, p. 39).

Dōgen arrived in China in April 1223 and had to wait aboard the ship for several days. During this time he encountered an elderly monk who was the *tenzo*, the head cook, of Ayuwang Mountain about 12 miles away. The *tenzo* had come to buy Japanese mushrooms from the ship for the next day's offering to the monks, and Dōgen, impressed with the old *tenzo*'s bearing and manner, invited him to stay and eat and further discuss the Way. However, the *tenzo* answered that it was not possible for 'if I do not take care of tomorrow's offering it will be done badly'. Not understanding the *tenzo*'s reasoning, Dōgen insisted and said: 'In your temple aren't there some workers who know how to prepare meals the same as you? If only one person, the tenzo, is not there, will something be deficient?' (Leighton, 1996, p. 41). The *tenzo* responded by stating that his responsibilities were 'wholehearted practice' and not something to be just 'given away'. Dōgen then asked:

> 'Venerable tenzo, in your advanced years why do you not wholeheartedly engage the Way through zazen or penetrate the words and stories of the ancient masters, instead of troubling yourself by being tenzo and just working? What is it good for?' … The tenzo laughed loudly and said, 'Oh, good fellow from a foreign country, you have not yet understood wholeheartedly engaging in the Way, and you do not yet know what words and phrases are.' … [Dōgen responds] 'Hearing this, I suddenly felt ashamed and stunned, and then asked him, "What are words and phrases? What is wholeheartedly engaging the Way?"' … The tenzo said, 'If you do not stumble over this question you are really a true person.' (Leighton, 1996, pp. 41–42)

Kodera remarks that the 'chief cook's reply disturbed Dōgen profoundly' and 'opened a wholly new path to enlightenment' in the 'radical shift from Dōgen's intellectual quest [to] the centrality of singleminded discipline' (Kodera, 1980, p. 38). To expand on this, the *tenzo*'s challenge can be read as a deconstructive corrective to the young Dōgen's hitherto intellectually based search, and the radical experiential shift is evident from the 'stunned' Dōgen's swift reply, 'What are words and phrases? What is wholeheartedly engaging the Way?' In other words, the *tenzo*'s negation of Dōgen's understanding is the deconstructive pivot of the dialogue: with one well-placed barb, Dōgen's dualistic ideas of 'wholehearted practice' or 'singleminded discipline' were deflated and he was 'suddenly ashamed and stunned'. Dōgen's intellectual perspective has linked the practice of *zazen* and studying or, in Zen terms, penetrating the words of the ancient masters, as being the 'method and wisdom' aspects of the way; however, there is a certain goal-orientated objectification inherent in Dōgen's questions which the *tenzo* rejects. Being an embodiment of the Way, the *tenzo* admits of no such dualisms and his response breaks Dōgen's dualistically founded conceptual link. Dōgen is stunned; however, he quickly recovers and in direct response to the *tenzo*'s challenge answers from what can be described as a 'not-knowing space' to reconstruct the question from a 'beginner's mind' standpoint.

In a commentary on this point, Zen master Ekai Korematsu refers to the *tenzo*'s challenge as 'feedback that teaches' and offers an evocative experiential description of Dōgen's *tenzo*-encounter that well illustrates the non-dual dynamics of the exchange:

> The *tenzo* is … presenting something, he is moving, 'cooking', and Dōgen shot at a point but he missed … [The *tenzo*] laughed at him and said you don't know and [Dōgen] reflected deeply on that. That is hard work trying to shoot something and aiming at the wrong position. [Dōgen was] stuck in a fixed notion of things. [But] … the most important thing was that he was able to immediately ask, 'What is wholehearted practice?' (Korematsu, 2001a)

Dōgen's question mis-aimed; not realizing the fact that the *tenzo*'s practice was in movement or, in Zen terms, in 'accord with reality', he aimed his question at what he perceived, from his own experiential framework, to be the *tenzo*'s fixed position. Ekai Korematsu continues:

> [The *tenzo* was] just bringing [Dōgen] back to the beginning, pulling apart the framework … in an understanding that that framework no longer works. It worked very well up to that point. Dōgen had accumulated knowledge and teachings but that framework has limitations. Dōgen had worked hard to get to this point, he had put his life into this quest [but] then it came to a point with the *tenzo* and it crashed. (Korematsu, 2001a)

And, according to Ekai Korematsu, those limitations were revealed in the *tenzo*'s deconstructive challenge that experientially undid Dōgen's fixed ideas of Zen practice:

> The popular term is to deconstruct, to deconstruct fixed ideas and notions of how things are … In his first exchange with Dōgen, the *tenzo* deconstructed Dōgen's fixed ideas of what practice is and that prompted Dōgen to really ask 'What is wholehearted practice? What are words and letters?' (Korematsu, 2001a)

In 'really asking' the question, that is, in asking the question from an 'unknowing space' free of previous conceptualizations and objectifications of practice, Dōgen 'hits' the non-dualistic 'mark'. The *tenzo* responds with an approving pointer for his questioner: 'The tenzo said, "If you do not stumble over this question you are really a true person"' (Leighton, 1996, p. 42).

The question has been asked of and for itself; direct questions cannot be 'stumbled over'. Questions that come from this 'not-knowing space' are key to the deconstructive processes that Zen teachings ignite. This point will be taken up in the phenomenological focus in part two. However, what is important to note here is Dōgen's fixed ideas or reifications of practice were undone by the *tenzo*, thereby enabling him to be in direct experiential response to the teaching in the here and now without intellectual objectifications. This is the point behind Zen master Linji's (d. 866) call for seekers to come to the teacher 'alone and free', that is, unencumbered with conceptualizations and objectifications of teachings; no matter how authoritative the source:

> These students of the Way who come from all over – there's never been one of them who didn't appear before me depending on something. So I start right out by hitting them there. If they come with a raised hand, I hit the raised hand … I have yet to find one who comes alone and free – they're all caught up with the idle devices of the men of old. (Watson, 1993, pp. 52–53)

The Ayuwang Mountain *tenzo* deconstructively 'hit' Dōgen where it hurt most; at the core of his intellectual understanding. This is an important shift in Dōgen's understanding of 'wholehearted practice' and a key facet of Dōgen's call for the 'liberation of words and letters' in the non-dualistic phenomenology of the *Shōbōgenzō.*

In the course of the *Shōbōgenzō*, Dōgen 'pushes medieval Japanese language to its expressive limits' (Kasulis, 1985, p. 68), often granting standard words and phrases new meanings and radically reinterpreting passages from Buddhist doctrine. Like Buddhist patriarchs before him, Dōgen considered his teaching to be in accordance with the 'correct Dharma' (*shōbō*), that is, with the essence of the Buddha's teachings. Dōgen's encounter with the *tenzo* showed him that intellectual expression of the way, no matter how eloquent, was in constant danger of reification. Buddhist teachings as fixed absolutes served to stultify the Dharma and objectify awakening as a 'thing' to be attained. The shattering of Dōgen's own epistemic frames in this encounter prompted him to ask, 'What is wholehearted practice? What are words and letters?' The first question was resolved in the centrality of the practice of *zazen* and the extension of *zazen*-mind (i.e., the dynamics of thinking; not-thinking and non-thinking) to all aspects of life. Dōgen resolved the second question in his ceaseless expression and re-expression of the non-dual nature and dynamics of awakening in his 'Voicing of the Way' (*Dōtoku*) in the *Shōbōgenō.*

As noted above, the young Dōgen's doubt was initiated by a passage on the Buddha-nature in the *Mahāparinirvāṇa sūtra* that traditionally read as 'Śākyamuni Buddha said: "All sentient beings everywhere possess the Buddha-nature; the Tathāgata exists eternally and is without change"' (Kodera, 1980, p. 25). In keeping with Dōgen's dynamic non-dual approach to 'voicing the way', this general Mahāyāna statement was reread in *Shōbōgenzō Busshō*[37] as 'all sentient beings-whole being *is* the Buddha-nature' (Waddell and Abe, 1975, p. 94, my italics). In this reading,[38] 'Buddha-nature as potentiality is construed as actuality, because sentient beings do not possess but are Buddha-nature, also "sentient beings", "whole beings" and "Buddha-nature" are non-dually one' (Kim, 1985, p. 64). However, for Dōgen, it is a non-dual oneness that is predicated on the non-duality of difference and identity. As Dōgen states in *Shōbōgenzō Zenki*,[39] 'though not oneness, it is not difference, though it is not difference, it is not sameness, though it is not sameness, this is not multifariousness' (Waddell and Abe, 1972a, p. 76). For Dōgen, all things are dynamically not-two.

As we have seen in Dōgen's non-duality of practice and enlightenment, Buddha-nature is understood by Dōgen as an ever-changing non-substantial reality that is realized inseparably from the transiency common to all beings. Dōgen's rereading of this text is underwritten by his breakthrough realization in which he non-dualistically affirmed that Buddha-nature is what sentient beings are. Hence, in the *Shōbōgenzō*, Dōgen's deconstruction of dichotomies works at the interface of identity and difference to show the mutually entailing nature of all dichotomous thinking and the interpenetrating non-dual nature of all things. 'To understand duality lucidly and penetrate it thoroughly within a nondualistic mode of existence' (Kim, 1987, p. 35) is the purpose of Dōgen's teachings and practice instructions in which practitioners' reifications of the Buddhist path are challenged and undone by Dōgen's articulation of the absolute non-duality and interpenetrating nature of identity and difference, ends and means and beings and Buddha-nature. For Dōgen, the dynamic 'not-two' nature of things is simultaneously confirmed and actualized in deconstructive practice of *shikantaza* which situates the practitioner at the cognitive interface of dualistic thinking and 'naturally' undoes adherence to either polarized 'extreme' in his or her actual experience.

Contemporary Masters

The practice of *shikantaza*, as formulated and articulated by Dōgen remains the central practice of the Sōtō school. To close this chapter, we will consider two contemporary Sōtō masters who both trace their lineages in the traditional manner to Dōgen, with the aim of highlighting the contemporary use and reformulations of these deconstructive teachings. Ekai Korematsu-oshō (b. 1948, known to his students as Ekai-oshō)[40] emphasizes the orthodox Sōtō practice of *shikantaza*, with an emphasis on body engagement and extending practice into all aspects of everyday life. The structures of the Zen Community that has formed around his teachings are based on the traditional Sōtō monastic model. Ekai Korematsu's explication of the process of *shikantaza* and his practice instructions are geared for Western Zen students and phrased in contemporary terms, his presentation of Zen thus offers a window into the deconstructive elements of *shikantaza* as practised today.

Hōgen Yamahata (b. 1935, known to his students as Hōgen-san)[41] also primarily teaches the practice of *shikantaza*. Hōgen Yamahata first taught in the West in the early 1980s and was struck by the challenging questions that Westerners asked, forcing him to re-evaluate his own practice and expression of Zen.[42] In response to such questions, Hōgen Yamahata's writings and teachings, while keeping *zazen* as the central focus, challenge 'blind adherence to religious organizations and dogmas' and urge students to 'discover and practice their personal life-questions' (Yamahata, 1998, p. 27). In contrast to Ekai Korematsu, who emphasizes a traditional Sōtō approach primarily based on practices and teachings laid down by Dōgen, Hōgen Yamahata's teaching presents us with an interesting fusion of traditional forms with contemporary influences and concerns. Hōgen incorporates teachings from non-Zen sources in his commentaries (Krishnamurti and Jung are two examples), teaches the practice of daily yoga exercises, and draws on insights from deep ecology in his presentation of Zen.[43] Hōgen thus affirms Dōgen's insistence on the centrality of *zazen* while opening traditional practice up to contemporary influences. Both Ekai Korematsu and Hōgen Yamahata teach in Australia, in English, to Western, primarily lay, practitioners.

Ekai Korematsu (b. 1948): 'Return to the spine'

During one of Zen master Ekai Korematsu's *teishō* (formal *dharma* talks) on Dōgen's non-duality of practice and realization, a student commented that: 'It's like a case of which came first, the chicken or the egg!' To which Ekai-oshō replied: 'What about if they both come together?' (Korematsu, 2001b).

Through a common witticism, the student throws into question the idea of anything 'coming first'. Which came first, the chicken or the egg, we can't say, although there is a fruitless search in the mental 'flip' between chicken, egg, egg, chicken and so on that could be said to be experientially illustrative of Buddhist ideas of the interdependence of all things (*pratītyasamutpāda*). Such an unanswerable question is in itself a deconstructive move that throws cause-and-effect relationships into question. But Ekai Korematsu's simple retort takes common consequential ideas of causality one step further: 'What about if they both come together?' The whole question of 'what came first' is suddenly turned on its head and questions of 'what came where' are swept away with this dynamic non-dualistic challenge to linear causality.

'Things coming together' is a metaphor for the mutual dependence or interdependence of all phenomena. As such, it is a common Zen deconstructive foil for ideas of linear timebound progression in practice, as it shatters any conceptualizations of *zazen* practice and realization being in a consequential relationship. As soon as a seeker falls into dualistic oppositions of before and after or ends and means, as in such projections like 'first I will practice and then I will be enlightened', he or she is shown that there is no 'first this then that'. With this simple statement that denies any 'first cause' and affirms Dōgen's undoing of the thought-constructed dualism that poses practice as means and realization as goal, Ekai Korematsu succinctly underlines the dynamic unity of practice and attainment as a ceaselessly unfolding process that is fully integrated with all aspects of temporality and concretely situates the practitioner 'right now and right here'.

According to Ekai-oshō, there are two aspects to practice: the physical body engagement [which] 'is very concrete, and in Zen the concrete aspect is very important', and the mental aspect, 'in which thoughts expand, wander and they are brought back'. However, 'it's not just sitting and watching the scenery, there is a deliberate effort'. In Ekai Korematsu's practice instructions, intention, in the form of 'effort', is important for the practitioner to keep the focus on the body. 'Any thoughts that you attach to, move you away from the body – moving away is not the required effort, the effort is to return – so how to return – not by thinking, no, just by paying attention to the spine, coming back, returning.' 'Returning to the spine' is the most essential element of the whole process and, according to Ekai-oshō, the 'closest and most accurate explanation that [the teacher] can give people is, "just sit with your back straight"' (Korematsu, 2000).

Ekai Korematsu's emphasis on the posture of *zazen* and the importance of formal practice highlights that, for practitioners, Dōgen's three 'thinking' distinctions – thinking, not-thinking and non-thinking – cannot be removed from his instructions for the physical position to be adopted in *zazen*. For Ekai-oshō, the 'essential art of *zazen*' is predicated on the 'steady, immovable sitting position'. In following Dōgen's precise and detailed physical instructions, the thought constructions of the conceptualizing mind are 'naturally deconstructed' by being allowed to fall back into non-thinking. In Ekai Korematsu's teaching, objectless, formal sitting practice (*shikantaza*) allows this 'undoing' of habitual thought patterns to occur and enables the practitioner to extend the non-dual body and mind engagement that begins with practice into all aspects of daily activities.

Speaking of the 'undoing' process of Zen practice, Ekai Korematsu comments that:

> … in Zen practice, habitual patterns and conditioning are naturally undone. Everyone without exception is made up of all kinds of habits or patterns, past conditions, all the packaging – and putting oneself in the sitting naturally unfolds this – unpacks these conditionings. But it doesn't mean that these conditionings go away, that is wrong, rather they become kind of free floating instead of fixed and solid. The mind is dynamic and flexible. Flexible means unfolding, unpacking but … it doesn't mean rejecting or destroying patterns. (Korematsu, 2000)

According to Ekai-oshō, the practice of *shikantaza* is an 'opening of the senses', not a concentrated 'closing down', and it is by 'being totally open' in practice that the undoing or the 'letting go' of the hold of thought-based constructions takes place:

> … *shikantaza* is openness, being totally open, all senses open. To concentrate is to close off, to only focus on one thing. To let go is a crude way of putting it, a crude level, because letting go implies trying, using the mind. You can't let go with the mind, you have to let go with the body and mind. Mind alone can't do it, it just becomes another construct. Body engagement is necessary. (Korematsu, 1999a)

A 'dynamic and flexible' mind can thus recognize and release thought-structured conditionings without falling to rejection. But 'mind alone can't do it', the 'essential thing' is to 'return to the spine': 'Zen practice is about the essential thing – simply erect your spine again and again and that which is beyond all conditioning will be slowly clarified' (Korematsu, 1999b).

Hōgen Yamahata (b. 1935): 'Why not now?'

At the beginning of a public talk, Zen master Hōgen Yamahata was asked to expand on one of his often-used teaching expressions: 'just this'. In reply, Hōgen-san, who was sitting in *zazen* posture, took a deep breath, extended his arm and intoned in a steady, strong voice: 'TTTHHHIIIISSS.' His reply was greeted by silence, and after a full minute or so he softly said, 'just this – only this – that's all', and returned to *zazen* posture (Yamahata, 2001).

By responding with a classic 'direct' demonstration of Zen, Hōgen Yamahata is following the traditional Zen emphasis on direct demonstration rather than verbal explanation. His 'answer', as simple and spontaneous as it was, had the effect of silencing his audience and placing them in immediate response to his teaching. Simply put, in the moment of his answer, in the 'now' of his response, all questions were 'frozen' in the sense that there was no space for the conceptualizing mind to 'kick in' and, in this sense, Hōgen-san's response was a direct presentation of the 'now and here' moments that Zen aims to ignite.

In the reading of this study, Hōgen Yamahata's demonstration is a deconstructive move to shift the questioner out of attempting to intellectually figure out what 'this' could mean or what are the qualities of 'this' to 'this' in concrete actuality. The 'concrete this' located in absolute 'now' is the deconstructive lynchpin of Hōgen Yamahata's teaching; where Ekai Korematsu would move a student away from conceptualizing reifications of *zazen* by bringing them back to the body, 'back to the spine', Hōgen-san moves to deconstruct all objectifications and projections of sequential constructions of practice by challenging his student with a 'now':

> [*Hōgen*]: The most advanced moment is now.
> Why not now?
> Why not?
> [*Student*]: Silence
> [*H*]: Will you be aware after this *sesshin* [retreat], is that it?
> Where are you now?
>
> (Yamahata, 1999a)

With the unanswerable question, 'Why not now?', Hōgen-san forces the questioning student into the elusive present moment, as there is no possibility of articulating a response; the only thing to do is to remain in 'now'. Taking advantage of the 'unanswerability' of his deconstructive move, Hōgen Yamahata further challenges the student's projections of attaining 'awareness' through mediation by confounding her ideas of 'before' and 'after'. If 'the most advanced moment is now' how can awareness be projected as something that is attainable in the future? 'Will you be aware after this retreat, is that it?' The student's projections are momentarily cut by being brought back to the immediate present.

In a restatement of Dōgen's core teaching of the non-duality of practice and realization, Hōgen Yamahata outlines for his students the nature of 'real' practice:

> What is real practice? We can easily assume the posture of zazen, but not actually practise. Real practice is very simple, and at the same time very profound. It is nothing more or less than freedom from concepts and beliefs about everything: even those about practice itself. Therefore, practice, to be free, is enlightenment. (Yamahata, 1998, p. 188)

In keeping with Nāgārjuna's warnings against reification of Buddhist insights, Hōgen Yamahata instructs his students to be free of concepts and beliefs about 'everything' including 'practice itself'. Given the centrality of practice, one of the greatest spiritual pitfalls for the Zen practitioner is the reification and objectification of the Buddhist path itself. Dōgen stresses the oneness of practice and attainment but a dynamic oneness in which practice cannot be substantialized and attainment cannot be reified. In his efforts to steer students away from reification and objectification, Hōgen Yamahata's deconstructive teaching targets these same dualistic pitfalls.

Both Hōgen Yamahata and Ekai Korematsu work to undo linear, dualistic ideas of goal-orientated practice in the experience of their students. In Hōgen-san's teaching, dualistic conceptual structures and bifurcated oppositional ways of thinking are targeted by situating the student in 'absolute now' and the 'concrete this' in which there is no 'room' for dualistic projections of ends and means or reifications of path and goal to reside. With a similar motive, Ekai Korematsu brings his students 'back to the spine' to move them away from attaching to thought-constructed projections that impede the 'natural unfolding' process of *shikantaza*. With these teachings, these contemporary teachers strive to deconstruct practitioner's dualistic views of self and world through practices that challenge unquestioned 'everyday' adherence to dichotomous 'extremes' which, according to Zen teachings, bind the practitioner to ideas of 'being' and 'non-being'.

Zen Buddhism Summary: 'Neither being nor non-being is to be taken hold of'

In practice instructions and discourses, Zen Buddhist masters challenge the dualistic assumptions of their students by throwing into question reified projections of the path and pointing them to the dynamic 'not-two' (*advaya*) nature of reality in which 'neither being nor non-being is to be taken hold of'.

In this chapter, I have focused on the non-dual philosophical underpinnings and deconstructive practice instructions that are important to the development of Sōtō Zen. As we have seen, Zen deconstructive strategies highlight the mutually entailing and dynamically reciprocal nature of dichotomies and strive to dislodge practitioner attachments to polarized 'one-sided' views. Based on the *Prajñāpāramitā*'s call to 'cut all ideas of duality at the root' and the *Laṅkā*'s 'mistrust of words to convey reality as it is', Zen teachings aim to liberate students' attachments to polarized dichotomies from their dualistic moorings by pointing out reality from 'both sides'. That is, dualities, such as 'practice and enlightenment', are shown to be in dynamic interplay rather than in a linear consequential relationship.

Thus the core problem for the Zen practitioner to overcome is the reification of polarized dichotomies. In Zen, either side of a binary opposition condemns the practitioner to a 'lopsided' view of reality and generates a substantialized ontology that binds the practitioner to a reification. In the *MMK*, Nāgārjuna's 'warnings' against reification well illustrate the substantializing trap of reifying pivotal Buddhist insights by 'falling to the extreme' of 'is-ing' them, i.e., granting them ontological status. According to Nāgārjuna, reification renders the Buddhist path unintelligible and impossible to actually practise. To *practise* the middle way, the aspirant should not adhere to polarized notions but should rather come to broader dynamic understandings of identity and difference through the non-dual prism of the 'two truths'. According to Nāgārjuna, ultimate and conventional realities or truths are also 'not-two' (*advaya*) and the ultimate is not taught apart from the conventional or relative.

This non-dual stance is taken up in Dōgen's thought where the ultimate and the relative are shown to be in a dynamic continuum of practice and enlightenment that is mutually entailing and, in the correct circumstances, i.e., the practice situation, mutually actualizing. Dōgen extends Nāgārjuna's equation of dependent co-origination and emptiness by fusing it with the Huayan doctrine of the mutual interpenetration of all things in which all dichotomous relationships are shown to be dynamically not-two. For the practitioner, this dynamic is actualized in the deconstructive practice of *shikantaza* which, as we have seen, is a physically precise yet objectless meditative practice that works to deconstruct conceptualizations on the non-thinking interface of the dichotomy of thinking and not-thinking. Exactly how this deconstructive dynamic functions is the subject of part two of this study; what is important to note here is that, for Dōgen, the physical and cognitive aspects of *shikantaza* cannot be separated and both contribute to the deconstructive process.

Zen masters refute all ideas of ultimates or absolutes including Zen's own 'highest' teachings as falling to an eternalist extreme and then they refute excessive negation as falling to a nihilistic extreme. For the student, Zen practice is situated in the interface of eternalism and nihilism wherein neither being nor non-being *can* be taken hold of. Shifting the practitioner into this non-dual awareness is the aim of Zen deconstructive strategies and, as we have seen, the liberative drive behind the philosophical articulations of Zen thought.

In this chapter I have been concerned to delineate the philosophical underpinnings to spiritual practices in Zen Buddhism and to highlight their deconstructive orientation. In Zen, as in Advaita, liberating understanding is non-dual understanding; however, as we have seen, the non-dual 'not different' (*advaitavāda*) understanding of Advaita differs from the Zen non-dual 'not two' (*advayavāda*). This difference is clear in their respective philosophical underpinnings; in particular the Advaita reality and appearance distinction and the Zen identity and difference template.

However, in their deconstructive practices, both traditions aim at overcoming dualistic modes of thinking and being in the actual experience of the practitioner. To this end, both traditions work with common deconstructive techniques (unfindability analysis; bringing everything back to the here and now; paradoxical problems; and negation) and target the same key dichotomies to be undone: cause and effect (ends and means); subject and object (self and other); and linear conceptions of space and time. Thus, for the practitioner, the critical realization in both traditions hinges on the undoing of dualistic conceptual structures and bifurcated oppositional ways of thinking that obscure direct non-dual insight. This contention is the subject of part two where the deconstructive techniques of Zen and Advaita are identified and the dynamics of experiential undoing are empirically explored.

Part Two

Deconstructive Techniques and Dynamics of Experiential Undoing

Chapter 4

Four Deconstructive Techniques Common to Both Traditions

Part one of this study identified and described the practice of deconstructive spiritual inquiry in the context of the traditional texts and in the teachings of selected contemporary masters of Advaita Vedānta and Zen Buddhism. Attention was paid to the philosophical foundations of tradition; how masters based their deconstructive practice instructions on these key philosophical tenets, and how dialoguing and questioning is employed in the practice situation. In part two, we move into hermeneutical and phenomenological analysis of practice experience. We will begin by hermeneutically examining the techniques employed by teachers in these dialogues and phenomenologically articulating the experiential impact on the practitioner in more depth.

For the purposes of exploring and articulating the dynamics of deconstructive spiritual inquiry, four deconstructive techniques, common to both traditions, have been identified: unfindability analysis, bringing everything back to the here and now, paradoxical problems, and negation. It is important to note that for the purposes of this study, these techniques are identified and analysed separately but in the actual practice situation they are not static devices, they function interdependently and are employed by teachers in constantly changing patterns and combinations.

As we have seen, the Advaita deconstructive practice of self-inquiry (*ātman vichara*) and the Sōtō Zen practice of just sitting (*shikantaza*) have two aspects: the 'internal' meditative inquiry, in which the practitioner internalizes the instructions and inquires into the boundaries of his or her personal experiencing, and the more 'external' aspect of questioning and dialoguing with a teacher. Thus, the deconstructive processes that these practices ignite takes place in a 'practice situation', that is, a context wherein the practitioner is in full existential engagement with a tradition, a teacher and a practice.[1]

From the Advaita perspective, the practitioner seeks to realize that ultimate reality (*brahman*) and self (*ātman*) are, in essence, not different. From the Zen practitioner's point of view, practice consists of realizing that, in essence, conditioned reality (*saṃsāra*) and unconditioned reality (*nirvāṇa*) are 'not two'. Common to both traditions is the assertion that, in essence, there is no duality between the conditioned and the unconditioned or the relative and the absolute.

Although predicated on different ontologies, the non-dual systems of Advaita and Zen both deny any bifurcation between self and non-self, subject and object, cause and effect and so on. Hence, in practice, both Advaita and Zen deny any bifurcation between categories because they both deny, for different reasons, the dualistic thought processes and structures that create oppositional categories in the first place.

To this end, in the evolving trajectory of spiritual practice, both Zen and Advaita teachers aim to move students beyond their 'everyday' dualistic thought processes and structures through ongoing deconstructive challenges to bifurcated categories and structures that support oppositional ways of thinking. Common to both traditions are the four key deconstructive techniques, identified above, that are employed in the practice situation to undo dichotomous epistemic frames and substantialized ontological boundaries in the experiencing of the practitioner.

In the following sections, the teacher–student dynamic and the use and dynamics of the four key deconstructive techniques of unfindability analysis, bringing everything back to the here and now, paradoxical problems, and negation will be described and analysed. The discussion will focus on how these four deconstructive techniques are used both individually and in combination to deconstructively challenge students' 'everyday' dualistic experience and to experientially undo key conceptual dualisms of self and other (subject and object), ends and means (cause and effect), and linear dualistic conceptions of space and time to instigate the experiential deconstructive 'shift' or 'movement' in the actual experience of the practitioner.

The Teacher–Student Dynamic

In teacher–student dialogues, dualistic ontological boundaries and epistemological filters that are impeding the student's insight are exposed by the nature of the questions asked, thus enabling the teacher to 'tailor' his or her deconstructive challenge to the particular dualistic construction that the student is displaying. In other words, the questioning/dialoguing process enables the teacher to identify the dualistic 'stumbling blocks' that the practitioner needs to 'move through'. Importantly, this 'undoing' also applies to dualistic attachment to or reification of the teacher–student relationship itself.

In the context of the practice situation, the student's relationship to the teacher is pivotal in keeping him or her concentrated and committed to the ongoing process of practice and inquiry. In Advaita and Zen foundational texts, the importance of the teacher is clearly emphasized. In *Upadeśasāhasrī* 3, Śaṅkara likens a teacher to a 'boatman', and claims that 'knowledge of Brahman is not obtained in any other way than through a teacher' (Deutsch and Van Buitenen, 1971, p. 125). Dōgen's stance on the importance of the *right* teacher is repeated throughout the *Shōbōgenzō* and unequivocally expressed in *Gakudō-yōjinshū*,[2] where he bluntly states: 'When you don't meet a right teacher, it is better not to study Buddhism at all' (Kim, 1987, p. 24).

Contemporary practitioners generally reiterate this stance. When asked how important is the teacher, Zen practitioners usually respond with 'essential'.[3] According to one practitioner, the teacher 'can see right through you, you can't hide anything from them. To me a good teacher is just one hundred per cent all the time just showing you your self' (InterviewJ20, 2001). In addition to this, another Zen practitioner claims that a teacher can 'point out things and straighten you out when there are problems' and is 'someone that holds [her] practice together' (InterviewB00, 2000).

Advaita practitioners also generally regard the teacher as essential but their emphasis is slightly different. In *satsang*, Advaita practitioners sometimes feel that the teacher is somehow generating the 'energy' in the sense that the focus of the collective practice is being 'held' by the teacher. Practitioners report 'feeling a strong stream of energy' (InterviewKC9901, 2000) that focuses their practice, which is generally attributed to the presence of the teacher.[4]

In both traditions, the teacher initially represents the non-dual 'state' of being that practitioners aspire to. However, the dynamic between teachers and students is more complex. Generally, teachers in both traditions are keen to deconstruct students' idealized projections of their role and thereby place the onus of practice onto the practitioner. But, given the traditional emphasis on the importance of the teacher, the teacher's function and status cannot be merely negated. Instead, teachers undo objectifications of their role by constantly problematizing the teacher–student relationship. This 'undoing' proceeds by deconstructive moves that serve to frustrate or 'deflate' students' dualistic expectations and to unsettle the respective 'positions' of teacher and student. This interplay of 'positions', that is, the 'absolute' non-dual view of the teacher and the 'relative' dualistic view of the student, is indicative of the dialectical function of the two truths in each tradition and reminiscent of the juxtaposition of affirmation and negation as found in the foundational texts of the *Prajñāpāramitā Sūtra* and the *Upaniṣads*. In plain terms, an overarching feature of deconstructive spiritual inquiry is the 'conflicting messages' on the role and status of the teacher that Zen and

Advaita teachers send to their students in the practice situation with the aim of undermining students' dualistic projections and expectations and placing the onus of practice on students themselves.

For example, to undermine his 'absolute' position, Zen master Hōgen Yamahata repeatedly tells his students that 'my role is to continually disappoint you' (Yamahata, 1999b) and, when speaking of the relationship to a teacher, the contemporary Advaitin Gangaji warns her students that she can only be of limited help; the final 'leap' must be taken alone. 'I offer you my shoulders. Stand on them for as long as they last to leap into what has never been known, never been said' (Gangaji, 2001).

These 'disclaimers' issued by Zen and Advaita teachers coupled with unfolding practice experience serve to alert the practitioner to the trap of dualizing the teacher–student relationship. It is from such 'disclaimers' that the undoing of the construct of 'getting anything from a teacher' begins. This undoing is well illustrated in the following comment from an Advaita practitioner who realized that

> … after all of my experience, after all this time I couldn't really get anything from a teacher anymore. I had rested my 'insights' on the authority of others, [and] it wasn't really serving me because faced with my own death or existential crisis it was just useless. (InterviewDO2, 2002)

In a similar shift, a Zen practitioner states that a teacher is

> … important at some junction. Everybody has times when they sit alone … and then times when you are with a teacher. [But] no matter what [the teacher's] attainment is I still have to do what I have to do so I can't rely on their attainment or their personality or whatever to do it for me. It's my present moment. (InterviewJ00, 2000)

This shift in the practitioner's relationship with the teacher is an important facet in the process of deconstructive spiritual inquiry. It is indicative of the necessity to move beyond the initial dualistic emotional attachment to the teacher, to a more complex dynamic in which the student realizes that a teacher 'cannot do it for me' but nevertheless still remains devoted to that teacher and his or her instructions.

Caught in the middle of the teacher–student duality, a Zen student of Hōgen Yamahata tells his teacher in frustration: 'If I had any sense, I would kick you and walk away, but I stay. Which one of us is the greater fool?' To which Hōgen replies, 'Your kicking, of course, makes me old, crippled, and happy'

(Yamahata, 1998, p. 176). Here, Hōgen subverts his student's frustration by affirming and approving it. In classical Zen 'style', which neither reproaches nor directly instructs, Hōgen 'addresses' his student's frustration by effectively telling him to 'Keep kicking!' and thereby placing the onus back on the student himself.

By undermining dualistic ideas of the teacher–student relationship, skilful teachers can employ the rising frustration that practitioners' unfulfilled expectations can provoke to deconstructive ends. In this example, a Zen student describes a personal interview (*dokusan*) in which he presented his 'understanding' and his teacher[5] responded by striking him with the *kyōsaku* stick.[6] A response that 'stunned' him:

> I came in and I did a presentation … but he didn't like it and I was stunned by his response and my mind was crazily trying to figure out the situation.[7] So off I went and the next few periods I just sat there with clouds of steam coming out of my ears and I was getting more and more angry. So I got in the *dokusan* [interview] line and all the [*dokusan*] line I was fuming and I burst in and he just went 'Hmmm'. Then the next day in *teishō* [formal *dharma* talk] … he talked about somebody coming in and having crazy eyes and he was kind of deriding me without naming names and so we went through this process and I got angrier and angrier and finally something broke and I just came into *dokusan* and said, 'I'm sorry' and he just smiled. (InterviewJ00, 2000)

Once again, the Zen teacher is neither affirming nor denying the student's frustration, but in this case, sends him back to the 'naturally deconstructive'[8] process of *zazen*. In the concentrated practice of retreat the student describes his release of frustration as: 'I think it's a process in as much as things change, [to] put it that way. It's kind of like being cooked – steeped or stewing in your own juice' (InterviewJ00, 2000). In this instance, by not directly acknowledging or responding to his student's anger, the teacher places the responsibility of finding a 'solution' squarely on the shoulders of the practitioner, thereby allowing the frustration to unravel in the practice of *shikantaza*. When asked how he overcame his anger, the student responded: 'It's more one's frustration I think and who is it and what is it that's frustrated?' (InterviewJ00, 2000).

Not being able to locate the experiencer, the 'I' that is experiencing frustration, difficulty, and so on, is a commonly reported experience in the practice of *shikantaza*. It is indicative of the breakdown of substantialized notions of self and, in this case, is a deconstructive 'by-product' of the teacher's refusal to directly engage his student in a linear discussion. It is, however, important to note that skilful teachers read their student's responses very closely and not all 'non-dual answers' are automatically approved. In the next example, Hōgen Yamahata challenges a student's seemingly 'correct' response to practice:

> [*Student*]: Whilst sitting in zazen, the question arose, 'Who is sitting in zazen?' In later contemplation, self asked self: 'Who is waiting for an answer?'
> [*Hōgen*]: Thank you for 'cooking' such a tasty treat. It smells good! But is your hunger really satisfied by your self-made answer?
>
> (Yamahata, 1998, p. 199)

As practitioners quickly learn, with skilful teachers, there are no static 'correct' non-dual answers. In the practice situation, both Advaita and Zen teachers work in response to the comments or questions of the individual student in front of them, deconstructively targeting objectifications and reifications of their own roles and of spiritual practice in general.

The Advaitin Poonjaji tackles his student's dualistic projections on the 'grace' of the teacher's 'presence' thus:

> [*Student*]: Through the grace of your presence we are now in silence. What will happen to us when you go away?
> [*Poonjaji*]: Because you saw me coming, you suppose that I will one day go away. I never come or go.
> [*S*]: But you are going away soon. What will I do in your absence?
> [*P*]: If you know how to create separation in the presence, why don't you create presence in the separation?
>
> (Godman, 1998c, p. 27)

The practitioner is attributing the 'silence' he is experiencing to the teacher's 'presence'. That is, he is creating a dualistic separation in the form of a productive relationship between the teacher and himself. Poonjaji rejects such a separation in two deconstructive moves. First, he negates the dichotomy of coming and going by claiming that 'he never comes or goes'. Second, he throws the onus back to the practitioner by pointing out that dichotomous ideas of presence and absence are creations of the mind. According to Advaita, such separations do not exist in reality. The problem is created by the practitioner himself: Poonjaji is actually present and the practitioner is creating absence. 'Why not', challenges Poonjaji, 'also create presence in absence?' This juxtaposition of dichotomies, in this example, coming and going, presence and absence, serves to place the practitioner 'right in the middle' of his own dilemma. His adherence to one side of a dualism (presence) has been challenged by his teacher saying that the other side (absence) would do just as well! The notion that there is no difference between them and that both are ultimately creations of mind effectively cuts the practitioner's line of questioning and undermines his reification that the presence of the teacher is somehow 'creating' or 'holding' the practice together.

The above Zen and Advaita examples are representative of the teacher–student dynamic in the practice situation. Both Advaita and Zen teachers strive to deconstructively point out to students the dangers of objectifying bifurcated categories and reifying oppositional patterns of thought and to experientially undo dualistic attachments and reifications projected onto the teacher–student relationship and the process of practice itself.

Four Key Deconstructive Techniques

As stated above, the process of experiential undoing evolves through the use of four key deconstructive techniques: unfindability analysis, bringing everything back to the here and now, paradoxical problems, and negation. These techniques and their experiential 'targets' are considered separately for purposes of analysis and clarity; however, in the actual practice situation they are not separate and function dynamically and interdependently.

Unfindability analysis

Unfindability analysis is a form of reductive analysis in which objectified reifications of entities and categories are deconstructed through a questioning process that challenges practitioners to precisely locate the entity or category in question. In this process of radical questioning, practitioners' assumed notions of the ontological 'solidity' of entities are undermined by showing the basis of such notions to be unfindable.

In the Advaita and Zen practice situation, the principal target of unfindability analysis is the practitioner's objectified and reified notions of self in the form of the objectified, individualized 'I' that is at the heart of the bifurcating self-and-other (subject/object) structures of personal identity.

(a) Advaita Vedānta

In Advaita dialogues the overall pattern is anchored to bringing the student back to the self (*ātman*). Accordingly, deconstructive spiritual inquiry in Advaita aims to experientially undo the distortions and obscurations of unquestioned superimpositions (*adhyāsa*) that students erroneously place on *ātman* by throwing into question the practitioner's constructions of 'I as doer', 'I as seer', 'I as knower' and so on.

In short, Advaitic deconstructive spiritual inquiry aims to catalyse self-realization in the experience of the practitioner by challenging the very fabric of constructions that supports the intimately personal conception of 'I as me'. To this end, one of the most effective deconstructive techniques employed by Advaita masters is to challenge their students to 'Find the "I"' that seekers so easily (mistakenly) identify as 'me', that is, a separate self that operates in an objectified world that is contingent and subject to change. In this technique, the Advaita teacher takes the student through a process of 'unfindability analysis' in which the student is challenged to 'find', that is, to precisely pinpoint, the 'I' that they are constantly referring to. In modern and contemporary Advaita (or neo-Advaita), the template for this exchange comes from the paradigmatic dialogues of Ramana Maharshi:

> [*Student*]: How to realize Self?
> [*Ramana Maharshi*]: Whose Self? Find out.
> [*S*]: Who am I?
> [*R*] Find it yourself.
> [*S*]: I do not know.
> [*R*]: Think. Who is it that says 'I do not know?' What is not known? In that statement, who is the 'I'?
>
> (Maharshi, 1984, p. 60)

'Who is it?' asks Ramana Maharshi, 'Who is it that says "I do not know?" "Who is the "I"'? This 'unanswerable' question provokes an experiential tension in which any notions of a substantial separate self that the questioning student may have are undermined again and again and serves to place the questioner in a experiential 'space' of 'unknowing' or 'not-knowing' that ignites the experiential undoing of the concept of self.[9]

The following dialogue from the contemporary American Advaitin, Gangaji well illustrates the Advaitic use of unfindability analysis and to this end is worth examining in full.

When questioned as to *how* to give up the empirical constructed 'I', Gangaji, echoing Ramana Maharshi, offers the following deconstructive challenge:

> [*Gangaji*]: Run headlong into that *I* that must be given up. Find it. Quickly, where is it?
> [*Student*]: It's in my head.
> [*G*]: Where in your head? In what part of your head is it hiding? Report from there immediately.

Can you find it? This *I* that has to be given up. Is it there? Quickly!

(Gangaji, 1995, p. 115, her emphasis)

Gangaji asks the seeker to locate the 'I', that she wants to give up. 'Where is it?' For the student, this 'I' is cognitive, 'It's in my head.' Gangaji quickly demands precision, 'In what part of your head?' and commands, 'Report from there immediately!' In this deconstructive challenge to 'find' the personal 'I' that is 'me', the seeker becomes 'cornered' by Gangaji's insistence on immediacy; 'Can you find it? Is it there?' 'Quickly!' Under pressure, unable to mentally locate this 'I', 'Where, exactly *am* I?' in her next response, the seeker enters a space of not-knowing: 'I don't know. It's a bunch of thoughts (laughter)' (Gangaji, 1995, p. 116). Here, the unsettling process is evident from the 'strangeness' of the seeker's Humean 'answer' – How can 'I' be reduced to a 'bunch of thoughts?' and the absurdity of her situation, 'How can I not find myself?' 'Yes,' replies Gangaji, 'this *is* rather funny! This is the joke! Where is this *I* that must be given up, if all you can find is the thought of *I*?'

[*S*]: I don't know. I've formulated it. I've –

[*G*]: In this instant, allow any one of those formulations to sink back into its place of origin.

(Gangaji, 1995, p. 116)

The student begins to conceptually elaborate on her 'not-knowing' and in doing so she has moved out of the 'not-knowing space' and into conceptualization: 'I've formulated it …' Gangaji quickly cuts this conceptual elaboration by employing the deconstructive technique of bringing the seeker back to the here and now. 'In this instant', urges Gangaji, without the mediation of thought 'allow any one of those formulations to sink back into its place of origin.' Here, the instruction is to move outside of thought and turn awareness to its source.

With thought-constructed conceptualization momentarily 'stalled' by this instruction, the student is ready for an experiential realization of pure Advaita; in turning awareness to its source, in the disclosure of *ātman-brahman*-identity awareness, nothing is lost and nothing is gained:

[*G*]: What is lost?

[*S*]: Nothing is lost.

[*G*]: When a formulation arises, what is gained?

[*S*]: Nothing really.

[*G*]: Excellent.

(Gangaji, 1995, p. 116)

According to Advaita teachings, thought formulations come and go but they do not impinge on awareness. In the instant of Gangaji's questioning the seeker recognizes the loss-less, gain-less nature of self-realization. Ramana Maharshi's account of *ātman-brahman*-identity realization describes a purportedly unbroken realization of this same insight:

> Absorption in the Self continued unbroken from that time on. Other thoughts might come and go like the various notes of music, but the 'I' [*ātman*] continued like the fundamental *sruti* note that underlies and blends with all the other notes. Whether the body was engaged in talking, reading, or anything else, I was still centered on 'I'. (Osborne, 1970, p. 8)

Thoughts are not stopped, they arise and they fall, but the *ātman-brahman*-identity realization continues as an unbroken substratum, unaffected by the engagements of the body-mind because the superimposition of an objectified 'doer' and 'knower' are no longer mistaken for the 'true self' (*ātman*). Ramana Maharshi elaborates on how being in the state of a 'knower' obscures one's true nature:

> One who is properly established in the Atman knows that nothing happens in this world, that nothing is ever destroyed. Something is felt to be happening only when we are in the state of the pramata, the knower. This state is not one's real nature. For the jnani [enlightened being], who has given up the idea of the knower, nothing ever happens. (Godman, 1998c, p. 219)

With the lessening of the individual's personal investment in the dualistic entity status of 'doer', 'knower' and so on, comes the understanding that 'nothing happens in this world'. Corollary to this is the Advaita tenet that the 'true self' (*ātman*) is neither an agent of action nor subject to the consequences of apparent action and change. Nothing ever happens – so how can *ātman* be affected by anything? Philosophically, ideas of action and change belong to a 'middle ground' reality that is taken as real until *brahmajñāna* dawns. This 'middle ground' or 'space' is conceptualized between the absolutely 'unreal' (*asat*: for example, the 'son of a barren woman' and other such impossibilities) and the 'absolutely real' (*sat* which is *brahman* alone) and is the experiential space in which the inquiry into *brahman* takes place. This space is the reality by 'courtesy only' or the 'useful fiction' which Śaṅkara defined in his three-levelled view of reality as '*sadasatvilakṣaṇa*', other than the real or unreal, or '*sadasadbhyamanirvacanīya*', indescribable as either real or unreal.

The key Advaita teaching that there is nothing to be lost nor nothing to be gained in self-realization is the philosophical thrust behind Gangaji instructing her student to allow thought formulations to 'sink back to their place of origin'. Thought formulations are not 'who we really are' but mere superimpositions (*adhyāsa*) on undifferentiated *brahman*. To think that *ātman-brahman*-identity realization can be gained or lost is a constructed overlay that Gangaji aims to experientially undo. 'What is lost' and 'what is gained' reiterates Gangaji, 'when thought formulations arise and are released?' The seeker repeats, 'Nothing' (Gangaji, 1995, p. 116).

However, the non-dual insight that in awareness there is nothing to be lost or gained is broken by the seeker's next comment: 'I know that, and I still do it' (Gangaji, 1995, p. 116). The formulations of a 'knower' and a 'doer' have arisen and the seeker is following them. Gangaji points this out:

> The formulation *I know that* has arisen. A knower has arisen as a formulation. Allow the formulation *I know that* to dissolve back into its unformulated state. With ending the *I know* formulation, where is the knower? (Gangaji, 1995, p. 116, her italics)

Does the 'I know' formulation have any enduring substance? When it is 'undone' or 'dissolved back into its unformulated state' is there a 'knower' that is 'doing' this knowing? The deconstructive move is, once again, the command to find this 'knower'. 'Where is the knower?' The student responds: 'It doesn't exist' (Gangaji, 1995, p. 116).

The questioner has shifted back to an 'unknowing' space. To ameliorate any fear of this 'unknowing', Gangaji reiterates the Advaita 'fact' that nothing can be lost in the undoing of the concept of the 'knower' because, in Advaita teachings, the concept of a 'knower' has no 'real' basis in reality:

> [*G*]: Has anything been lost in the dissolution of the thought of *knower*?
> [*S*]: There's nothing lost.
> [*G*]: There is nothing to lose. What is fear now?
> [*S*]: Right now, nothing.
>
> (Gangaji, 1995, p. 117)

In the instant of now, the questioner recognizes that if nothing is lost then there is nothing to fear. Gangaji then advises her to be still and release all mental activity; to undo all conceptual formulations, even the formulation of undoing formulations:

> Be still then. Be quiet. Every time a formulation arises, even the concept that you have to get rid of the last formulation, recognize it as mind activity, as

> noise. Rather than embellishing upon the previous formulation, let all mental activity cease.
>
> (Gangaji, 1995, p. 117)

In full insight into non-duality, the undoing process itself must be undone in an ongoing deconstruction of deconstruction deconstructing itself. In other words, epistemic deconstruction in itself is not enough; insight into non-dual *brahman* requires the deconstruction of the process of epistemic deconstruction. This is what Ramana Maharshi was indicating in this practice instruction:

> [*Student*]: How will the mind become quiescent?
> [*Maharshi*]: By the inquiry 'Who am I?' The thought 'Who am I?' will destroy all other thoughts, and like the stick used for stirring the burning pyre, it will itself in the end get destroyed. Then, there will arise Self-realization.
>
> (Godman, 1992, p. 56)

'The stick used for stirring the burning pyre' eventually is consumed just as the question used to question the very process of questioning will undo itself in the dawning of self-realization. Gangaji leaves her student by pointing beyond formulations to 'open mind'.

> Living life through formulation doesn't work, does it? You have tried endless amounts of formulas, but, finally, you reach a certain point where you realize there is nothing to be gained by any formula of who one is. At that point, there is a natural quieting of the grasping tendency of mind. Mind can open, mind can rest. Open mind is no different from pure consciousness. At the instant of opening, the truth of limitless consciousness is not veiled by mental formulation. (Gangaji, 1995, p. 117)

As we have seen, the practice of self-inquiry, advocated by Ramana Maharshi and widely taught by contemporary Advaitins, hinges on the deconstructive question 'Who am I?' the challenge being for the student to find the 'I' that he or she unquestioningly attributes entity status to. In dialogues and in the meditative practice of 'Who am I?' one of the key deconstructive techniques employed is unfindability analysis. Unfindability analysis most often takes place, and is most easily identified, in dialogues such as the Gangaji encounter presented above. In such examples a questioner is forced to doubt the reality of his or her thought-constructed conception of 'I-as-something else' by simply being unable to coherently define it or to precisely locate it. This moment of doubt, that I have referred to above as a 'not-knowing space', can be phenomenologically read as an opening or a 'shift' in the practitioner's experiencing to a non-dual 'space' in which taken-for-granted ontological assumptions and fixed epistemic frames are shifted in the experience of the practitioner. This non-dual experiential space that deconstructive spiritual inquiry opens will be fully explained and argued for in the next chapter where the dynamics of such openings will be explored in more depth.

(b) Unfindability analysis in Zen Buddhism

In Zen, the overall pattern of practice and dialogues is centred on undoing practitioner attachments to substantialized ontological categories and reified polarizations of dualisms. To this end, Zen teachers work to disclose the mutually entailing and dynamically reciprocal nature of dichotomous categories of thought in the practitioner's experiencing by challenging the dualistic assumptions that support them. Accordingly, the deontologizing orientation of deconstructive spiritual inquiry in Zen aims to undo practitioner reifications of self by throwing into question seekers' constructions of the substantialized entity that they commonly refer to as 'self'. When challenged in this way, either directly by a teacher or in the objectless meditative process of *shikantaza*, practitioners find that they cannot actually locate this substantialized 'experiencer', that is, the 'I' that they so readily attribute entity status to.

In the following dialogue, in response to a student having difficulty with the practice of *shikantaza*, the *rōshi*[10] advises that 'it might be better to ponder a question' and sets the deconstructive question 'Who am I?' as a *kōan*.[11] This interaction is a good example of the teacher–student dynamic in Zen and presents interesting parallels and contrasts to the Advaita dialogue examined above. The beginning of the interaction runs thus:

> [*Rōshi*]: Who are you? [No answer.] Who are you!
> [*Student*]: [pausing] I don't know.
> [*R*]: Good! Do you know what you mean by 'I don't know'?
> [*S*]: No, I don't.
> [*R*]: You are You! You are only You – that is all.
> …
> [*R*]: When I said that I would ask you who you are, I didn't want you to reason out an answer but only to penetrate deeper and deeper into yourself with 'Who am I?' When you come to the sudden inner realization of your true nature, you will be able to respond instantly without reflection.
> What is this [suddenly striking tatami mat with baton]?
> [No answer]

> Probe further! Your mind is almost ripe.
>
> (Kapleau, 1989, p. 153, square brackets in text.)

The *rōshi* has set the question to provoke an inner realization. The student's 'not-knowing' is approved as 'a good sign' and he is encouraged to penetrate the question further. The gesture of suddenly striking the mat and asking, 'What is this?' is a classic Zen technique to unsettle fixed definitions of things. The student is thus sent away, unable to answer, with the *rōshi* encouraging him to 'probe further' into this not-knowing.

At the next *dokusan*, the dialogue continues:

> [*Student*]: I have been asking and asking, 'Who am I?' until I feel that there is just no answer to this question.
>
> [*Rōshi*]: You won't find an entity called 'I.'
>
> [*S*]: [heatedly] Then why am I asking the question!
>
> [*R*]: Because in your present state you can't help yourself. The ordinary person is forever asking, 'Why?' or 'What?' or 'Who?' … [The question] is an abstraction … There is no real answer to 'Who?' 'What?' or 'Why?' Why is sugar sweet? Sugar is sugar. Sugar!
>
> [*S*]: You told me earlier, 'You are You!' All right, I am I – I accept that. Isn't this enough? What more need I do? Why must I keep struggling with this question?
>
> [*R*]: Because this understanding is external to you – you don't really know what you mean by 'I am I.'[12] You must come up against the question with the force of a bomb, and all your intellectual notions and ideas must be annihilated. The only way to resolve this question is to come to the explosive inner realization that everything is ultimately reducible to Nothing. If your understanding is merely theoretical, you will forever ask, 'Who?' 'What?' and 'Why?'
>
> (Kapleau, 1989, pp. 153–154)

The student's efforts to 'answer' the question have moved him out of the 'not-knowing space' that his teacher approved of earlier. As with the Advaita student in the dialogue above, he is focusing on 'figuring out' the 'problem' and has moved into conceptualization. When told that the entity 'I' that he is looking for is unfindable, the student questions the validity of the exercise: 'Why am I asking the question!' He challenges his teacher by asserting that he accepts the 'answer' 'I am I' so what more does he need to do. His teacher retorts that theoretical understanding is not realization and only generates more dualistic 'who', 'what', and 'why' questions. The *rōshi*'s point here is to undermine any idea of a substantialized experiencer by reinforcing the unfindability that the student is struggling with. The student is thus 'cornered' in his own structures of knowing that, according to this teacher, must be 'blown apart' by the inquiry 'with the force of a bomb'.

One Zen practitioner describes the twin dynamic of finding no answers and having no answers accepted as being '*stuck*'. 'You get stuck and then you say, "I don't know"' (InterviewJ00, 2000). That is, the questioner is trapped in his own logical process with no apparent conceptual 'exit':

> Your brain has a process to work something through logic. You reach a point where the logic just doesn't work and you'll walk in, present something and he'll go 'sorry!' and there's nowhere to go, there's no avenue of escape. (InterviewJ00, 2000)

Moreover, this practitioner further describes the process of being stuck as a not-knowing: 'you get stuck and then you say "I don't know" and that's also a very radical space to be in' (InterviewJ00, 2000). This 'radical space of not-knowing' represents an experiential 'stillpoint' in both traditions. The experience of 'stuck-ness' is the experiential 'endpoint' of the mind scrambling around for an answer that is unfindable within the usual epistemic framings. Since all conceptualizations are rejected or refuted by the teacher, the student experiences his dilemma as being 'stuck'. It is important to note that the experiential quality is not only mental; there is an ontological aspect in which the mind is not felt as separate from the body and the student experiences this 'stuck-ness' as 'a physical thing right through my whole body' (InterviewJ20, 2001). Not only is thinking 'stalled' by the recognition of its own limitations, but also there is a physical sense of being 'stuck' in this 'not-knowing space'.

The Zen application of the technique of unfindability analysis is most obvious in the question-and-answer dynamics of *dokusan* as outlined above. The Zen master's point being that no matter how (or where) the student 'looks' he or she will not find the everyday substantialized 'I' that entity status is attributed to. Every attempt to 'fix' such an entity results in the student becoming experientially 'stuck' in the pincers of a not-knowing from which there is no conceptual 'escape'. In addition to this dialogical challenge, a striking facet of the objectless meditative practice of *shikantaza*, wherein the student has nothing to lean upon, is a felt deconstructive process in which practitioners are unable to 'find' any solid sense of self. In speaking of *shikantaza*, Zen practitioners commonly report that the boundaries of self and non-self seem to dissolve: 'You can't find your self or anything solid.' And when an interviewee was asked 'How can you not find you?' she replied: 'A whole lot of things fall apart. You don't seem to need what you thought you needed. What was indispensable just doesn't seem so solid' (InterviewB00, 2000). This loss of a sense of self is experienced as a 'falling apart' or 'disassembling':

> All those walls that you've happily built up over the years they just fall apart and you kind of disassemble there somewhere and you have to make sense of it. On retreat you get a lot deeper because a lot more of that happens – you do disassemble! (InterviewB00, 2000)

This ontological 'disassembling' is experienced as disorientating and 'scary':

> Getting yourself off familiar ground is a scary thing – you don't know what to do. I've thought, 'I don't know who this person is – Who the heck am I?' 'What am I doing? Why am I doing it? Who is doing what?' (InterviewB00, 2000)

The practitioner's disorientation, her unfamiliar entry into a not-knowing experiential space, has produced a series of radical deconstructive questions indicative of her inability to 'find' her usual unquestioned 'solid' sense of self. 'Who is doing what?' is a primary deconstructive question that signifies the beginning of a 'no-subject' state in which no stable sense of 'self as subject' nor 'other as object' is recognized.

The meditative practice of *shikantaza* initiates a process of unfindability analysis in the immediate experiencing of the practitioner in which 'self seeks self' and is unable to conceptually 'find itself'. This internal problematizing of substantialized ideas of self produces a radical and paradoxical self-questioning along the lines of the 'Who is doing what?' example (given above). According to Zen master Ekai Korematsu, this is the 'naturally deconstructive' process of *shikantaza* in which:

> … habitual patterns and conditioning are naturally undone. Everyone without exception is made up of all kinds of habits or patterns, past conditions, all the packaging – and putting oneself in the sitting naturally unfolds this – unpacks these conditionings. But it doesn't mean that these conditionings go away, that is wrong, rather they become kind of free floating instead of fixed and solid. The mind is dynamic and flexible. Dōgen Zenji simply said that this kind of mind knew nothing. (Korematsu, 2000)

In this analysis, 'sitting still' in the prescribed Zen manner discloses a dynamic and flexible mind that does not seek to create substantialized ontologies.[13]

Dualistic ontologized conditionings are naturally 'unpacked' and are understood as being dynamic and 'free floating'. In the following report, a practitioner describes a practice experience of the 'naturally deconstructive' process of *shikantaza* manifested in the felt 'dissolution' of notions of identity, action and location:

> [During] sitting it felt like a wave came out of nowhere and hit me. My connection to where I was, what I was doing, who I was, suddenly seemed to dissolve under the impact of? What? I don't know. It felt like I had been turned upside down and shaken. The 'wave' seemed to come from within me yet it was also outside of me. But all that was, was somehow riding this wave with me. (InterviewKC9901, 2000)

Unfindability analysis is a deconstructive technique, employed by Zen teachers in dialogues and ignited through the practice of *shikantaza* that experientially discloses to students the 'unfindability' and thus nonexistence of substantialized ontologies. Through this process, the student finds that she cannot 'answer' such elementary questions as 'Who am I?', 'Where am I?', and 'What am I doing?' with any ontological certainty.

In both Advaita and Zen the empirical, dualistic 'I-as-subject-operating-in-a-world-of-objects' is disclosed as being unfindable. In this process, both traditions work to experientially disclose to the practitioner the ultimate 'unreality' of any bifurcation between dualisms. Hence, the difficulties that the undoing of dualistic categories and entities pose for the student are very similar; often culminating in an experience of being existentially 'stuck' and phenomenologically entering a non-dual experiential 'space' that can be described as *not-knowing*. Of course, the ontological status of the 'real and true I' differs in each tradition, but despite the supreme ontological status of the Advaita 'self' and the non-ontology of the Zen 'self', the processes and techniques employed to undo dualistic constructions and the experiential impact on the student are very similar.

Bringing everything back to the here and now

The deconstructive technique of 'bringing everything back to the here and now' serves to cut practitioner projections of linear causal notions of time and space by vigorously situating the inquiry 'right here' and 'right now'. In both traditions, this technique has the experiential effect of 'cornering' the student in the absolute present moment in which there is no 'room' for conceptual projections of the future or abstractions from the past to take hold and proliferate.

(a) Zen Buddhism

As we have seen, by logically demonstrating that *nirvāṇa* and *saṃsāra* are 'not two', Nāgārjuna showed that the locus of liberation is 'right here' and 'right now' – a liberative insight that was expanded and extended in the teachings of Dōgen, who located the practice of *zazen* 'in the dynamics of the absolute present, in and through which all time and existence are realized' (Kim, 1987, p. 68). In this teaching, of utmost importance is the place-and-time, the here-and-now in which one actually is. This absolute immediacy is experientially conveyed to students in the dynamics of the practice situation wherein linear abstractions and dualistic projections of time and space are countered by the teacher's insistence that there is only here and only now. Accordingly, Zen master Ekai Korematsu dismisses questions on the 'best' time to begin practice thus:

> The idea of starting comes with our linear sense of time. This present time actually contains endless past and endless future but if we treat them as separate, if we single out the linear forms of past and present and future, we fall from the Way. We only exist in this present so why do you wait? How can we wait? I'll start tomorrow I'll get everything worked out – that's how we think. (Korematsu, 2000)

In a similar instruction, Hōgen Yamahata equates any abstraction or projection of time that moves one away from the encounter of 'here-now' as 'ignorance':

> Ignorance is whenever you ignore this encounter of HERE NOW. That is it. That is the only ignorance. Because whenever we settle for, or grab, any assumptional ideas, we already slip from this encounter of here now. This is nothing other than ignorance.
>
> We usually make lots of assumptions, like: 'if this happens I will be happy,' or 'if that happens I will be miserable'. But what is your reality NOW? When you have such an assumptional viewpoint or concept, you are not HERE NOW. You are somewhere else, millions of miles away from THIS. When you have so many assumptional ideas, with endless questions, at that time you don't meet with THIS real life. In this way, we are ceaselessly escaping and wandering off, so that we miss this one moment of deep peace. This one moment of deep peace is the very arrival at the very end, and at the same time, the real starting point of new life. But we miss it. (Yamahata, 2004b)[14]

According to Hōgen-san, being fully present in the here-now of each encounter is the non-dual beginning and end of 'this' real life. On retreat, during a formal *dharma* talk (*teishō*), Hōgen instructs his students to practice outside of concepts in 'now-by-now':

> Real awareness of now is better than any future enlightenment.
> Now cannot be measured by time – time is a concept.
> Now is outside of concepts.
> If I meet you now then it is a life encounter – without baggage of past present future – just now!
> If you make a concept out of now it's already rotting – no longer fresh.
> Real now – now by now is always new – fresh: that's why it's a life encounter.
> (Yamahata, 1999b)

Here, Hōgen articulates the dynamic of now. In this instruction, he empties the absolute present of any substantiality and locates it outside of the usual dualistic concepts of time consisting of duration and progression. According to Hōgen-san, now that is not reified as a fixed concept is 'fresh' always 'new' and it is in the now-by-now of these new, fresh moments that life encounters, i.e., authentic meetings, really occur. As 'real awareness' of now is not dependent on the linear objectification of time as past, present and future, but rather in dynamic movement on the beginningless and endless continuum of dependent co-origination, now is ever-present and ever-fresh.

When a student asks: 'Can you describe this here now encounter? What it is to be in the here now encounter? Is there any word you can use to describe it?' Hōgen answers: 'Ah yes, shall I give it to you? (Hōgen strikes the bell …) This is it!' (Yamahata, 2004b)

In Zen, the response, 'this is it!' is perhaps the most direct presentation of the here and now that a teacher can offer. Hōgen emphasizes the importance of understanding that 'This' present moment 'is it!' by recounting his first meeting with his master in which Hōgen asked: 'What is life?' 'What is life? What is my life? What is the real meaning of life?', provoking a direct demonstration of Zen:

> Suddenly, he grabbed my shoulders and shook them 'THIS IS IT!' In his answer, he gave me all of himself, his life itself. His answer was not intellectual at all, he replied with just life itself. His eyes were very straight and very serene, and very strong. I was deeply shocked, but I still stuck to my intellectual level. My intellect was not satisfied but I felt something directly in my innermost depths. (Yamahata, 2004a)

Not all students can immediately intuitively 'grasp' the direct teaching, Hōgen notes that the response 'shocked' him but it wasn't enough to experientially 'push' him into the here and now.

The emphasis in Zen on bringing everything back to the here and now serves to problematize dualistic understandings of self and things as permanent, independent entities functioning in linear ideas of time. In addition to this, it works to cut practitioner projections of future attainment in practice and ideas of past successes or failures. If the practitioner is 'just doing this', whatever 'this' may be, then there is no conceptual 'room' for oppositional modes of thinking or reification. According to Dōgen, 'the time right now is all there ever is, each being-time is without exception entire time ... Entire being, the entire world, exists in the time of each and every now'[15] (Waddell, 1979, p. 118) and an experiential understanding of this is what the key Zen deconstructive moves of 'This is it!' and 'Why not now?' are attempting to ignite.

(b) Advaita Vedānta

The modern Advaita master Poonjaji begins a *satsang* by negating the idea of practice as cause and freedom as effect. According to Poonjaji, this dualism only serves to postpone what is available *now*:

> We have a conception that by practice we shall become free. Such a person is postponing his freedom. We become enlightened in this instant only and not as a result of ten year's practice. Freedom is available now. (Poonja, 1992b, p. 35)

In another instance, he stresses the urgency and the unique nature, the 'new-ness' of the task by stating that 'we have not done this at any time before' (Poonja, 1992a). Since Poonjaji gave this teaching towards the end of his life, and is speaking at a *satsang* full of long-time devotees, it is safe to assume that most people in the room have certainly done this 'Who am I?' practice before. However, what Poonjaji is emphasizing here is that there is no 'before' or 'after' in this practice, for the question to be fully existentially asked there is only the moment of asking; the *now* of the inquiry that cannot be postponed.

> So who are you? ... You will have to ask the question, 'Who am I?' This is what we have come here to understand, and we have not done this at any time before. This question must be solved, but we have postponed it, everyone has postponed it for millions of years. We will not postpone this here. (Poonja, 1992a)

According to Poonjaji, if the inquiry is really performed 'here and now, in this instant' then there is no need for a method. For Poonjaji, self cannot be anywhere else or at any other time:

> There is no method to practice. Simply find out, 'Who am I?' This is not a method or practice or *sadhana* [spiritual practice]. This can be done here and now, in this instant, because the Self is here. (Poonja, 1992a)

Like Zen master Hōgen, Poonjaji accuses his students of postponing what is available now. Poonjaji then moves from a straightforward negation of spiritual methods with their accompanying baggage of ends and means, to fixing his students' awareness in the immediate present moment –meditation is a move away, thought is a move away, a move away into a nonexistent projected future. The instruction is to 'stay quiet in now':

> Do not think. Do not even meditate. Meditation means postponing for old age or at least for next year that which is available now. Meditation means rejecting the rose flower and hunting for the thorn. Don't meditate here. Just now! Sit quietly! (Poonja, 1992a)

Coming to the end of his instruction, Poonjaji confronts his students with a series of powerfully deconstructive questions that undermine any timebound dualistic projections of cause and effect: 'Why postpone this until some other moment? Have you ever seen the next moment?' Here the challenge is to bring everything back to the here and now:[16]

> Don't think! Whenever you meditate, you are postponing Now! Why postpone this until some other time, until some other moment? Have you ever seen the next moment? Why not now? Isn't it available now? What kind of meditation do you need? (Poonja, 1992a)[17]

Despite the differing ontological underpinnings, the Advaita master Poonjaji and Zen master Hōgen, ask the same deconstructive question of their students: 'Why not now?'[18] This unanswerable question serves to narrow the student's temporal experiential parameters to the point where there is no 'room' for linear dualistic projections and abstractions of time. Any attempt to conceptually approach the key deconstructive question 'Why not now?' existentially corners the seeker in the very 'now' that he or she is seeking. The 'strangeness' of the question itself is well expressed in this Advaita practitioner's response: 'What kind of event is this, here, now? ... There is something strange in the difficulty of even formulating this question' (Odell, 2004).

Both Zen and Advaita admit of no linear notions of before and after, here and there. According to both traditions, we only 'really' exist in the 'now' of the present moment. In Advaita, self is always present and the practitioner cannot ever be separate from that self. In Zen, self is never fixed and dualistic conceptions of time and space are attempts to reify and polarize entities and categories that, in reality, are fluid and mutually entailing. The deconstructive technique of bringing everything back to the here and now is employed in both traditions to undo any goal-orientated bifurcations of linear ideas of time by situating the practitioner *right here* and *right now* and thus allowing no experiential 'room' for temporal and causal conceptual abstractions and projections of here-and-there, before-and-after and now-and-then.

In the experiential trajectory of practice, the techniques of unfindability analysis and bringing everything back to the here and now serve to existentially 'corner' the student in the moment of questioning. In both traditions, the student experiences being 'pinned down' by the immediacy of the inquiry with no conceptual room to manoeuvre. Practitioners report that attempts to 'answer' the key deconstructive questions of 'Who am I?' and 'Why not now?' result in an experiential sense of being 'stuck' which is described as a 'radical space' of not-knowing.

One of the most effective ways that the practitioner is shifted into this 'not-knowing space' is through problematizing ontological and epistemological adherence to either side of a dualism. For instance, in the examples given above, subject–object distinctions are experienced as 'blurred' in the undoing of self and other in the 'Who is doing what?' experience of *shikantaza*, while presence and absence are both shown to be constructs of mind in Poonjaji's subversion of the dualism of coming and going.[19] When analysed separately, unfindability analysis and bringing everything back to the here and now can be said to do the 'preliminarily deconstructive work' of problematizing the student's attachments to dualisms by focusing on 'unanswerable' deconstructive questions that challenge and confront practitioner's taken-for-granted dualistic patterns of knowing and relating:

> Practice really confronts you. It makes you doubt things that you think you know, it pushes you up against the way we define everything. What [it does] is … really show you where you get caught, where you're hooked by ideas about things, relationships to things. (InterviewJ00, 2000)

The experiential sense of being 'stuck' or 'caught' is indicative of the challenge that these non-dual understandings pose for 'commonsense' reliance on either/or patterns of thinking and results from the practitioner's inability to find an 'answer' to these deconstructive questions without falling into contradiction and paradox.

Paradoxical problems

With the deconstructive techniques of paradox and negation, we begin to move into the heart of the dynamics of the experiential undoing of habitual oppositional ways of thinking. Paradox intensifies the deconstructive process in the sense that the student's taken-for-granted dualistic constructions are thrown into question and experientially undone through the undermining of the very notions that support them. The use of paradox both exposes the limits of dualistic structures and their ultimate relativity. For the student, still in the grip of dualisms that 'everyday' life is driven by, this can be an epistemologically unsettling and ontologically challenging experience. In the practice situation, Zen and Advaita teachers further 'develop' the undermining of practitioner adherence to dualisms by exploiting the rising sense of paradox and contradiction that the practitioner experiences when familiarly structured either/or patterns of thought are problematized by non-dual understandings.

In Advaita and Zen dialogues, 'paradoxical expressions issue from the discontinuity between ordinary awareness or conventional truth and enlightened awareness or ultimate truth. The discontinuity becomes manifest and paradox begins to emerge wherever and whenever a human being who participates in conventional truth begins to seek ultimate truth' (Wright, 1982, p. 327).[20] In this discussion, we will describe how paradox arises when the dualistic 'conventional' view of the seeker 'collides' with unfolding non-dual understandings and explanations. This is paradox in 'its first and most basic ... etymological sense, something that is contrary to ordinary expectation, a startling statement that is literally "against the opinion" of conventional thought' (Wright, 1982, p. 326).

In the practice situations of both traditions, paradox emerges when the student attempts to frame the unfolding non-dualistic understandings within dualistic frameworks. That is, non-duality is perceived as contradictory and paradoxical when the practitioner is operating from a dualistic point of view. In the following exchange, Ramana Maharshi makes this point clear:

> [*Student*]: What are the obstacles which hinder realisation of the Self?
> [*Ramana Maharshi*]: They are habits of mind (*vasanas*).
> [*S*]: How to overcome the mental habits (*vasanas*)?

[*R*]: By realising the Self.
[*S*]: That is a vicious circle.
[*R*]: It is the ego which raises such difficulties, creating obstacles and then suffers from the perplexity of apparent paradoxes. Find out who makes the enquiries and the Self will be found.

(Maharshi, 1984, p. 4)

In keeping with the Advaita insistence on the student having to find out for himself, Ramana refuses to enter into a theoretical discussion regarding problems and methods. When the student complains that Ramana's 'answer' is a vicious circle, Ramana responds from the absolute viewpoint; the student's difficulty arises from obstacles raised by the ego which is then subject to the perplexity of apparent paradoxes. According to Ramana, if the seeker insists on creating a duality between an un-realized self and a future realized self then paradox will emerge. From the perspective of the non-dual self, in keeping with the Advaita distinction between reality and appearance, these paradoxes are 'apparent', that is, they have no bearing in reality.

In a similar vein, when Zen students complain that Dōgen's practice instructions are contradictory, Ekai Korematsu reminds them that Dōgen is 'pointing out the essentials', that is, the ultimate non-duality of opposites:

> Dōgen explains things from all ways – this way and then that – pointing out the essentials of *zazen* – what this is and what this is – no separation … always turning, complete. Dōgen Zenji also says, 'when opposites arise the Buddha-mind is lost' – when one side of things come up, the other side, the back part is hidden. Like a piece of paper with two sides turning, always changing, not static. We may think in opposites like that but as soon as we make a certain type of effort we see that opposites come and go, always in movement. Dōgen Zenji is pointing this out. (Korematsu, 2000)[21]

The 'effort' that Ekai-oshō is referring to is the practice of 'sitting like a mountain' or *shikantaza* in which, it is claimed, dualities are experientially disclosed to be mutually entailing or not-two. According to this teaching, when the student realizes the dynamic nature of opposites then she will not fixate on one side of a polarization and be free of notions of contradiction. Ekai continues by referring directly to Dōgen's use of the two truths; 'our tendency is to … get stuck in one truth – the relative truth – but Dōgen Zenji is using both truths to point out one'. According to Ekai-oshō, the crux of the problem is either/or patterns of thinking: 'We think in such dualistic ways; if it's not absolute it's relative; if it's not relative it's absolute. If it's not conditioned, it's unconditioned.

Dōgen Zenji works with these ... two aspects of reality that both complement and complete each other' (Korematsu, 2000).

In the above two examples both teachers instruct from the 'absolute' viewpoint and maintain that contradictions, vicious circles and other paradoxical problems will cease to bother the student once non-dual insight arises. This is the simplest, most direct answer that teachers can give their students; however, it is usually not sufficient to move the student out of his or her 'conventional' habitual dualistic viewpoint. A further deconstructive move that takes the student into the heart of dualistic paradoxes is required to unsettle and begin to unravel the practitioner's habitual adherence to dualistic patterns of thought.

The deconstructive point in both traditions is not to resolve or remove apparent non-dualistic paradoxes, but rather to situate the student in an experiential *aporia* that 'traps' the seeker in the heart of his or her own bifurcatory processes. From the student's viewpoint, the unfolding non-dual understandings are found to be irreconcilable within conventional oppositional structures of thought, which creates an experiential tension that is deconstructively exploited by the teacher to strike at the dualistic foundations of habitual oppositional thinking.

For example, the Advaitin Poonjaji problematizes the dualism of 'presence and absence' in the dialogue quoted above by challenging his student with the question, 'If you know how to create separation in the presence, why don't you create presence in the separation?' (Godman, 1998c, p. 27). Hence, according to Poonjaji, there is no presence and absence outside of the student's own mental fixations on such opposing categories. The required view is not to adhere to either for, according to Advaita, there is no presence and no absence. Poonjaji emphasizes this by concluding with the deconstructive question: 'If you don't allow the mind to create a distance, who goes and where does he go?' (Godman, 1998c, p. 28). Here, Poonjaji augments his paradoxical negation of presence and absence by pointing out the ultimate unfindability of the separated self that is subject to the dualisms of coming and going.

Ekai Korematsu also stresses the paradoxical nature of the unfindability of separations between dualisms by telling his Zen students that 'the infinitely large, infinitely spacious, and timeless is the same as the infinitely small, the barriers fall apart and that is the central focus of Zen' (Korematsu, 1999b). Thus, according to Ekai Korematsu, the infinitely large and the infinitely small are not-two; the focus of Zen is not on dualisms such as 'large' and 'small' but rather on the barriers between such oppositional dualistic categories 'falling apart'.

Experientially speaking, the key dualistic problem that both Ekai-oshō and Poonjaji address in the above instructions is bifurcated oppositional ways of thinking that obscure direct non-dual insight. In both cases, students are instructed that there is no 'correct' side of a dualism to adhere to because in

Zen neither being nor non-being is to be taken hold of and in Advaita, *brahman* admits of no relationships. Both are 'outside' of either/or adherence to dualisms. In both traditions, to favour 'presence' over 'absence' or to differentiate 'large' over 'small' is to adhere to one side of a dualism and to be trapped in the pincers of dichotomous either/or patterns of thought.

In these instructions, Poonjaji and Ekai-oshō are undermining two of the mainstays of dualistic thinking: the law of contradiction and the principle of the excluded middle. This undermining serves to place the student in a 'felt' paradoxical 'knot' between dualisms which cannot be undone within conventional dualistic patterns of thought. In both examples, teachers are striving to move practitioners away from either/or ways of thinking and into the dynamics of non-dual understandings.

The use of paradox is thus taken directly into the practice situation in both Advaita Vedānta and Zen Buddhism, where, along with negation, it is employed and exploited as a key deconstructive strategy to 'open' the paradoxical space between dualisms in the experiencing of the practitioner. Thus, in many ways, paradox and negation represent the hinge on which experiential undoing turns. In the following sections, we will primarily concentrate on how paradox arises and is employed in the Zen and Advaita practice situation to subvert the law of contradiction. The subversion of either/or lines of thought or the 'trap of the excluded middle' will be described and analysed in the following section on negation, which plays a sister role to paradox in Advaita and Zen deconstructive strategies.

(a) Advaita Vedānta

In the Advaita practice situation, the dualistic contradictions that arise from the Advaita insistence that ultimate reality or *nirguṇa brahman* is beyond conventional predication and discursive thought are employed and exploited by teachers to experientially place the student in the heart of their own dualistic bifurcations and ignite the *ātman-brahman*-identity realization. From the student's point of view, this emphasis situates him or her in the contradictory situation of receiving teachings and practices that, by definition, can never lead him to the liberation that he seeks. The basic 'problem' from this point of view is that since *nirguṇa brahman* admits of no predications or qualities and transcends all dualities, nothing can 'really' be said of it and no practice or teaching can 'really' indicate it. As we have seen, the Advaita solution is that the seeker must realize that 'nothing ever happens' and, as a consequence of this fundamental teaching, that there is 'nothing' to seek and 'nothing' to be attained.

Working from the above presuppositions, the Advaita master Poonjaji articulates the non-duality of seeker and sought by reiterating his core deconstructive instruction of 'You are not to do anything':

> We must touch emptiness whatever we do. We can't do without this empty moment. We ignore this moment because it is so readily available. You are not to do anything.
>
> It [i.e., the empty moment] happens between thought and thought also, when the mind takes a rest. Two thoughts cannot happen at the same time. Think. Stop. Next thought.
>
> Always you are surrounded by that which you seek outside. You are inside that thing. And outside also; it is the same thing. Only we have to pay a little attention. (Poonja, 1992b, pp. 68–69)

Here, Poonjaji locates the 'empty moment' in the space between 'thought and thought'. In this teaching, Poonjaji begins by indicating the ever-present nature of the 'moment' that the seeker is looking for. What is being sought is here and now, readily available, yet ignored by attaching to thoughts. According to Poonjaji, the ever-present realization can be ignited by turning attention not towards thoughts but towards the empty space between the rising and falling of thoughts.[22]

After pointing this out, Poonjaji then enters into the heart of the student's objectification of seeking liberation 'outside' self by employing the non-dual 'both/and' deconstructive move to blur his student's constructions of searching inside or outside self: 'You are inside … and outside too … it is the same thing.' Hence, being 'inside' and 'outside' at the same time is not contradictory for, according to Advaita, 'it is the same thing'.

Here, Poonjaji is asking his student to realize that in the empty moment, which by extension is all moments, there is no opposition between 'inside' and 'outside'. The instruction is 'felt' to be contradictory or paradoxical only when the student adheres to the separation generated by thought. Adhering to one side of a dualism is what substantializes thought and keeps generating contradictions for the practitioner to become 'stuck' in.

In an experiential account of this point, a contemporary Advaita practitioner offers a felt 'solution' to the problem of becoming 'stuck' in contradictions. In this case it is the contradiction generated by the Advaita insistence on immutable, undifferentiated reality and the empirical 'fact' of manifestation:

> Reality is appearance and appearance is reality. There is nothing else either of them could be. And yet, as appearance it is subject to a continual unfolding and self-revelation, and endless disillusionment, while as reality it never

changes at all. This is sublimely unproblematic simply because reality is no longer opposed to appearance. (Odell, 2004)

Since, according to Advaita, there is nothing but *brahman* then there are 'really' no differences, in any sense, anywhere. Differentiation is the result of oppositional patterns of thought. In this experiential 'meltdown' between the boundaries of opposites the practitioner can suddenly 'see' reality and appearance as being identical yet different, different yet identical, and there being no contradiction in this.

(b) Zen Buddhism

In the Sōtō Zen practice situation, teachers admit no separation between the practice of *zazen* and realization, for, according to Sōtō teachings, the very act of *zazen* is a phenomenological expression of enlightenment. As we have seen, given the centrality of practice, one of the key dualistic 'problems' to be overcome in Zen is the practitioner's tendency to substantialize *shikantaza* as a 'thing' that leads to realization and to reify realization as a 'thing' that can be attained. Contemporary Sōtō teacher Taigen Dan Leighton warns his students against such two-way reification in the following instruction: 'Just sitting [*shikantaza*] is not a meditation technique or practice or any "thing" at all. "Just sitting" is a verb rather than a noun, the dynamic activity of being fully present' (Loori, 2002, p. 1). Based on Dōgen's non-dual insight that spiritual practice and spiritual awakening are one (*shushō-ittō*), Sōtō Zen instructional discourse works to actualize insight into the interrelated, interpenetrating, empty nature of all things in the practitioner's immediate experiencing. To this end, a non-dual dynamic that deconstructs the boundaries of polarized dichotomies by turning, juxtaposing, and/or reversing practitioners' dualistic notions of identity and difference is one of the most effective Sōtō challenges to reification. Dōgen's description of the relationship of the one and the many, the different and the same, in *Shōbōgenzō Zenki*[23] highlights the importance of dereifying both sides of dichotomies: 'though not oneness, it is not difference, though it is not difference, it is not sameness, though it is not sameness, this is not multifariousness' (Waddell and Abe, 1972a, p. 76).

According to Heine, Dōgen's 'paradoxical identity-in-difference ... reveals the middle path [as] unbound by, yet giving rise to, all polarities' (Heine, 1982, p. 56). For Dōgen, all things are dynamically not-two, and for the practitioner to experientially understand this dynamic not-twoness, 'the sameness of things' differences and the differences of things' sameness' (Waddell and Abe, 1972b, p. 130) must be 'penetrated' (i.e. non-dualistically understood) in practice. In other words, the dualistic sense of contradiction that the practitioner encounters when told that all things, including practice and realization, are 'identical in difference' and 'different in identity' must be undone by highlighting the creatively dynamic interplay between both perspectives. In Heine's view, 'two or more meanings seen in a single phrase may not imply contradiction, but indicate that in Dōgen's understanding there are multiple and paradoxical dimensions of impermanence' (Heine, 1982, p. 46).

In a commentary on Dōgen's multi-dimensional and multi-perspectival vision, Ekai Korematsu states that in Zen thought and practice 'nothing is in contradiction to anything else – everything is moving in a dynamic relationship'. Ekai-oshō refers to practice instructions that indicate this dynamic relationship as 'reversals' that represent 'the turning of the *dharma* [which] is the meaning of impermanence – always reversing or turning ... In practice, you turn *dharma*, *dharma* turns you' (Korematsu, 2000).[24]

Ekai-oshō's description of the two-way turning of *dharma* is experientially echoed in this practitioner's insight into the non-dual 'stillness' of *shikantaza*:

> The stillness is still but it's not always the same stillness. There is still movement in the stillness – it's a funny expression. It's all the same thing when you talk about stillness and emptiness and space and there's still everything in there, the movement and whatnot. (InterviewB00, 2000)

In this report, 'stillness' is not perceived as being in opposition to 'movement'. The practitioner finds that 'there is still movement in the stillness' and that 'talking about stillness and emptiness and space' does not mean that 'movement' is excluded. In this description she has hit upon the 'dynamic stillness' of *shikantaza* in which the dichotomous boundaries of movement and stillness are in dynamic interplay rather than rigid opposition.

The unhinging of clear-cut definitions of identity and difference and the pointing toward their ultimate dynamic interplay has the paradoxical experiential effect of leaving aspirants with no 'solid ground' on which to predicate objectifications and reifications. In this process, things are shown to be 'not-two' by experientially opening the paradoxical space between dualisms wherein both sides of a dichotomy can be simultaneously affirmed and negated in the practitioner's experiencing without apparent contradiction.

The Zen and Advaita deconstructive use and exploitation of contradiction are similar in effect in spite of the fact that their respective strategies are 'launched' from differing ontological positions. Based on Dōgen's vision of the non-dual interpenetration of all things, Zen 'aims' to ignite a 'difference in identity' and 'identity in difference' understanding in the practitioner's immediate experiencing. In contrast, Advaita emphasizes an experiential understanding that hinges on highlighting the ultimate non-validity of oppositional manifestations of difference and identify in the all-encompassing 'identity-of-identities' that is *brahman*.

In the practice situation, Zen and Advaita teachers deconstructively challenge practitioners' dualistic notions of identity and difference by problematizing adherence to *both* sides of a dualism and 'leaving' the practitioner in the paradoxical 'space' between contradictions. Thus, both Zen and Advaita aim to destabilize oppositional modes of thinking by blurring the strict cognitive demarcation between bifurcations and placing the student in the contradictory 'middle space' between oppositional categories. For the purposes of this study, the point to follow is that once dualistic oppositional modes of thinking lose their stability and everything is experienced as being either in perpetual non-oppositional flux (Zen) or perpetual non-oppositional permanence (Advaita), the principle of contradiction becomes experientially irrelevant and philosophically inoperable.

Negation

Along with paradox, the deconstructive technique of negation is one of the driving forces of deconstructive spiritual inquiry. Since both Advaita and Zen claim that the fundamental characteristic of reality is non-dual and unconditioned, negative expressions are a common feature of instructional discourse in both traditions. As we have seen, such negative pointers as non-grasping, no-mind, unborn, non-thinking, and not-knowing (among others) are emphasized in the foundational texts and frequently employed by teachers to refute students' dualistic attachments to reified concepts of self and path.

In Zen, a paradigmatic example of such negation is seen in this early dialogue from the Tun Huang caves:

> Questioner: If we wish to enter the Path, what Dharma should we practice, what Dharma should we study, what Dharma do we seek, what Dharma do we experience, what Dharma do we attain, in order to proceed toward enlightenment?
>
> Answer: No Dharma is studied, and there is no seeking. No Dharma is experienced, and there is no attaining. No Dharma is awakened to, and there is no Path that can be cultivated. This is enlightenment.
>
> (Cleary, 1986, pp. 107–108)

Before embarking on the path, the student has asked for the key categories of practice, study, cultivation, experience and attainment to be outlined and explained. In keeping with the experiential emphasis of Zen, and with the aim of 'nipping' any potential reification 'in the bud', the teacher negates all these 'indispensable' categories with a series of apophatic 'answers'. Such a response serves to place the inquiry outside the either/or structures of the discursive mind and alert the student to the dangers of substantializing the path.

In Advaita, Poonjaji's simple negation of all spiritual methods serves the same purpose:

> [*Student*] Please tell me how to realise the Truth.
> [*Poonjaji*] You don't have to do any practice. You don't have to chant any mantras. You don't have to do any yogic *asanas*, and you don't have to go on any pilgrimages. You simply have to look within at your own Self. In no time at all you will see that you have always been free, but you didn't realise it before because you were always looking outwards.
>
> (Godman, 1998b, p. 62)

When asked for a method, Poonjaji immediately moves to situate the student outside of the 'ends and means' dichotomy. Here, he negates all the standard forms of Hindu spirituality: no practice, no chanting, no yoga, no pilgrimages, and then negates the question itself by stating that the questioner is already 'free', he is merely 'looking in the wrong place'.[25] The questioner is superimposing the idea of method onto *brahmajñāna* and Poonjaji responds by negating all possible superimpositions.

In both examples, the questioners are adhering to the bifurcation that they are unenlightened and will become enlightened by or through some method. Both Poonjaji and the Zen master negate this polarized adherence by answering that the path and the methods are not 'things' to be substantialized and the 'goal' cannot be subject to reification.

Although Zen and Advaita deconstructive use of negation displays parallels to the classical mystical path of the *via negativa*, negation as a deconstructive technique functions in more nuanced and complex ways than straightforward denial or a simple cancelling of an affirmative. In the practice situation, teachers are concerned to experientially negate students' adherence to bifurcated categories without privileging one component of the bifurcation over the other. Thus, in both traditions, teachers are wary of propelling the student into ontologically affirming, and by extension, reifying, the opposite of what is being denied and thereby establishing yet another dualism.

Practitioners often misinterpret dereifying negation as an instruction to 'fall to the other extreme' and fixate on the idea that spirituality or practice is 'about' eliminating some 'thing' or 'getting rid' of concepts. In Advaita, Poonjaji confronts his student's dualistic emphasis on eliminating or 'getting rid of concepts' in the following way:

> [*Student*]: When I ask myself what this whole spiritual journey is about, I say it is nothing more than getting rid of all concepts. Am I right?
> [*Poonjaji*]: Spirituality doesn't tell you to get rid of anything. What will be removed? Where will you put it? In this world there are mountains and rivers and animals. If you get rid of them, where will they go? They have to stay here. It is better to stay with everything and with love, not to reject or accept.
> (Poonja, 1992b, p. 36)

The student is interpreting the Advaita negation of conceptual thinking as an instruction to 'get rid of all concepts', a dualistic stance that Poonjaji rejects. 'What will be removed?' he asks, and then 'Where will you put it?' Outside the duality of accepting or rejecting, what space exists to 'put any "thing" in or to take any "thing" out?' Here, Poonjaji's deconstructive questions render a reply based on either/or lines of thinking impossible. 'What will be removed?' is indicative of the Advaita tenet that nothing 'really' exists in the way that we suppose, hence, from the Advaita point of view, the student is proposing to 'take nothing from nothing'. Equally, any attempt to 'answer' 'Where will you put it?' further problematizes privileging one side of a dichotomy by revealing the mutually entailing nature of the components that comprise such an antithesis. From the student's point of view, the mutually entailing nature of opposites is experientially revealed by the mental 'loop' that Poonjaji's question ignites. If the student thinks that he must 'get rid of all concepts' then, according to Poonjaji's deconstructive challenge, he is accepting the idea that he must reject all concepts and rejecting the idea that he must accept all concepts. The added twist to this is that, according to Poonjaji, both pincers of this dilemma are nothing but conceptualizations anyway. When Poonjaji states that 'everything has to stay here' and the student should 'neither accept or reject', he is indicating that both accepting and rejecting are superimposed conceptualizations that have no bearing on reality as Advaita understands it. The point here is that in Advaita teachings, *ātman-brahman* realization admits of no dualisms such as accepting and rejecting, coming and going, and so on. Hence Poonjaji's next question: 'If you get rid of them, where will they go?'

In a similar vein, Hōgen Yamahata responds to the question 'Should everything be abandoned?' with: 'Abandoning everything is an extra head on your head! You don't need to abandon one thing. Just sit! Exhale! That's enough. Do not add anything. Just do "this", whatever it may be. "This" is the one way to peace in any practice' (Yamahata, 1998, p. 181). In Hōgen's presentation of Zen, 'just this' is not to be placed in the either/or dichotomy of 'this or that', nor is the dynamic of just sitting to be confused with the dualistic act of abandoning or adding any '*thing*'. Here, Hōgen insists that ideas of 'adding' or 'abandoning' are 'extras' that separate the student from insight into emptiness.

In Mahāyāna Buddhism, following the deconstructive manoeuvres of the Mādhyamika dialectic, teachers often employ negation to initiate a deontologizing process that is based on keeping practitioners oscillating between extremes. In this process, first one side of a dichotomy is negated and the student is allowed to fixate on its opposite. At a later stage, the new fixation is negated. In this way, the oscillation between dichotomies is progressively reduced and the 'either/or of the excluded middle' is then further destabilized by the 'two-way undoing moves' of the bi-negations. In Zen, this strategy is most evident in the classical Chan/Zen encounters where a common deconstructive device is to send a questioning student 'running' from one master to the other in the hope of getting his question answered.[26] For example, a student could first be told 'mind is Buddha' by one master then 'no-mind is Buddha' by another master and on and on in a spiral of affirmation and negation which, in many instances, culminates in the Zen performative 'version' of 'neither mind nor no-mind is Buddha'. In such encounters, the questioning student eventually finds himself trapped or stuck in his own bifurcations with no conceptual room for the 'either mind or no-mind' dichotomy to function. The Tang Dynasty master Mazu Daoyi[27] was one of the best exponents of this technique and his deontologizing strategy is well illustrated in the following exchange. 'A monk asked: "Why do you say that the very mind is Buddha?" Mazu answered: "I simply want to stop the crying of children." "Suppose they do stop crying?" asked the questioner? "Then not-mind, not-Buddha," was the answer' (Fung, 1948, pp. 257–258).[28]

In both traditions, teachers move to correct and reject 'reification of their own negating activity in any objective, referential manner' (Kim, 1985, p. 77). In this way, they work to undo the mistaken supposition that if reality is not characterized by one side of a dichotomy then it is characterized by its opposite. In this context, the Chan master Sengzhao's (c. 5th-century) warning is well taken for both traditions: 'When you exclude an assertion, be sure not to include an assertion of the contrary' (Faure, 2004, p. 36). In the foundational texts, this type of two-way negation is a mainstay of the desubstantializing formulas of the *Prajñāpāramitā* literature and found throughout the *Upaniṣadic* teachings to indicate the absolute non-dual status of *brahman*.

This two-way negation is best seen in the practice situation of both Advaita and Zen by variations on the use of the neither/nor negating process. The neither/nor negation or bi-negation is a multi-dimensional form of negation and represents the most direct challenge to either/or oppositional patterns of thought. Bi-negation is chiefly employed in both Advaita and Zen teaching strategies as a double negating move that capitalizes on the contradictory 'position' that the student finds him or herself in once adherence to both sides of a dualism have been rendered problematic by constant refutation.

In the previous section, we have seen how the use of the 'both/and' contradictory affirmation of both sides of a dichotomy serves to place the student in an experiential *aporia* that precludes either/or attachment to individual components of dualistic categories. As a kind of mirror image to the 'both/and' deconstructive strategy, teachers also employ the two-way 'neither/nor' negation to bring the student to an impasse where either/or adherence to dualities is not possible. Thus, the point behind such instructions as Gangaji's 'Neither follow, nor deny. This is the secret' (Gangaji, 1995, p. 81) and Hōgen Yamahata's 'You cannot get it or lose it!' (Yamahata, 1999b) is not to push the student to follow or deny, to 'get it' or 'lose it', but rather to situate him or her outside of the dualistic either/or framework.

Hence, when a student asks Poonjaji what he should do to 'jump', i.e., to take the final step to self-realization:

> [*Student*]: I get to the edge and my head tells the feet to jump but my feet don't go. The courage doesn't get to the feet. Is there anything I could do, or not do, that might get the courage to the feet?
> [*Poonjaji* admonishes him with:]: Neither! Neither doing or not doing. Do not allow your mind to abide anywhere, not even in the nothingness.
> (Poonja, 1992b, pp. 27–28)

In this instance, Poonjaji is issuing the warning that realization or the 'jump' cannot be dependent on the dualism of doing versus not doing. For Advaita, the self (*ātman*) that the practitioner is seeking is self-evident, that is, already fully present. In negating both sides of the doing/not doing dichotomy Poonjaji is pushing the student out of the trap of the excluded middle with the further warning against reification that mind should not abide anywhere, not even in the nothingness.

When 'both/and' deconstructive combinations are combined with the neither/nor negation the pincers of either/or thinking are experientially 'tightened' and the student finds himself in an experiential bind that further detaches him from the principle of the excluded middle by 'opening' the intermediary space between contradictions. In contrast to situating the student outside the framework of the excluded middle, the following Advaita use of the bi-negation experientially pushes the student *into* the trap of the excluded middle to create an experiential bind that cannot be resolved within dualistic categories or frameworks.

In this exchange, Poonjaji is in dialogue with a questioning student who is attempting to 'figure out' what he should or should not be doing, that is, what spiritual action would bring him the best 'result'. Poonjaji is countering this dualistic fixation on action and result by insisting on the key Advaita tenet that spiritually 'there is nothing to be done' other than to give up the dualistic fixation of action and result that is binding or blinding one. In other words, this dialogue is a deconstruction of causation, an undoing of the relationship between ends and means and is a good example of the experiential bind that a sudden both/and, neither/nor insight can provoke. Interestingly, the both/and, neither/nor dilemma is posed by the questioning student himself:

> [*Poonjaji*] If you don't do anything and give up the idea of doing anything, where do you return?
> [*Student*]: Right here.
> [*P*]: So stay right here in this present instant. What doing or not doing is involved?
> [*S*]: Yes. Or no. Both doing and non-doing or neither doing nor non-doing is involved. (Poonjaji laughs) It is like a child's puzzle. Each way I turn is a trap.
> [*P*]: Whose trap is it? Who set this trap? 'I want to do something is a trap.' 'I want to do nothing is another trap.' This is your imagination only. Can you show me this trap?
>
> (Poonja, 1992b, p. 84)

According to Advaita teachings, it is the dualistic mind that is trapped, Poonjaji has taken the dichotomy of doing/not doing and moved the questioning student into the heart of it; caught in the duality of doing or not doing the student is frustrated by the 'turning' of this dichotomy; suddenly, 'everything comes at once', both doing and non-doing, and neither doing nor non-doing are involved – how can that be?

In conceptual terms, Poonjaji's deconstructive challenge has placed the student in the midst of the dilemma of the excluded middle, the student knows that the answer cannot be *either* doing or not-doing; this is a dualism. But how can it be *both* doing and not-doing or *neither* doing nor not-doing? Poonjaji's instruction to 'stay in the present instant' is from the absolute perspective; he then moves to the relative by asking an either/or question, 'what doing or not-doing is involved?' The Advaita point is that being in the present moment admits of no duality; the student's shifting sense of both/and, neither/nor places him in a radically non-dual experiential 'space' in which the dualizing mind is stopped, or in the words of the student is 'trapped', on the hinge of non-dual knowing which is the beginning of an experiential shift or an existential 'trap' in which dichotomous patterns of thinking begin to be undone.

Interestingly, Poonjaji is quick to move against the student fixating on or reifying the conceptualization of 'a trap' by pointing out to the student that it is his own fixation on 'a trap' that is 'trapping' him: 'Who set this trap?' Poonjaji rhetorically demands. More importantly, he points out the dualistic trap of positing traps by negating the very dualism that prompted the seeker's original question: 'I want to do something is a trap. I want to do nothing is another trap', says Poonjaji. Then, with a final pointer to the unfindability of the seeker's constructions, Poonjaji demands, 'Can you show me this trap?'

From the student's point of view, there is no standard frame of reference in which Poonjaji's question can be answered. Such radical deconstructive questions bring the seeker to a stillpoint of not-knowing that is not driven by the usual demands of familiar semantic structures or the securities of standard ontological certainties. The conceptual conflict that generates such a 'space' is stilled by the mind having 'nowhere to go' and precipitates experiential openings into non-dual understandings in which both 'the conceptual conflict of the mind and the paradoxicality of the imperative vanish' (Cheng, 1973, p. 92).

In Sōtō Zen, the use of neither/nor negation is philosophically and experientially underpinned by Dōgen's particular emphasis on the absolute dynamic, mutually interpenetrating, non-duality between practice and enlightenment and, by extension, all bifurcated dualisms. Dōgen's elevation of the practice of *shikantaza* to a phenomenological expression of realization informs the Sōtō use of bi-negation with a different non-dual nuance that has significant ramifications for the experiencing practitioner.

As we have seen throughout this study, both Zen and Advaita acknowledge the inadequacies of language to express the 'highest non-dual truth' (*paramārtha*) and counter this inadequacy by various deconstructive rhetorical, semantic and structural manipulations in the practice situation. However, as Ruegg (1977) notes, and as we have seen in the discussion above, the neither/nor sentence can be 'pressed into service in an attempt to indicate or reveal the *paramārtha* because it constitutes the closest linguistic approximation available to the semioticized silence of the Ārya [Sage], the only kind of "sign" that conforms to ultimate reality as it really is' (p. 19). The point is particularly relevant to the practice of *shikantaza* but also offers further light on the use of the bi-negation in Advaita.

For example, when Poonjaji insists 'neither reject nor accept, neither do nor not do', and so on, he is both pointing the student beyond the bifurcations of the excluded middle and indicating the non-relational 'status' of *brahman*. In this sense, the neither/nor configuration is in itself non-dual, as it is both the pointer and what is being pointed to, the method and the 'result'.

In Sōtō Zen practice, 'the only kind of "sign" that conforms to ultimate reality as it really is' is not only employed by teachers to indicate 'things-as-they-are' but is also the nature of the neither affirming nor negating space that the practice of *shikantaza* discloses in the practitioner's awareness.

For example, in *Shōbōgenzō Genjōkōan*, Dōgen outlines 'things are present' as: 'This way and this place are neither great nor small; they are neither subjective nor objective; neither have they existed since the past nor do they appear in the present; and so they are present like this' (Nishijima and Cross, 1994, p. 36). According to Dōgen, 'things-as-they-are-present' are neither this nor that but present just as they are 'like this'. That is, 'things-as-they-are-present' are not in a dichotomous relationship with 'things-as-they-are-absent' or anything else. In the 'now by now' dynamic of dependent co-origination, things are neither subjective nor objective, neither have they existed in the past nor do they appear in the present but are just present 'now'. This is the point of the *Rōshi* in the 'Who are you?' dialogue above[29] when he states 'You are You! You are only You – that is all.' There is no either/or bifurcation to adhere to, nothing to compare to or differentiate against; according to this teaching, the practitioner is present 'just like this'.

Being present 'just like this' is indicative of the thinking, not-thinking, non-thinking dynamic of *shikantaza* that, according to Dōgen and Zen practitioner reports, actualizes a neither affirming nor negating phenomenological space in the immediate experiencing of the practitioner which *allows* things to be present 'just as they are'. The neither/nor configuration is thus the pointer to this space and the actual nature of the awareness that the space ignites in the experiencing of the practitioner. This is significant for the practitioner because the bi-negation is experienced as being both prescriptive and descriptive. In this sense, it is the closest one can get to describing both the process and the effect of *shikantaza* and is an experiential confirmation of Dōgen's core teaching that practice and realization are one (*shuhō-ittō*).

In the Advaita use of the bi-negation, teachers are concerned to break down student adherence to bifurcation by deconstructing ideas of difference based on the underlying reality and appearance template. In the above examples, Poonjaji highlights that being absent or present, doing or not doing, and so on, are all differentiated tricks of the mind that have no bearing on immutable, undifferentiated *brahman*. Since *brahmajñāna* is knowledge of non-difference and nothing ever really changes or arises, deconstructive use of the bi-negation in Advaita pushes the practitioner towards the insight that there are ultimately no differences to adhere to. *Brahman* is neither present nor absent, neither dependent on doing nor not doing. *Brahman* is not above, below, behind, inside or outside, for as the very undifferentiated nature of all things *brahman* admits of no relation to any thing (or non-thing). In effect, we can say that Advaita use of the bi-negation stresses the absolute non-relational status of *brahman*. But, when we talk of the non-relational status of *brahman*, it must be remembered that 'this reality [Brahman] is not the mere unity underlying the diversity of the universe, for unity and diversity are relative to each other, and it is impossible to retain the one as real while rejecting the other as appearance' (Hiriyanna, 1994, p. 371). As the non-phenomenal ground (*nirviśeṣa-vastu*), *brahman* is non-relational in the sense of having nothing to do with conceptions of reality and appearance or any other relational dichotomy. Hence, 'really and truly' speaking, *brahman* is actually neither related to things nor not related to things. This is the felt paradox that, by definition, *nirguṇa brahman* ignites in the experiencing practitioner and which, as we have seen, is exploited and employed in the Advaita practice situation to deconstructively 'jog' students into and out of dualistic bifurcations of trying to 'know' *brahman* and into realizing immediate identity with *brahman* where neither knowing nor not-knowing holds sway.

In contrast, for Dōgen, all things are intimately and incorrigibly interrelated and interpenetrating on the ever-turning continuum of dependent co-origination, but also *non-dualistically* so. In other words, for Dōgen, things-as-they-are both transcend and embrace dichotomous reified oppositions and are dynamic. There is no inside or outside the flow of reality; reality 'just is'. The practice of *shikantaza* is the actualization of this 'just is', that is, an experiential space in which all things 'just are' in their non-dualistic, impermanent, related-ness. Dōgen's 'identity in difference and difference in identity' non-dual template nuances the realization towards the practitioner understanding that realization is ongoing and not-two and the practice of *shikantaza* experientially confirms this. According to Dōgen, practitioners 'should know that ongoing enlightenment is neither the process of practice nor the result of enlightenment … it is neither manifestation nor hiddenness, neither giving nor depriving'[30] (Kim, 1987, p. 83). Thus, when a contemporary Sōtō practitioner describes the felt experience of opposites breaking down as 'a little bit like one side tends to negate the other and then laugh at it' (InterviewJ00, 2000) he is indicating the felt dynamic process of the neither affirming nor negating space of *shikantaza*.

As we have seen in this chapter, although predicated on differing ontologies, the four key deconstructive techniques are employed in similar ways in the practice situations of Zen Buddhism and Advaita Vedānta. Zen and Advaita teachers challenge their students to find the 'I' that is so readily referred to and further confront linear projections of time by demanding 'why not now?' Both traditions employ and exploit paradox and negation as deconstructive devices to move students into and out of the *aporia* that often precedes an experiential shift into a 'not-knowing space' from which experiential undoing ignites. Also, in both traditions, the bi-negation is both prescriptive and descriptive. That is, it is employed by teachers as a compelling deconstructive device and experienced as the nature of the non-dual space that experiential undoing discloses (particularly in Zen). This non-dual phenomenological space will be further delineated and analysed in the next chapter.

In this chapter I have focused on how the four key deconstructive techniques are used both individually and in combination to deconstructively challenge students' 'everyday' dualistic experience and to experientially undo key conceptual dualisms of self and other (subject and object), ends and means (cause and effect), and linear dualistic conceptions of space and time to instigate the experiential deconstructive 'shift' or 'movement' in the actual experience of the practitioner. Thus, the point to follow from our detailed discussion here is that the deconstructive processes of both traditions exhibit structural and experiential similarities because they are reacting against the same thing: practitioners' habitual bifurcation between dualistic categories and structures of thought.

Chapter 5

Dynamics of Experiential Undoing

From the discussion thus far, we can see how deconstructive spiritual inquiry in both traditions targets the habitual disposition of the mind to bifurcate and conceptualize and works to undo practitioner adherence to conventional dualistic structures of discursive thinking. In this chapter, we will endeavour to further identify and describe the deconstructive dynamics that underlie the process of the experiential undoing of dualities by paralleling practitioners' experiential reports with philosophical analysis. In this way, we will attempt to integrate the philosophical, observational and phenomenological data described, analysed and explicated in the preceding chapters. This experiential paralleling or mapping will proceed in two steps. For the purposes of our inquiry, we will identify practitioners' reported shifts of understanding as a shift into, or a disclosure of, a non-dual phenomenological space. This conceptualization is employed as a heuristic explanatory device that correlates with practitioners' felt experience of shifting into a more open cognitive space and with practice instructions that point to the 'non-thinking' that is not dependent on thinking and not-thinking (Zen), and the empty space between thoughts that is not dependent on the rising and falling of thoughts (Advaita).

In the second section of this chapter, we will attempt to enter into the multi-dimensional nature of the dynamics of deconstructive spiritual inquiry by mapping the experiential impact of deconstructive spiritual inquiry on two veteran Advaita and Zen practitioners against the key philosophical tenets and deconstructive practice instructions of the traditions. This experiential mapping both highlights the ontological differences between the non-dualistic *advaitavāda* (non-different) path of Advaita and the non-dualistic *advayavāda* (non-two) path of Zen and draws attention to the phenomenological similarities of their experiential impact.

Non-dual Experiential 'Space'

In his discussion of meditative inquiry, Gangadean notes that 'the meditative narratives characteristically present themselves as moving beyond the space of ordinary conventional thought and discourse to a higher space where reason is silenced' (Gangadean, 1993, p. 5). For the practitioner, the space of ordinary, conventional, dualistic thought is problematized again and again in the ongoing practices of meditative inquiry and dialoguing with a teacher. As the practice unfolds, students are challenged to recognize and undo increasingly subtle levels of dualistic structuring. At various points in this ongoing deconstructive process, practitioners begin to disengage from familiar adherence to dualistic patterns of thought, and, in the unfamiliar experiential 'space' of being unable to fix on one side of a dichotomy, report an experience of being 'stuck'.

In both traditions this experience of being 'stuck' precipitates an experiential state of not-knowing, described by practitioners as 'radical'. This 'not-knowing' state is a 'stillpoint' in the trajectory of practice that serves to hold or steady the practitioner in a neutral non-reifying space. As we have seen in the exchanges between teachers and students in both traditions, practitioners endeavour to move out of the 'stuck-ness' by reverting to familiar epistemological framings and ontological stabilizations. But, as teachers deconstructively point out, this dualistically motivated mental 'scrambling' – to either 'grab an ontological foothold' (substantializing) or 'make epistemological sense' (reifying) of 'not knowing' – plunges students further into conceptualization and shifts them out of this 'not-knowing space'.

This phenomenological space is felt as being radical because it is a not-knowing or a 'don't know' that is not dependent on, or part of, the dichotomy of knowing and not-knowing. In Advaita, according to Poonjaji, the state of 'don't know' 'denotes a real experience outside of objective knowledge' in which there is no 'comparing' (Godman, 1998b, p. 270). In addition to this, Poonjaji states that this 'real experience of don't know … is neither knowing nor not knowing nor anything in between. It is something that cannot be known' (Godman, 1998c, p. 41). In Zen, the oft-quoted turning phrases of Luohan's 'not-knowing is most intimate'[1] and Nanjuan's 'the Way is not a matter of knowing or not-knowing'[2] are indicators for the same 'space'.

In experiential terms, the shift into this 'not-knowing space' places the student in the heart of his or her own dualistic bifurcations without the possibility of privileging either side of a dichotomy. In this sense, this is the non-dual neither/nor space that, in dialogues and foundational texts, both traditions point the student to. As we have seen, in the Sōtō Zen deconstructive practice of *shikantaza*, the dynamic non-thinking space of *zazen* is posited as a neither affirming nor negating experiential space. Experientially, this neither/nor space actualizes a non-positional neither affirming nor negating attitude or view in which, it is claimed, the pure presence of things-as-they-are is disclosed. While in Advaita, Poonjaji and Gangaji point their students to the 'distance between thought and thought' which is the 'ever-present, empty space' (Poonja, 1992b, pp. 23–24) and only realized when 'thought formulations are dissolved back into their unformulated states' (Gangaji, 1995, p. 116).

This distance, space, or gap between thought and thought is the non-dual undoing space from which 'nothingness' unfolds (Advaita)[3] and in which emptiness is actualized (Zen). Poonjaji's pointer to the 'empty space' between thoughts phenomenologically echoes Dōgen's instructions for *zazen* in *Fukanzazengi* in which non-thinking is posited as the dynamic turning space between thinking and not-thinking: 'Think of not-thinking. How do you think of not-thinking? Non-thinking [*hishiryō*]. This in itself is the essential art of zazen' (Waddell and Abe, 1973, p. 123). For the purposes of this discussion, the point to follow here is that in both traditions students are instructed that thoughts come and go but practitioners should not attach to them. Rather, thought should be turned to its source which is not part of the dichotomy of thinking and non-thinking but in the empty space 'between' and underlying the rising and falling of thought (Advaita) and the empty impermanent 'turning' that is the mutually entailing space 'between' thinking and not-thinking (Zen).[4]

In contrast to Poonjaji's articulation of the emptiness between thoughts which is philosophically representative of Advaita's teaching of *ātman-brahman*-identity as the universal formless substratum, Dōgen's phenomenological unpacking of the thinking process is representative of the basic Buddhist teachings of impermanence and dependent co-origination. In keeping with the impermanent continuum of dependent co-origination, Ekai Korematsu's practice instructions work from Dōgen's space where thinking/not-thinking alternates on an ever-turning non-directional continuum, while Poonjaji is pointing his student towards the distinctionless space that 'persists through all states' where *brahmajñāna* is realized.

Despite these important 'bottom-line' ontological differences, from the point of view of the inquiring practitioner both teachings are representative of the non-dual phenomenological space that is 'opened' or disclosed in awareness through the process(es) of problematizing or undoing the boundaries of bifurcated dualisms. In effect, movement into this space is analogous to what Puhakka identifies as a 'shift from thinking into awareness' in which 'subject and object coincide fully and their distinction collapses altogether' (Puhakka, 2000, p. 24). The phenomenological similarity of this shift for Advaita and Zen students is indicated in the following reported descriptions of the undoing of subject–object boundaries:

> You notice when you are sitting that the boundaries between yourself and whatever don't seem to be there anymore. The boundary between you and the wall in front of you – like you are looking at each other! (Zen Practitioner;[5] InterviewJ20, 2001)

> You lose all phenomenal distinction you can't really find any individual self that ends or [is] opposed to other people. (Advaita Practitioner; InterviewDO2, 2002)

Before examining practitioner reports of shifting or moving into this non-dual phenomenological space, it is important to note that, ultimately neither Zen nor Advaita admits of any 'in-between space' or the bifurcation of a dualistic space and a non-dual space. Indeed, Poonjaji rejects the idea of a 'boundary situation' as yet another concept because 'You are never at the end, and you never start from anywhere else' (Poonja, 1992b, p. 75). Similarly, Dōgen's 'continuous practice' (*gyōji*) in which 'there is not even the slightest gap between resolution, practice, enlightenment, and nirvana'[6] (Abe, 1992, p. 103) also allows for no such bifurcation. However, from the practitioner's point of view, the undoing of bifurcations *is* experienced as an existential shift into a more open or less constricted cognitive 'space'. Hence, for the purposes of this discussion, the heuristic frame of a non-dual phenomenological space offers the most fruitful conceptualization to explore the dynamics of the experiential impact of Advaita and Zen non-dual practice instructions.

Experiential Mapping: Practitioners in the Space

In the following sections, we will parallel practitioners' reported shifts into this space and make some observations to identify the deconstructive dynamics that underlie the process. This attempt to integrate the philosophical, observational and phenomenological data is aimed at entering into the dimensions of the experiential impact of these teachings and practices more fully. In other words, by looking at the personal challenges involved or placing ourselves 'on the receiving end' of these practices, a window can be opened on the intra-psychic dynamics of these non-dual forms of inquiry and transformations in identity and worldview can be identified.

Experiential undoing in Advaita Vedānta

As Advaita masters continually caution, merely parroting the question 'Who am I?' will not disclose *ātman-brahman*-identity; this is one of the reasons that at some point in a seeker's quest, dialogue with a teacher seems to be essential. Interaction with and guidance from a teacher can serve as a form of 'reality check' (as it were) for the practitioner and assist in cutting the objectifications and reifications that can be projected onto spiritual practice and experience itself. For example, in the following dialogue, Ramana Maharshi succinctly deflates his questioner's objectifications of the teacher as an 'enlightened being' that 'knows all' and cuts reification of a future 'enlightened state' that the seeker is projecting:

> A man asked Sri Bhagavan [Ramana Maharshi]: Sri Bhagavan can know when I shall become a jnani [knower of Reality; enlightened]. Please tell me when it will be.
> [*Ramana Maharshi*]: If I am Bhagavan then there is no one apart from me to whom jnana [non-dual knowing] should arise or to whom I should speak. If I am an ordinary man like the others then I am as ignorant as the rest. Either way your question cannot be answered.
>
> (Maharshi, 1984, p. 519)

The dualistic assumptions of the question are exposed in Ramana Maharshi's reiteration of the core Advaita tenet of non-difference; if all is undifferentiated *brahman* then how could a separate knowledge arise in a differentiated individual? How could Ramana consider 'himself' or any other 'self' to be a *jñāni* when no other 'selves' exist? Conversely, if Ramana considers 'himself' to be an 'ordinary' individuated entity then how could he 'answer' a question from the viewpoint of *jñāna*? Simply put, Ramana Maharshi is indicating that *brahmajñāna* is undifferentiated knowing; there are no viewpoints or divisions, and the questioner's dualistic projections are dismissed. In pointing out the misguided presumptions inherent in the question, Ramana moves the student away from the thought-based projections that he has imposed on spiritual experience and points him to a 'not-knowing space' wherein direct inquiry into the self can unfold.

To cut such thought-constructed objectifications and reifications as given above, interaction with a teacher is almost always essential. However, when the internal, meditative inquiry into the deconstructive question 'Who am I?' is practised, a non-dual 'not-knowing space' can be catalysed in the experience of a practitioner without the immediate intervention of a teacher. To explore and explicate this experiential journey we will map a long-time Advaita practitioner's reported experiential entry into this 'space' against the teachings and philosophical underpinnings of his tradition.

The practitioner begins by noting his 'obsession' with the 'Who am I?' practice: 'I was pretty obsessed with "Who am I?" because I thought that there was something that I actually could find or some little knot that you would get to [with it]' (InterviewDO2, 2002). Here, the impetus to practice comes from the idea that one can actually locate 'something' or 'come to some little knot' that 'answers' the question 'Who am I?'

According to this practitioner, the process is one of 'honing the subject down to a small point' by 'turning off' as many 'false ideas of the self' as possible:

> I just sit there quietly ... trying in as subtle a way as possible, try[ing] to turn the focus of attention to the subject ... I know it can't really be done but I like to just see how close I can get to doing it. How many false ideas of the subject I can kind of turn off. I try to hone it down to a small point. (InterviewDO2, 2002)

The seeker is aware of the subtle nature of the inquiry; first he attempts to be quiet and then tries to turn the focus of attention to its source. The apparent paradox of awareness seeking its source is clear to this practitioner: 'I know it can't really be done but I like to just see how close I can get to doing it.' Here, he realizes that he is using intentional awareness to undo the very structures of thought that support it. The attempt to 'turn off false ideas of the subject' hinges on throwing into question or 'doubting' the 'commonsense' dualistic notions of self-as-subject and world-as-object that we 'normally' operate from. Questioning these taken-for-granted ontological and epistemological 'certainties' is the beginning of Advaitic deconstructive strategies; this questioning coupled with a 'cutting away' of dualistic ideas of self initiates the processes of negation that deconstructive spiritual inquiry hinges on:

> ... it is a kind of negative thing, cutting away all this stuff. I've done these 'Who am I's?' [for years] ever since I was a child really and I've noticed that ... you carry a kind of existential energy with it to varying degrees and you don't have much control over that energy. (InterviewDO2, 2002)

The 'existential energy' that this negative practice of 'honing down' or 'cutting away' generates is outside of the immediate thought-constructed intentionality of the practitioner's asking of the 'Who am I?' question. The crucial turn from a mind-based questioning of the status of an individual self, i.e., a '*me*' to a broader existential questioning of the entity 'self' is a movement into a non-dual 'space' in the direct experience of the practitioner that is felt as an existential energy which 'carries' the inquiry in a more intense, concentrated way. This excitation or 'energy' is a movement or shift outside of habitual dualistic patterns of thought. As Advaita masters stress, if 'Who am I?' is asked with the mind alone then the process will be a movement of mind. That is, the process will be a product of the dualistically conceived categories of subject and object, cause and effect, and so on. But, if in the space of the inquiry the actual premise of the question has shifted from the individual's habitual investment in the constructed thought-bound notion of 'I' and is carried or asked with full existential force or energy, in the manner of Ramana Maharshi's spontaneous 'Am I this body?' then the question is 'energized' in a different way. In dialogue with a student, Poonjaji elaborates on this important point:

> If you make a process of self-enquiry, you stay in the mind. You make it a series of linked thoughts. You look outside and remember that you should be looking inside. This is a movement of the mind. Next, you try to turn your mind inwards. You try to look at yourself, or you try to see where your 'I' is coming from. This searching and this looking are just thoughts and perceptions that are attached and linked to each other. The result of such activity will be more thoughts. Thoughts cannot result in no thought. If you have an experience as a result of this kind of enquiry, it can only be an experience of a thought, of a state of mind, not a state of no-mind. So long as you stay in the mind, experiences and thoughts are the same. (Godman, 1998b, p. 281)

Here, Poonjaji is indicating the substratum of the space between thought as the 'place' from which the deconstructive question of 'Who am I?' must be asked. He is also commenting on exactly the point of our practitioner's doubt – 'I know it can't really be done' – because searching with the mind alone is still linking and attaching thoughts and perceptions to each other and creating more conceptualizations to be undone. Our practitioner describes this mind or intellect-centred practice of 'Who am I?' as 'thin': '... if you are just sitting there going "Who am I?" "Who am I?" it tends to be very thin, [and it's] almost [an] intellectual kind of energy that goes into it' (InterviewDO2, 2002). But if the question is asked at a 'crucial' moment, at a very intense, focused, open or 'spacious' moment then 'exactly the same question' can be experienced in a very different way:

> Whereas if [the inquiry] occurs at some very crucial or felicitous moment then somehow you are gifted with this tremendous ... force of curiosity,

> this tidal wave of doubt ... that carries that question and then exactly the same question unfolds into an enormous kind of opening. And it is the same question but there's a very different energy behind it [that] you don't have that much control over. (InterviewDO2, 2002)

This 'tidal wave of doubt' that 'carries the question' is a movement away from the habitual dualistic patterns, attachments and linking processes of mind. This is one of the dimensions of Poonjaji's admonishment to 'move away from the mind'. For, according to Advaita teachings, in the ordered links that we impose on our thoughts there is the idea of control: energy and effort is marshalled and 'put to some use', we plan to do something and then we carry it out. Trying to 'turn your mind inwards' is a paradox that always remains in the constructions and projections of mind. However, in the paradox of turning thought in this way in 'sawing off the branch on which one is sitting' there appears to be the possibility of unfolding the question in awareness in a different way. 'The tidal wave of doubt' as reported by this practitioner is a movement that questions the very foundations of habitual patterns that support the linking and reification of thought and, most importantly, that undermines the very processes and relevance of the 'Who am I?' question itself:

> I was ... going through this 'Who am I?' and suddenly ... this immense tidal wave of doubt swept over me and I realized that I couldn't even ask that question. That to ask 'Who am I?' presumed that there was an 'I' to ask about, presumed that I knew that I was alive, that I knew that I was some kind of entity asking some sort of question and that just got rushed around and there was a flip into a completely different state of awareness that was no longer separate – I can't really describe it. (InterviewDO2, 2002)

The practitioner has hit upon a key non-dual realization. To even ask the question 'Who am I?' is to assume a dualism of seeker and sought. To posit an 'I' that is asking the question is to grant this 'I' entity status as a subject seeking an object. This dualistic assumption is what initially carries the question; however, once this assumption begins to unravel, the inquiry moves into a vortex of infinite regress: 'Who am I?' 'Who is asking?' 'Who is asking who is asking?' 'Who is asking who is asking who is asking?' and on and on. '[The] question ... just got rushed around and there was a flip into a completely different state of awareness that was no longer separate.' The shift from taking the notion of 'I' as a findable, recognizable entity that can be inquired into, to the recognition of the inherent dualistic presumption that any sort of 'I-inquiry' necessarily entails, is one of the key realizations in the practice of Advaitic self-inquiry.

The existential doubt that this practitioner is experiencing is the beginning of the undoing of the attributed entity status to the personal pronoun 'I'. To ask 'Who am I?' is to presume that there is a separate individual 'I' that can be differentiated from other entities and inquired into. The experiential impact of this recognition of the 'non-separateness' of things is a major lynchpin in the experiential undoing of dualistic notions of self. The newly energized question is experienced as an 'opening' in which the practitioner's 'small' inquiring self is no longer separate from the force of the inquiry. The questioner becomes the question:

> But when this question is truly energized then there's this kind of opening and a recognition of this energy … [that's] fantastic. And I don't think that you can distinguish yourself from that energy ever. But again you have no control over it in the ordinary sense of control. (InterviewDO2, 2002)

The energized 'space' that the seeker has 'opened' is experienced as absolutely real, indeed, '[that energy] is the only thing that's real in the world'. And when asked if we would call this awareness a 'knowing', the interviewee replied, 'Yes, a knowing' (InterviewDO2, 2002). But a 'knowing' of a different kind:

> In every ordinary kind of knowing there's always an awareness of a … doubtful element, I could be dreaming … there's a tiny little shadow that clings to everything and I guess that's the normal way we function. We couldn't function without that little bit of free space where someone can actually move. It appears to be this but it's actually that. So no matter how sure we are that it's this, there's always a tiny little margin in which just doubt or, I don't know, scepticism or something, an empty margin in which if we [are] forced to re-evaluate what [something] is, it completely changes. (InterviewDO2, 2002)

According to this practitioner, in 'ordinary' knowing phenomena are evaluated and re-evaluated into a succession of categories or entities that we label and relabel as 'this' or 'that'. This knowing operates on a dualistic relational basis, things are either this or that, subject to change as our relationship to them changes, or definable and redefinable by their relationship to us. The 'empty margin' that the seeker refers to grants a 'behind the scenes' contingency to our epistemic grasp of reality in which the self as subject moves in an objectified differentiated world. However, in this highly energized absolutely 'real' knowing, the epistemic 'margin' which allows the relational re-evaluation or reframing of the object known appears to fall away: 'But in this other state everything was just as it is, as it appears, there was no kind of 'behind the scenes' reality to things' (InterviewDO2, 2002).

In this experiential opening, the practitioner reports that phenomena just *are*, without epistemic overlays or ontological boundaries that obscure the parallel 'is-ness' of awareness:

> It was to some extent a 'consciousness-only'. [In this state] everything is just made of consciousness. So there is no backing, there's nothing. Everything is just as it is, and the quality of awareness was one in which the place where those empty margins were was now filled with this tremendous kind of 'self-ness', totally full, a totally full sense of existence you could say (that's not quite right, but like that), 'I' just 'I' [that is] in a more cosmic sense. (InterviewDO2, 2002)

Reality has no 'backing' – in this non-dual knowing the quality of awareness is reported as 'a tremendous self-ness' in which existence is '"I" just "I"'. This 'totally full sense of existence' and the extended 'cosmic' sense of 'I' is one aspect of the Advaita teaching that 'the world is in you' and the impetus behind Ramana's statement concerning the relationship between world and self: 'The Self does not move. The world moves in it' (Maharshi, 1984, p. 208). This 'tremendous self-ness' is an experiential description of the Advaita relationship between world and self wherein the seeker realizes that *all* is non-differentiated self or consciousness. In the following dialogue, Ramana Maharshi elaborates on the absolute non-differentiation of consciousness:

> Reality must be continuous and eternal. Neither the unconsciousness nor the self-consciousness of the present is the Reality. But you admit your existence all through. The pure Being is the reality. The others are mere associations. The pure Being cannot be otherwise than consciousness. Otherwise you cannot say that you exist. Therefore consciousness is the reality. When that consciousness is associated with upadhis [adjuncts] that you speak of – self-consciousness, unconsciousness, sub-consciousness, super-consciousness, human-consciousness, dog-consciousness, tree-consciousness and so on. The unaltering factor in all of them is consciousness. (Maharshi, 1984, p. 544)

Ramana reiterates Śaṅkara's[7] argument for the existence of the self – 'you cannot say that you do not exist' and as this existence is admitted as an 'unaltering factor' through all other mere associated states it is 'continuous and eternal'. According to Ramana Maharshi, this continuous sense of existence cannot be other than the continuous substratum that is all – i.e., consciousness, pure being, or *brahman*. However, Ramana's questioner still 'feels' a difference:

> [*S*]: But a dog-consciousness is different from my consciousness. I cannot read the Bible to a dog. The tree again does not move whereas I move and act.
> [*R*]: Call the tree a standing man; and call the man a moving tree.
> (Maharshi, 1984, p. 544)

In non-dual *ātman-brahman*-identity, the objection does not stand; Ramana Maharshi breaks identification with differentiated entities by reversing fixed definitions: 'Call the tree a standing man, call the man a moving tree.' Ramana's point is that, according to Advaita teachings, the seeker's query, based as it is on dualistic differentiation, takes him no closer to self-realization. If all is consciousness why is the questioner blocking his own realization by stubbornly adhering to mere associations and unreal differences? In this instance, Ramana's reply is a deconstructive move to cut the questioner's identification with dualistic differentiation by 'flipping' his descriptive categories, 'call the tree a standing man' and pointing him back to the self.

Our practitioner indicated this point when he described this experience of 'consciousness-only' as a 'kind of flip from positive to negative' in which everything, even 'things that are normally thought of as being doubtful or in shadow were totally full of this unnamable sense of self [that] was absolutely rooted in my own being' (InterviewDO2, 2002).

This 'unnamable sense of self [that] was absolutely rooted in my own being' is the beginning of a recognition of the role that awareness plays in self-realization. When everything is seen as located, 'rooted' in one's own being, then reality 'unfolds' in a different way:

> This thing unfolded – all kinds of revelations of the unreality of matter and this kind of stuff. It actually stopped when I got to the point of thinking that I could turn my attention to anything and kind of unfold it. I could turn my attention to my little self and all of the psychological quirks that have formed this little self would kind of just automatically unfold and I got frightened – I didn't want to see all that. I wasn't ready to unpack that structure completely. (InterviewDO2, 2002)

The 'unfolding' of matter in non-dualistic awareness is indicative of the Advaita dictum that the only 'real' reality is awareness (*brahman*). In this practitioner's experience the structures of phenomena are felt to be unpacked (or deconstructed) by turning this concentrated, heightened sense of awareness to them. Constructions that we place on reality are 'unfolded' in the focus of this 'energized' attention including the structures and 'quirks' that constitute one's self-identity. Faced with the prospect of undoing his own 'bundle of thoughts' that holds the personal I-structure together, our practitioner steps back, 'I wasn't ready to unpack that structure completely.' Although, in spite of the fear, the experience left him 'with a feeling of tremendous freedom' that was centred on the 'inside-ness' of reality.

> I just had to put my attention onto anything and it would ... unfold in that way ... I was ... amazed at everything and thinking how incredible it is that anyone could believe in the reality of matter as some kind of outside, totally opaque thing. I was left with a tremendous feeling of freedom which lasted several weeks. And ... everything was just totally OK – nothing could go wrong. (InterviewDO2, 2002)

The non-dual insight here is, once again, that the 'world is in you'. 'How could anyone believe in the reality of matter as some kind of outside, opaque thing?' In this insight difference is unreal, as is the fact that, no matter how intense and 'frightening' this insight may have been, 'everything was just totally OK', indicating that, in Advaita teachings, liberating knowledge is knowledge of non-difference. There is, however, an apparent paradox in this non-differential state:

> It is paradoxical – it's a very immersed state and yet it's somewhat separate. You might be focused on something but there is a strong kind of peripheral awareness as well; everything is kind of chorusing around this moment but that which is aware of it is so free in relation to the objects that it isn't identified with any of them. I suppose there's this sense of tremendous freedom as well because if I wanted to I could turn my attention to something else. I'm not bound to anything. (InterviewDO2, 2002)

The practitioner is experiencing a paradoxical state that he describes as 'very immersed and yet separate'. He reports a knowing of that which is aware. The immersed/separate paradox is generated by the non-dual experience of awareness becoming what it is focused on and a simultaneous 'awareness' of awareness-being-aware. According to this practitioner, 'that which is aware of it is so free in relation to the objects that it isn't identified with any of them'. This insight is indicative of the non-relational, undifferentiated nature of *brahman*. This state is both immersed and separate. In other words, it is not experienced as being subject to oppositional structures of thought; rather, it is an undifferentiated state that has nothing to do with the dichotomy of differentiation and non-differentiation. For this practitioner, it is a freedom that cannot be identified with any objects and wherein he is 'not bound to anything'.

The practitioner goes on to describe the relationship between his body and this 'sense of tremendous freedom'. He reports being 'blissed out – it was so beautiful that my heart was being turned. And looking at things and feeling them in your body – it's really strong!' (InterviewDO2, 2002). However, the body and phenomena are not experienced as 'one' but rather as 'transparently interlinked' and as 'smoothly interrelating':

> The body and the world are kind of transparently interlinked and you are a little bit apart from it and that's what enables it so smoothly interrelate. These things are not experienced in a complete physicality; they are sort of outside. (InterviewDO2, 2002)

The practitioner's inside/outside observation is yet another reconfiguring of a dichotomous relationship. He reports, 'looking at things and feeling them in my body' and 'whatever I put my attention on I become' and yet 'these things are sort of outside' and 'not experienced in a complete physicality'. He is experiencing both 'being inside and outside' and finding no contradiction in that. This is the point behind Poonjaji's non-dual description of 'inside and outside' and his instruction to 'pay a little attention'. 'Always you are surrounded by that which you seek outside. You are inside that thing. And outside also, it is the same thing. Only we have to pay a little attention' (Poonja, 1992b, pp. 68–69).

Our practitioner sums up by noting the paradoxical process of turning attention to its source in which attention 'takes a U-turn' (so to speak) and becomes aware of its empty nature which, according to this practitioner, 'is the reality of one's own being'.

> To some degree we know we exist but we can't really say how we know we exist. Somewhere in there, there is some little ability to pivot around and try to turn attention to what it is that's actually alive, or attentive or aware. And it's just an emptiness to what is normally taken to be objective but it's an emptiness that's tremendously real and you can't deny that reality because it's the reality of your own being. (InterviewDO2, 2002)

In an experiential echo of Śaṅkara's argument for the existence of the self – you can't deny the reality of your own being – the practitioner notes the 'tremendously real emptiness' of that which is aware. In this insight, the practitioner has experientially undone objective conceptual superimpositions that are habitually placed on awareness and confirmed the Advaita point that *brahmajñāna* is not a matter of knowing but a matter of being. An insight that is the impetus behind Ramana Maharshi's core admonishment to students: 'Be as you are! That is the whole instruction' (Godman, 1992, p. 11).

Experiential undoing in Zen Buddhism

As we have seen in the discussion of Nāgārjuna and Dōgen, Zen thought and practice works to highlight the fundamentally empty, impermanent and mutually interdependent nature of all phenomena. In keeping with this orientation, deconstructive spiritual inquiry in Sōtō Zen is deontologizing and dereifying in intent. From the point of view of the practitioner, to perceive all things as mutually interdependent and empty requires a shift from the conventional dualistic mode of perception that binds one to an ontologized, reified view into a multi-dimensional, dynamic interpenetrating vision that allows things to be present 'just as they are'.

In Sōtō Zen, the practice of *shikantaza* is claimed to be a phenomenological actualization of a neither affirming nor negating space that allows practitioners to directly experience this vision of 'things-as-they-are'. Furthermore, the Sōtō Zen emphasis on the absolute non-duality of practice and realization/actualization and, by extension, practice and daily life is felt by Zen practitioners as a 'blurring' of the boundaries between the non-dual experiential shifts of formal *zazen* practice and 'flashes' of non-dual insight in daily life. In this sense, Dōgen's continuous practice (*gyōji*) is not only experientially actualized in the practice situation but also expressed in action in practitioners' everyday activities.

In this lengthy interview selection a Zen practitioner, with over twenty years' practice experience, reports on the shifts or turns experienced in the practice of *shikantaza* and comments on the 'spilling over' of such shifts into her daily life. As with the Advaita practitioner, we will follow this Zen practitioner's experiential 'shifts' or 'turns' into this non-dual 'space' and, once again, attempt to make some observations on the personal challenges involved and identify the shifts in dualistic worldviews that this practice can ignite.

First, this Zen practitioner reflects on the reason she came, and continues to come, to practice:

> The reason why we've come to practice is because we've sensed something deep down and the practice confirms it or somehow brings it to the surface but the process of bringing things that are already there to the surface does involve a lot of undoing [of] other ways of thinking. (InterviewJ20, 2001)

To this practitioner, Zen practice springs from an inner felt-knowledge that is confirmed in the process of practice. However this 'confirmation' or 'process of bringing things to the surface' involves an 'undoing of other ways of thinking', implying that our normal dichotomous ways of thinking somehow block or obscure a 'below-the-surface' knowing. When asked what exactly it is that practice 'undoes', she replied:

> Habits I think. Habitual ways of thinking, ingrained ideas about myself as someone who needs to fight to be acknowledged as a separate identity … Ways of thinking that really are just habits and ideas. Nothing is tangible or fixed and yet we fix it. We act as if [things] are [fixed] and because of that we get ourselves in all sorts of strife because things are not fixed. (InterviewJ20, 2001)

The practitioner identifies habitual ways of thinking and ideas of the tangibility and substantiality of phenomena as the cause of our problems ('strife') and asserts that even though we take phenomena to be static and solid they are not. She further identifies this process as a cognitive 'recognition' that self and world are not dependent on thought and that this can be seen by looking at 'what is actually happening' with our minds:

> For me it's a recognition that I am not just what I think and that everything else is not what I think it is either. It's just a real process of just looking at my mind and what's actually happening with it. (InterviewJ20, 2001)

Speaking of her very first Zen retreat (*sesshin*), this practitioner notes her lack of Zen vocabulary; she 'hadn't really read anything' and 'didn't know the expression "boundaries disappearing"' that the teacher Robert Aitken-rōshi[8] used:

> I'd gone into *dokusan*[9] with him and I'd said something about being turned. Like my inside felt like it was on the outside and the outside felt like it was inside. And he said … yes the boundaries disappear and that's what it [was], although at the time it felt like I was turned inside out. (InterviewJ20, 2001)

To this practitioner, the lessening of ontological boundaries 'felt like my inside was on my outside and my outside was on my inside'; an initial non-dual experience that well describes the undoing of the taken-for-granted ontological solidity that is usually ascribed to the notion of 'self'. Aitken-rōshi had supplied the ontological description of 'boundaries disappearing' but experientially the practitioner had felt 'turned inside out'.

> I didn't know that expression and he related that to [the *kōan*] *mu*[10] and this was the first time that I'd ever heard *mu* and at that moment there was a magpie calling outside and we'd both heard it at the same time and we looked at each other and I know that he knew that I'd heard it but then my mind kicked in and I started thinking about *mu* and I said 'well, actually I've got no idea what *mu* is'. But it was there already, it was totally unspoken and I'd never heard the word before but the magpie was there and that was it! (InterviewJ20, 2001)

The mutual, unspoken recognition of the magpie calling was, in Zen terms, already *mu*. Both teacher and student were in full existential response to the spontaneous timeliness of the magpie's 'answer'. Phenomenologically, this unspoken recognition represents an empty moment in the sense that the student is not positing *mu* as an object to be defined or discerned by thought. However, the student reports a shift in this awareness as her 'mind kicked in' and she began to think about *mu*, that is, to posit *mu* as an object of thought. Here, the practitioner's description of her mind 'kicking in' represents the epistemological attempt to frame a conceptualized answer. Consequently, her admission to having no idea what *mu* is breaks the immediacy of the moment and plunges the inquiry back into conceptualization.

After many years of *kōan* practice, primarily with *mu*, our practitioner changed teachers and moved to the practice of *shikantaza*. 'Now it's more just sitting, no *mu*, no nothing, just pure *shikantaza*' (InterviewJ20, 2001). When asked to describe the difference in these practices she replied:

> I've often wondered what the difference is. Sometimes when I've been doing *mu* I've felt like I'm not doing *mu*. I'm doing something else – I'm doing *shikantaza*. But don't ask what the difference is because there isn't really a difference, but there is! … I guess with *mu* there is *mu* whereas with *shikantaza* there is just everything. (InterviewJ20, 2001)

The practitioner's observation that in *shikantaza* 'there is just everything' is indicative of the experiential spaciousness that the objectless meditative practice of *shikantaza* discloses.[11] In addition to this, she acknowledges that 'doing *mu*' can dissolve into an objectless experiential state that is akin to the practice of *shikantaza*.[12] From this report, it seems that at some point in *kōan* practice, the duality of the practitioner as a meditating subject confronting *mu* as an object of meditation 'drops away' and practitioners shift into a subjectless/objectless *shikantaza*-type experience. Her struggle to pinpoint the difference between practices – 'there isn't really a difference, but there is!' – is indicative of the felt 'meltdown' of dualistic divisions of identity and difference that these practices initiate. 'There isn't – but there is!' is an appropriate experiential 'summary' of the desubstantializing formulas of the *Vajracchedikā Prajñāpāramitā Sūtra* and much of Dōgen's *Shōbōgenzō* 'reversals' in which things are affirmed, negated and reaffirmed in a newly energized, deontologized status.

Continuing on this point, when asked 'Would you say that both practices undo habitual ways of thinking?' the practitioner answered:

> No. I think with *shikantaza* there is a sense of there's nothing really to undo. It's things – I know what I'm trying to say but I can't say it. I've gone blank! I'm just trying to get a sense of what I am feeling and then try and put it out. I'm trying to say that *shikantaza* just presents things as they are. There's nothing that's been undone but – it's like the difference between saying it's a cup [pointing to the cup] and it's a cup! I can't say it! It doesn't make sense! (InterviewJ20, 2001)

The difficulty in formulating a statement describing what *shikantaza* 'does' is indicative of the neither negating nor affirming nature of the practice itself. In 'trying' to say 'that *shikantaza* just presents things as they are', the practitioner is fighting substantializing the practice of *shikantaza* as a 'thing' that presents or produces other things. The practitioner is intuitively aware that *shikantaza* cannot be reified as a 'subject' that is undoing or presenting any 'thing' or any 'self'. Ekai Korematsu warns against this exact reification by stating that it is in 'the process of *zazen* or the phenomena of *zazen*' that habitual structures or patterns are recognized and unfolded, it is not *zazen* as a 'thing' that is 'doing' this unfolding. 'If you say *zazen* as subject then it becomes difficult – you begin to make wrong effort' (Korematsu, 2001a).

The practitioner is struggling with the attempt to frame a non-dual insight within the dualistic framework of identity and difference. The mutually entailing quality of things-being-present-just-as-they-are and habitual ways of thought undoing 'doesn't make sense' to her in the conventional context of trying to explain it. That is, she cannot epistemologically frame these felt process(es) of practice without dualistically separating them as categories that can be identified and compared. The practitioner likens the differentiation to 'it's like the difference between saying it's a cup [pointing to the cup] and it's a cup!' By paradoxically stating difference as identity – 'it's a cup and it's a cup' – this practitioner offers an experiential restatement of Dōgen's identity-in-difference and difference-in-identity that 'doesn't make sense' in either/or structures of thought.

This 'difference-in-identity' is reflective of the neither/nor space of *shikantaza* in the sense that it represents a non-oppositional experience of the categories of difference and identity. Here, 'difference and identity' are experienced as dynamic and mutually entailing rather than being in dualistic opposition. This non-oppositional differentiating is the driving force behind much of Dōgen's non-dualistic 'turning' expressions of identity and difference in which he 'reveals the middle path [as] unbound by, yet giving rise to, all polarities' (Heine, 1982, p. 56).

In an experiential example of this point, our practitioner describes the non-oppositional and mutually entailing phenomenology of *shikantaza* (sitting) with the following observation:

> You notice when you are sitting that the boundaries between yourself and whatever don't seem to be there anymore. The boundary between you and the wall in front of you – like you are looking at each other! (InterviewJ20, 2001)

She elaborates on this point by describing a retreat experience where 'the boundaries between herself and "whatever" didn't seem to be there anymore', and she began to have problems with her eyes, 'they were out of focus and I kept seeing things moving – like seeing everything all at once'. She asked about this in *dokusan* and was told by the teacher that 'it's a good sign'[13] (InterviewJ20, 2001).

The practitioner further reports that the experience 'flipped her sense of reality' in that 'things weren't behaving in the way that [she] was used to' (InterviewJ20, 2001). Moreover, she describes the experiential tension of the breakdown of the boundaries of oppositional ways of thinking thus:

> It was like seeing two sides of the same coin at the same time and being confused by it but at the same time feeling it was perfectly OK. It felt like I got the turn between the two things and … I was getting both at the same time but it was turning too quickly and I was getting dizzy! But that was interesting that was a physical thing right through my whole body … It finally lifted and it was like a calm lake. (InterviewJ20, 2001)

'Getting the turn between things' is an apt experiential description of Dōgen's multi-dimensional and multi-perspectival vision of the interpenetrating nature of all dichotomies. Moreover, it is indicative of the turning space of non-thinking which, according to Ekai Korematsu, is the 'dynamic of thinking and not-thinking' (Korematsu, 2000). This turning dynamic is experienced by the above practitioner as a mental and a physical 'thing' that initially made her 'dizzy' but then 'lifted and it was like a calm lake'.

The practitioner continues by noting the physicality of the experience and linking it to Zen conceptions of the two truths: 'I went for a walk in the bush [i.e., woodland] and I had the realization two feet but one body! Just walking. Just that relative and absolute connection there. How the two both fit together and how they are actually separate' (InterviewJ20, 2001). The practitioner has realized the mutually entailing connection between the relative and the absolute that allows her insight into their simultaneous difference and identity. Her above description of the experience as 'seeing two sides of the same coin at the same time' is also reflective of the mutually entailing and interpenetrating absolute and relative connection in Zen, while her initial confusion is reflective of attempting to frame the 'turning' within static dualistic understandings.

Further to this, her experience of the relative and the absolute being 'together yet separate' is phenomenologically reminiscent of the Advaita practitioner's feeling 'immersed' in the non-dual experience 'yet somehow separate'. The point to follow is that, for both practitioners, non-dual insight is not dependent on dualisms such as relative and absolute, together and separate and so on. The experience is confusing within the epistemic framings of oppositional structures of thought but 'tremendously free' (Advaita) and 'like a calm lake' (Zen) when these structures are experientially loosened or undone.

In a commentary on this point, Ekai Korematsu notes that the Zen practitioner's experience of the simultaneous difference and identity of things is really 'not anything special', it's just the flow of life without the separations of oppositional thought structures:

> It's very difficult to see things as undivided – in their many aspects and dimensions – it's just life ... not anything special – just do it. Nothing to think about it – in the morning you get up, do you wait to clarify that beforehand? [laughter] Already you are beyond the point of clarifying or not clarifying – that which makes you do that, that which is behind that natural movement is realization itself – you don't need to realize it, it's there. (Korematsu, 2000)

The Sōtō insistence on the physical flow of actualized realization 'already being there' is evident in the practitioner's realization of 'two feet but one body! Just walking.' According to Ekai-oshō's commentary 'that which makes you do that, that which is behind that natural movement is realization itself'. In Sōtō Zen, non-oppositional thinking, best expressed in direct action, is 'already beyond the point of clarifying or not clarifying'. In this sense, what the practitioner has experienced is not a resolution or even a merging of opposites but a penetration of the dynamic between opposites in which action just flows.[14] Hence, the 'turning' of contradictions that previously made her feel 'dizzy' and 'stuck' were no longer experienced as a 'problem' once oppositional structures were experienced as being loosened or undone in the practice of *shikantaza*.

The non-dualistic 'reality' of the mutually interpenetrating and non-oppositional nature of all 'things' does not stop the 'fact' that practitioners *do* experience thoughts and phenomena as rising and falling in dichotomous patterns and, according to Zen teachings, this (false) experiencing has to be recognized and undone. In the practice of *shikantaza* the non-dual nature of things as Zen understands it is not revealed by stopping thoughts or denying their perceived dichotomous relationship but rather by just allowing them to arise and fall without granting this movement in and out of thought any particular credence.

For this practitioner, *shikantaza* just presents 'things-as-they-are', which allows 'you to be as you are':

> If *shikantaza* is things just presenting themselves the way they are then that is also what you're doing, just allowing yourself to be as you are. You're just – it's a willingness to sit with it – it's not turning off or turning on, it's being with ... I don't even know if you can say it's being present; it's more a sense of flowing with things from moment to moment. (InterviewJ20, 2001)

According to this report, the practice of *shikantaza* is allowing yourself to 'be as you are' without the overlays or interference of thought constructions. This phenomenological description of the intention required in *shikantaza* echoes the Advaita instruction to 'be as you are' and is indicative of the similar experiential effects of undoing bifurcations between dichotomies. In both traditions, practitioners are instructed not to aspire to being 'this' or 'that' but rather to just 'be as they are' in the moment. Thus, for our practitioner, the intention required in *shikantaza* does not involve 'a turning off or a turning on, it is being with ... just – a willingness to sit with things'. This is also an apt experiential description of the neither affirming nor negating awareness that is described by Zen teachers as the 'now by now' of the arising and falling of phenomena on the ever-turning continuum of dependent co-origination.

In her reluctance to identify the experiential dynamics of *shikantaza* with 'being present', the practitioner hits upon a key Zen non-dual insight: 'being present' cannot be reified as an ontologized state of being. As indicated above, her description of *shikantaza* as a process of 'flowing with things from moment to moment' is indicative of her experience of reality as a flowing dynamic process rather than a series of isolated substantialized happenings. In this sense, as Zen teachers stress, to practice *shikantaza* is to be in 'accord' with things-as-they-are, and not, in the words of another long-term Zen practitioner, 'to pour our minds over the top of everything' (InterviewB00, 2000).

'Being present' or 'things being present just as they are' are standard Zen terms that Sōtō practitioners often use in descriptions of *shikantaza*. As Sōtō teachers point out, and practitioners themselves acknowledge, there is an inherent danger of reifying the idea of 'presence' and ontologically substantializing the notion of 'things just being present'.[15] Although subtle, this point is important and can lead to what Ekai Korematsu identifies as 'wrong effort' (Korematsu, 2000).

In keeping with the *Vajra Sūtra*'s[16] deconstructive attack on all ontological 'supports', the practice of *shikantaza* is often described by teachers as the practice of no support in which 'mind has nothing to lean on' (Kapleau, 1989, p. 132). That is, in the actual sitting, practitioners are phenomenologically 'just there' in a totally open cognitive space without affirming or negating thoughts. Hence, a significant aspect of wrong effort in Zen is reifying the process of practice by projecting ontological 'overlays' that attempt to stabilize the dynamic space of *shikantaza*.

According to Ekai Korematsu, this habitual ontologizing tendency is undone and Dōgen's non-dual expression is experientially clarified by the 'limited conditions of just sitting in the correct posture' of *shikantaza*:

> As far as *shikantaza* is concerned it is better to limit the conditions. Everything Dōgen Zenji talks about is in the phenomena of just sitting in the right posture – nothing else ... Sitting in the correct posture is the prerequisite, then all his use of words, his expression of phenomena, all his pointing out of realities becomes clear. Understanding that naturally is affirming using *zazen*, correct *zazen*. (Korematsu, 2000)

As we have seen, 'Dōgen came to believe that the mode of consciousness in *zazen* is fundamental in all modes of consciousness' (Kasulis, 1985, p. 69) and this fundamental mode of consciousness is actualized in the phenomenology of formal *zazen* practice. In Sōtō instructional discourse, the 'essential art of *zazen*' is predicated on the 'steady, immovable sitting position'. According to Sōtō teachers, in following Dōgen's precise and detailed physical instructions the thought constructions of the conceptualizing mind are 'naturally deconstructed' by being allowed to fall back into non-thinking. For example, practitioners cannot 'think' not-thinking nor can they concentrate on eliminating all thinking because either of these 'options' would be falling to the extreme of ontologizing one side of a dichotomy. The point hinges on the kind of effort involved in the practice of *shikantaza* and exactly how practitioners deploy their attention.

According to this practitioner, in the practice of *shikantaza* you are 'making effort' but 'doing nothing'.[17] When asked what is the difference between *shikantaza*'s 'doing nothing' and what we would all recognize as 'doing nothing', our practitioner replied: 'The doing part. The doing nothing. It's a process, it's something that you are doing. Whereas if you're vague-ing or vegging out you are not really doing … I might be sitting with a nice straight back but actually I might as well be asleep!' (InterviewJ20, 2001).

She elaborates on this 'doing nothing' by linking it to a change in awareness:

> I think it's more an awareness that you are actually a part of what's going on. It's more of an awareness that you are physically there and your body is physically being affected by things in very subtle ways and also you are more aware of surroundings too, you are really paying attention. (InterviewJ20, 2001)

'Really paying attention' seems to be the difference between practising *shikantaza* and sitting with a 'nice straight back' but 'being asleep'. Since *shikantaza* is objectless, what is attention focused on? The practitioner describes being 'focused' in *shikantaza* as a physical sense of being centred rather than a mental sense of focusing on an object: 'It's a sense in your body of being comfortable, relaxed, like someone could knock you over and you would just bounce back. Your centre really has shifted' (InterviewJ20, 2001). Furthermore, this shift involves a change in one's 'sense of self'. The practitioner describes feeling 'less connected to my own self but … maybe it's the feeling that the weight of myself becomes less, the weight of who I am is just in balance with everything else rather than having a heavy sense of me' (InterviewJ20, 2001). Here, the practitioner gives another example of the lessening of rigid subject–object boundaries. 'Self' is experienced as 'in balance' with phenomena rather than a weighty individual in sharp relief.

However, this bodily sense of feeling focused and balanced does have a mental corollary in the constant need to 'reign thoughts in' by focusing and refocusing on the immediate moment by the effort of 'coming back':

> Just the effort to keep coming back to breathing to coming back to … yeah, what *are* you supposed to be doing? (laughing) There's no point in doing it if you're just going to vague off. (InterviewJ20, 2001)

In a commentary on the practice of *shikantaza*, Ekai Korematsu describes the dynamics of the Zen process of 'coming back':

> At the beginning we are habituated to think and we have to think hard to come back [laughter] but that process becomes shorter and shorter. You are more present. It doesn't mean that you are rejecting what's happening, you don't need to reject or grasp – without doing that you come back – that happens all through the *zazen* process. (Korematsu, 2000)

The physical posture – the 'nice straight back' – is maintained by a mental effort to bring wandering thoughts 'back' to a focal point of attention. But first, practitioners have to 'settle' themselves both physically and mentally:

> Yeah you have to settle, balance yourself, focus. If you try and arrange your body too much then it doesn't work. I think your body has a sense of where it's balanced. I usually close my eyes in the beginning to let things settle and then open them. (InterviewJ20, 2001)

According to this practitioner, intention cannot come from the mind alone. 'If you tell your mind to stop chattering then it chatters even more.' For her, body and mind work together in this process:

> I think in the same way that your body knows what to do your mind knows what to do as well. If you have that intent to be aware, the intent just to settle, the intent just to find your centre, if your body can do that your mind can do that as well without having to direct it too much. If you tell your mind to stop chattering away it chatters away even more but if you allow it to chatter away also with an intent to settle then it will settle. You know, trying to stop thinking produces a lot of thinking! (InterviewJ20, 2001)

The intent to settle, the intent to be aware, is different from intending to 'follow' practice instructions and thereby enter into a 'non-thinking' space as described by Dōgen. The practitioner 'centres' her body and mind by 'not directing it too much'. Beginning the practice of *shikantaza* is often said to be akin to playing a musical instrument, in the sense that repeated practice brings some ease to the physical position and the mind does seem to 'fall in with this' more easily over time. In other words, once there is some competence with the physical 'technique' then 'things just flow'. However, the practice of *shikantaza* operates on more subtle levels. As a second practitioner notes, the 'practice makes perfect' analogy only has a limited relevance:

> You have to do a lot of practice in anything to feel comfortable in what you do and I don't think that Zen is any different except that it's a different type of practice. It's on much subtler levels than learning how to play an instrument … It's not like you touch an object, it's more something that envelops you or you envelop it. (InterviewB00, 2000)

For committed practitioners, the subtler levels of Zen practice are explored in the concentrated atmosphere of retreat (*sesshin*). For our first practitioner, the purpose of intensive practice in a retreat situation is 'time for a really concentrated effort at letting the mind settle down [and] giving yourself the space and the time to be able to do that' (InterviewJ20, 2001). According to this practitioner, the effort to settle begins by dealing with racing thoughts:

> I guess it's all in the head. Thoughts racing always starts off in the head and it's an effort to get that refocused ... The same thoughts will turn themselves on and sometimes I feel I'll just let them run their course and they'll settle down, and other times I really have to ... quite often I'll just go back to counting my breath to really refocus. (InterviewJ20, 2001)

When asked if counting the breath is a reliable and efficient way to refocus she replied:

> Yes and no. Sometimes even breathing becomes hard to do. Sometimes I feel that things are just stuck here [chest area], some block that stops me breathing or makes me want to stop breathing completely. And I sometimes find that in chanting if I'm not focused, if breathing isn't just breathing itself, then the voice won't come either. (InterviewJ20, 2001)

From this description, we can infer that the focusing of *shikantaza* enables 'things to just do themselves'. The practitioner observes that if she is not focused 'if breathing isn't just breathing itself', then she is blocked and in conflict with the practice. She further notes that:

> The Zen saying, 'You begin by doing this practice and this practice ends up doing you' is so true. In the beginning you are breathing but in the end breathing is just breathing itself. Breath just breathes. Things take care of themselves. (InterviewJ20, 2001)

The key seems to be to employ the technique of 'returning' to the breath or to posture as a 'thought clearing space' that removes the pressure of conceptual conflicts and *allows* whatever is happening in the practitioner's experiencing to unfold without the affirming or negating overlays of thought: 'Things [just] take care of themselves.'

However, 'things [just taking] care of themselves' and 'just sitting with what is' are not experienced as a flat disengaged state of being. Practitioners are certainly affected by intense emotional shifts in practice and such shifts are an integral part of experiential undoing in Zen. According to our practitioner:

> Sometimes in sitting there's floods of joy, floods of sadness, floods of emotion because you are open. It's all coming out and that's followed by this intense period of fear; your pulse starts speeding up and your heart starts thumping. You are in a panic, you get really hot or really cold and you are *sitting still*. Sometimes I get a sense that I'm standing on top of a cliff and you just have to step and not being able to step and half stepping and getting frightened [of] that drop and panic. (InterviewJ20, 2001)

'Being open' and 'it's all coming out' are experiential descriptions of dualistic subjective boundaries and ontological 'certainties' undoing in the practice of *shikantaza*. The practitioner's sense of 'standing on top of a cliff and not being able to take the final step' is indicative of the resistance that practitioners experience when 'everyday, commonsense' dualistic patterns of thought are challenged by unfolding insight into non-dual understandings. In another instance, our practitioner reports that once, in intense retreat practice, 'I did have a sense of coming up against brick walls, and a sense of being in a box and beating my head against these brick walls endlessly and knowing that the brick walls weren't there. I just wasn't able to let them go' (InterviewJ20, 2001). In this insight, she acknowledges that the 'brick walls' are of her own making. They 'weren't there' but she 'just wasn't able to let them go'. This struggle with 'enemies of her own making' gave her a sense of 'what she was up against'. She reports:

> I think that was the first time where I really had a sense of the part your mind plays, just the real grip that it can have and what it really means to let go of something. I think that that was one of the questions that I'd asked him [the teacher], 'How do you let go? How do you let go?' and he wouldn't tell me; he'd just pick up his stick and drop it! 'How do you pick up your stick and drop it? I can't do it!' That retreat gave me a sense of what I was up against, of what I was dealing with. (InterviewJ20, 2001)

Speaking on this resistance and the required shift towards 'opening', or 'letting go' of such mind-constructed dualistic 'obstacles', Ekai Korematsu notes that:

> If there's anything unresolved it comes up in practice because it's naturally opening and reconstructing it – in the process these conditionings appear and are naturally deconstructed – all the power goes out of them and people get fascinated by that – body is feeling it, mind is feeling it *bahm, bahm, bham*. (Korematsu, 2000)

As Ekai-oshō observes, the mental and physical aspects of *shikantaza* are interrelated – 'body is feeling it, mind is feeling it'. In an experiential description of this point, our practitioner notes that 'it does take a 'mental effort to shift yourself into gear' but this mental effort also 'feels like your mind has shifted a gear physically, like your mind has gone clunk! It's dropped' (InterviewJ20, 2001). In addition to this, the practitioner observes that 'at the same time as being a downward movement it's also an expansive thing ... it's an opening up. It's where you're not – it's not me sitting here in the centre of things – it's more connected; maybe that's a better word ...' (InterviewJ20, 2001). 'It's where you're not' is another succinct experiential description of the lessening of subjective ontological boundaries. Here the practitioner has experienced a deepening sense of knowing and an expansive sense of being that is not dependent on her 'usual' subject–object boundaries. However, she also notes that conceptual structures in the form of thoughts have not been eliminated, just the connection to them has changed: 'there's nothing really that's changed; the thoughts are still there but the attachment to them is not the same' (InterviewJ20, 2001).

Thoughts and emotions certainly arise, but for this practitioner the 'attachment to them is not the same'. The key is not to 'follow' them but just to acknowledge that, 'whatever is going to happen while you are sitting there is OK and not to get too carried away with what is happening, just to recognize that this is what's going on, this is how it is – thoughts, emotions, pain whatever' (InterviewJ20, 2001). Furthermore, for this practitioner, after sitting 'a few *sesshins*', the emotional shifts become 'normal' and are not to be accepted or rejected but seen as processes to be 'gone through':

> You've gone through all the convolutions, all the different ways you can go through a retreat. Nothing new is going to come up, it's going to be the same round of pain and feeling bad and feeling good and emotions and the whole thing but that's just normal, so just go through it and [do] not think this is good or this is bad. (InterviewJ20, 2001)

In the practice of *shikantaza*, practitioners do not 'pour their minds over' what they are experiencing by thinking 'this is good or this is bad'. Instead, they 'allow' things to just present themselves and 'allow' themselves to be just as they are in the presence of whatever 'arises'. By not rejecting or grasping they 'come back' to 'where they are'. In other words, emotional shifts and conditioned conceptualizations are experienced and recognized but the personal investment in them and the dualistic attachment to these thought-constructed dualistic overlays is weakened or undone.

Shikantaza can be experientially described as the act of sitting still in a precise physical position with an alert mind that is pulled taunt by the mental act of returning. Returning to the physical position, to counting the breath, to the thumb tips touching and so on, are heuristic focusing devices that serve to bring the practitioner out of thought and into a more 'spacious' awareness in which the mind and body are felt to be not-two. Importantly, the non-dual neither affirming nor negating awareness that the practice of *shikantaza* discloses is not limited to formal *zazen* practice. For many practitioners this sense of 'practice' infuses with direct action in their daily activities. According to our practitioner,

> To me, the sitting practice and the everyday life part of practice are totally inseparable. The sitting practice helps to reinforce what's happening in life and life helps – gives you grist for the mill. If you take the time to pay attention to everything that you are doing that sense of weightlessness or balance can be found, can be seen [in daily life]. (InterviewJ20, 2001)

According to this practitioner, 'you can be sitting in the *zendō*[18] and not practising and you can be walking around in everyday life and practising' (InterviewJ20, 2001). She further states, 'I think that the really important part of the process for me is putting it together with life and that's when things begin to confirm each other. And you can't say which does which to which' (InterviewJ20, 2001).

For this practitioner, insight into non-duality is not confined to the formal practice of *shikantaza*, as non-dual understandings also manifest in daily life. In fact, formal Zen practice and daily activities cannot be posited as separate experiential realms. In 'putting practice together with daily life', the practitioner has tapped into the non-duality of practice and actualization. According to Ekai Korematsu, the deconstructive elements of Zen practice is 'to be in touch with the zero, no engaged activity – you know, no trying to make sense out of things, you don't need to try to make sense out of anything' (Korematsu, 2001a) but the reconstructive elements of practice are manifested or actualized in daily life. In a succinct encapsulation of the dynamics of practice and actualization, Ekai-oshō observes that:

> Human nature has a tendency, to try to make things permanent, to fix a permanent position; that's how concepts and ideas work. Then we find ourselves in a stuck position. Then we lose the sense of being in absolute non-dual time. Reconstruction is a kind of meeting in a way with reality – relative reality, which was met before deconstruction but now it no longer meets so now we need a reconstruction. Actually as a whole, taking that kind of course

> we build a notion of self and people and ideas and we need to deliberately undo it and so it is an ongoing process. (Korematsu, 2001a)

Like Dōgen's pivotal meeting with the *tenzo*[19] in which his fixed, intellectual grasp of practice was experientially deconstructed by the *tenzo*'s well-placed non-dual 'barb', Zen practitioners need to 'correct' their fixed relative positions and reconfigure their 'positions' to move in accordance with absolute reality. In Zen understandings, direct experience of reality is a non-linear series of ongoing mutual meetings in which fixed notions of self and world are deconstructed and reconstructed in newly energized relationships that dynamically converge with reality-as-it-is. This is the experiential thrust behind the desubstantializing formulas of the *Prajñāpāramitā Sūtras* and the import of Dōgen's encounter with the *tenzo*.

Moreover, the practitioner's description of 'things beginning to confirm each other, and you can't say which does which to which' is an experiential account of Dōgen's non-dual descriptions of the mutually confirming, interpenetrating nature of all phenomena. As we have seen, both Nāgārjuna and Dōgen demonstrated that *saṃsāra* and *nirvāṇa* or the relative and absolute are intimately connected and ultimately non-dual[20] – here our practitioner has experientially confirmed the two-way confirmation of the relative and the absolute and the intimate connection between them. Zen teachings admit of no duality between practice and daily life and the practitioner's sense of mutual confirmation is indicative of this.

Indeed, it is in the relative realm of daily activity that the practitioner finds the demarcation between practising and not-practising blurred and that what she is 'missing' or searching for in practice is 'right here'. In an experiential echo of Nāgārjuna (*MMK* XXV: 20),[21] our practitioner states:

> When are you not sitting that line between sitting and not sitting is not so rigid. The thing that has always been missing is right here! But it's a journey that you have to take, you've got to take the steps, but a lot of times you just come right back in a big circle where you started from! (InterviewJ20, 2001)

For Nāgārjuna, as for our practitioner, the conventional is the only means to the ultimate; moreover, properly understood, there is no difference between them.

In keeping with the non-directional flow of dependent co-origination, insight into the rising and falling of phenomena or 'now by now moments of clarity' is never ending. Dōgen's 'everything is just a flashing into the vast phenomenal world' (Suzuki, 1984, p. 105) is well taken here, in the sense that 'flashes of clarity' are not cumulative but ongoing and never-ending. On this point the practitioner gives the following account:

> I did a practice at Green Gulch with Reb Anderson and Norman Fischer[22] and Reb Anderson was asked: 'Do those moments of clarity get bigger?' And he answered 'Well no you just have more of them!' That flash in the dark is always just a flash in the dark but you get more of them! I think you think that you've seen this and you're going to build on it but actually you don't – you see it again and again. And you can see it again in every single moment and that's when it can seem like this huge thing. And then everything starts connecting. (InterviewJ20, 2001)

Phenomenologically, every moment is new and interdependent. The 'flashes of clarity' are not static and discrete and cannot be dualistically 'built on'. The non-dual insight here is that these flashes of clarity can be 'seen' again and again in a continuous 'now-ing' that is not dependent on linear constructions of duration and enduring essence. When this dynamic movement is 'seen in every single moment' then the interdependent nature of all things can be perceived and, according to this practitioner, 'everything starts connecting'.

To this practitioner, in an echo of Dōgen's continuous practice (*gyōji*), Zen practice is ongoing and multi-dimensional. In her words, practice is 'never one thing' and it is never a separate activity that is distanced from daily life. She sums up by stating that 'As far as the process [of practice] is concerned you can't ever step out of it, you can't ever not do it anymore. It becomes the most important thing that you have to do' (InterviewJ20, 2001).

In the deconstructive practice of *shikantaza*, the non-dual 'point' is the experiential disclosure that subject and object are not-two. As a corollary to this, self and all phenomena are experienced as dynamically interrelated and in continuous change. In the Advaita deconstructive practice of self-inquiry, the non-dual 'point' is the experiential disclosure that subject and object are not different. As a corollary to this, self in absolute identity with *brahman* is experienced as unchanging, undifferentiated and immutable. In keeping with their differing non-dual ontological orientations, the Advaita and Zen practitioner that this chapter focused on reported differing 'experiential undoings' of common dualistic notions of self. The Advaita practitioner reported an experiential sense of everything being 'filled with a tremendous self-ness' in which there was '"I" just "I"' while the Zen practitioner reported 'less of a sense of self' and feeling more 'in balance and connected to everything'. In this key sense, these practitioner reports are reflective of the core 'all-self' and 'no-self' ontologies and the *advaitavāda* (non-different) and *advayavāda* (non-two) non-dual paths of their respective traditions.

Despite these ontological differences, the experiential trajectory of deconstructive spiritual inquiry in Advaita and Zen displays some striking phenomenological affinities. Phenomenologically speaking, in both traditions, experiential undoing is an opening or emptying of the dualistic concept of 'oneself' into the immediacy of the moment beyond bifurcations of 'this and that'. In Zen, this phenomenological moment is ever-changing; in Advaita, never-changing. In both cases it is experienced as a timeless moment not dependent on subject and object, unmotivated by the cause-and-effect chain, and articulated as a non-dual 'not-knowing space' from which experiential undoing unfolds.

Experientially, the major shift that both practitioners report is the non-dual perception of things 'just as they are'. That is, with no epistemic overlays or ontological boundaries. This is indicative of the breakdown of the structures of dualistic experiencing and the lessening of practitioner adherence to bifurcated dualisms that these practices ignite. In both traditions, the phenomenological space that is 'opened' in the practitioner's experiencing is not dependent on either polarity of a dichotomy and admits of no bifurcation between categories. In this sense, shifting into this space is an experiential movement away from the structures of thought and into non-dual awareness.

Conclusion

Deconstruction of Reified Awareness

A thing becomes an object when it is limited by time, space, and causation.
Śaṅkara (Vireswarananda, 1993, p. 4)

For the practitioner, the spiritual path is a lived experience. In the non-dual practice traditions of Advaita Vedānta and Zen Buddhism, engagement with a spiritual practice represents an ongoing process of applying oneself to a form of inquiry in which fundamental dimensions of what it is to be a human being are claimed to be revealed. In the practice situation, Advaita and Zen teachers both invite and challenge their students to clarify and confirm the central philosophical and experiential claims of tradition by testing the validity of their previously unquestioned, 'everyday', personal frames of experiencing against unfolding non-dual understandings.

Deconstructive spiritual inquiry in both traditions targets the primary dualisms of subject and object, cause and effect, and linear conceptions of space and time. Despite their different ontological underpinnings, we have seen how both traditions employ the deconstructive techniques of unfindability analysis, bringing everything back to the here and now, paradoxical problems, and negation with the same deconstructive aim: to experientially undo the limiting effects of adherence to objectified bifurcated dualisms, thereby shifting the practitioner out of dualistic structures of thought and into non-dual awareness.

In Sōtō Zen, the undoing of bifurcations does not indicate a resolution of opposites nor does it instigate the 'falling to the extreme' of privileging one side of a dichotomy. The instructional 'point' and experiential 'effect' of Sōtō practice instructions is to shift the practitioner into a non-dual penetration of the dynamic between oppositional categories in which the trap of the excluded middle holds no sway. In the practice of *shikantaza*, this dynamic penetration of opposites is experienced as a non-dual neither affirming nor negating space where neither being nor non-being *can* be taken hold of. As we have seen, practitioners describe this experience as 'getting the turn between things' and 'everything coming at once' and report a realization of the fundamental interconnectedness of all things 'just as they are'. That is, without objectified ontological backing or reified epistemic overlays.

In Advaita Vedānta, the undoing of bifurcations is also not representative of a resolution of opposites, nor does it instigate a merging with the 'real' in the sense of admitting any opposition of reality and appearance. For the Advaitin, 'nothing ever happens' and *brahman* cannot be experienced by merging with one polarization of a dichotomous relationship. As the beginningless and endless non-dual emanation that is the substratum 'between thought', *brahman* admits of no shadings or aspects of differentiated oppositions. In the unravellings of self-inquiry, this non-dual understanding is experienced with the insight that reality has no phenomenal oppositions; *brahman*, as the non-phenomenal ground, is neither reality nor appearance. That is, *ātman-brahman*-identity is not a realization of identity as opposed to difference, nor is it a merging with reality as opposed to appearance. For Advaita, *ātman-brahman*-identity is ever present and 'just is'.

As we have seen, in many ways instructional discourse and reported experience in the practice situation reflects the core ontologies and non-dual nuances of each tradition. Advaita teachers direct students to the 'space between thoughts' that is the never-changing, non-relational substratum of *brahman* and Zen teachers point to the dynamic between thinking and not-thinking which is the ever-changing, always relational, ever-turning continuum on which all dichotomies rise and fall. Zen practitioners offer experiential descriptions of the rising and falling of phenomena which are articulated and experienced as impermanent, momentary 'flashings in the vast phenomenal world' (Suzuki, 1984, p. 105) and report a 'lessening of the sense of self'. Advaita practitioners report the ontological 'fullness' of things and report a 'tremendous sense of self' in an experience of an unlocalized and immutable awareness that is, in philosophical terms, not different from *brahman*.

From our discussion we have also seen that the deconstructive point in both traditions is that the choice between any dichotomous pairing, doing and not-doing, self and other and so on, is only binding as long as there is attachment to the law of the excluded middle. Thus, deconstructive spiritual inquiry in both traditions works to subvert either/or patterns of thought that support dichotomous epistemic framings and objectified ontologies. Despite the 'all-self' ontology of Advaita and the 'no-self' (empty) ontology of Zen, both traditions reject any objectification of their ultimate non-dual expressions: *brahman* in Advaita and *śūnyatā* in Zen. It is this rejection of objectification that underpins the phenomenological similarity of the non-dual experience in both traditions and allows for an affinity in scope and purpose of key deconstructive techniques. Simply put, whether deconstructive spiritual inquiry is orientated towards a *deontologizing* (a dynamic experiential 'emptying') that admits of no reification in which the non-dual dynamic self is disclosed or a *reontologizing* (an all-encompassing experiential 'fullness') that undoes 'mistaken' reified ontologies in which the non-dual permanent self is disclosed, the dualistic 'targets' and the experiential impact are the same.[1]

In part one of this study, we examined the philosophical underpinnings of deconstructive spiritual practice in Zen and Advaita. We traced how deconstructive spiritual inquiry has been taught in Zen and Advaita and outlined how these key philosophical tenets are 'put into action' in the instructional discourse of each tradition. An 'old masters' approach was taken in which we concentrated on the deconstructive implications of the teachings and practice instructions of foundational figures and contemporary teachers in interaction with students.

In part two, a dynamic interactive methodological framework was employed that enabled analytical movement between the deconstructive intent of the teacher's instructions and the experiential impact on the questioning student. In this way, the experiential trajectory of practice could be approached and a window was opened on the challenges that these practices present to previously unquestioned personal dualistic ontological structures and epistemological framings. In this way, the personal challenges experienced and insights gained in the practice situation were further explored and delineated. In part two, we concentrated on the hermeneutical and empirical exploration of modern and contemporary practitioners who are 'on the receiving end' (as it were) of these practices in practice situations that are specifically tailored for their implementation. We studied the external dynamics of deconstructive spiritual inquiry by identifying four key deconstructive techniques, common to both traditions, and examined how Zen and Advaita teachers employ these techniques, both individually and in combination in the practice situation. The internal dynamics of deconstructive spiritual inquiry, specifically in the practices of self-inquiry and *shikantaza*, were explored by mapping the reported practice experiences of two veteran Zen and Advaita practitioners against the philosophical, observational and phenomenological data explained and presented in part one. From this mapping the intra-psychic dynamics of the ontological shifts that these dynamic non-dual practices generate for practitioners were brought into relief and some insight into the transformation of identity and worldview experienced by practitioners was gained.[2]

This study can be summed up by revisiting the astute insights of two scholars into the philosophical and phenomenological relationships between practices in Advaita Vedānta and Buddhism. The first insight, advanced by Dasgupta is philosophical. In pointing out the philosophical similarities between Śaṅkara's *brahman* and Nāgārjuna's *śūnya*, he notes that 'it is difficult indeed to distinguish between pure being and pure non-being as a category' (Dasgupta, 1992b, p. 493). The non-dual key to this insight is that both traditions reject the trap of the excluded middle with the accompanying either/or polarizations of oppositional thought. Pure being and pure non-being are not seen in oppositional relationship in either tradition. *Brahman* is all-being with no relationship to the dichotomy of being and non-being. *Śūnyatā* is empty non-being that is not dependent on the dichotomy of non-being and being. Both 'ultimates' are pointed out to students in the practice situation as being *neither* this *nor* that and *both* this *and* that. That is, *brahman* and *śūnyatā* are not to be dualistically objectified as attainable, reified entities.

The second insight, advanced by Loy, is phenomenological. In pointing out differences of non-dual orientation in the spiritual practices of Advaita and Zen, Loy notes that 'experientially reducing to nothing or expanding to everything brings us to the same point' (Loy, 1988a, p. 204). As we have seen from practitioner reports, the subjective experience of 'self as everything' or 'self as nothing' provokes the same insight into the connectedness or non-separateness of all things. Zen practitioners report the 'emptiness' of things and Advaita practitioners report the 'fullness' of things; however, the experiential point that these insights reveal is that reality 'has no backing'. That is, reality cannot be reduced to any form of ontological objectification or epistemic reification.

As stated in the introduction, our primary objective here was to clarify how language and other communicative techniques are used in the spiritual practices of Advaita Vedānta and Zen Buddhism and how the boundaries and barriers of conceptual thought and personal dualistic experiencing are subverted, reconfigured and deconstructed to disclose a purported non-dual knowing that both traditions claim is somehow innate but unrecognized. In doing this, we have identified a non-dual phenomenological 'space' that the practices of self-inquiry and *shikantaza* 'open' in the practitioner's experiencing. As we have seen, practitioners experience this non-dual space as a stillpoint of not-knowing in which the dualistic ontological boundaries and epistemic framings that provide a 'backing' to reality are deconstructed or undone. For the purposes of this discussion, this space is indicative of practitioner shifts from dualistic thought structures into non-dual awareness wherein the paradoxical 'empty fullness' of *brahman* or the 'full emptiness' of *śūnyatā* is experienced without contradiction. Deconstructive spiritual inquiry in both Zen and Advaita experientially 'moves' practitioners into this 'space' wherein the boundaries and barriers of conceptual thought and personal dualistic experiencing are felt to be lessened or undone and an already-present non-dual sense of 'knowing' is disclosed in the actual experiencing of the practitioner.

Notes

Introduction

1 Potter, 1981, p. 222.

2 J. Zen master Wanshi Shōgaku (1091–1157).

3 For the classic exposition of 'insider/outsider' approaches see N. R. Reat's seminal 1983 article 'Insiders and Outsiders in the Study of Religious Traditions'.

4 A full, technical treatment of the methodologies can be found in chapter five of my doctoral thesis, *Deconstructive Spiritual Inquiry: Dynamics of Experiential Undoing in Advaita & Zen*, Deakin University, Australia, 2005, and in my forthcoming article 'Inquiring into Non-dual Spiritual Experience: Research Methodologies and Hermeneutical-Phenomenological Strategies' (Davis, 2010).

5 Ninian Smart identified six dimensions of religion: ritual, mythological, doctrinal, ethical, social, with the dimension of experience underlying the previous five. He thus viewed religion as a 'total organism separable for the purposes of analysis and comparison'. The religious traditions of Advaita and Zen certainly admit all these dimensions; however the focus here is on the experiential dimension. See Smart, 1977, p. 21.

Chapter 1

1 'This *brahman* is the self' (*ayam ātmā brahma. Bṛhad-āraṇyaka Upaniṣad* II:5.19).

2 *Brahman* is 'One without a second' (*ekam evādvitīyam, Chāndogya Upaniṣad* VI:2.1).

3 Zen master Eihei Dōgen quoted in Suzuki, 1984, p. 105.

4 Central to the development of Zen and, arguably, the most important Mahāyāna philosophy.

5 One should be careful here: Mādhyamika cannot be said to posit or assert non-duality as it claims to make no positive claims whatsoever. Nāgārjuna's project is to refute all philosophical positions and conceptual distinctions, not to posit an Absolute, non-dual or otherwise.

6 Unless otherwise indicated, all quotations from the *Upaniṣads* are from Radhakrishnan, 1994.

[7] Unless otherwise indicated, all *MMK* quotations are from Inada, 1970.

[8] Potter notes that 'frequently Advaita texts read as verbatim reports of teacher–pupil interviews' (Potter, 1981, p. 8) and the Mahāyāna *Prajñāpāramitā Sūtras* often depict the Buddha being questioned by a *bodhisattva*. This is echoed and developed in Chan/ Zen literature where a key element is the 'encounter' between a master and student. See Yanagida, 1983.

[9] Shunryu Suzuki (1904–1971) went to the United States in 1959 to minister to a small Sōtō Japanese-American congregation in San Francisco. He attracted many American students and eventually established one of the most influential Sōtō centres in the West, the San Francisco Zen Center, and the first Sōtō monastery in the United States, Tassajara. Suzuki's teachings can be found online at suzukiroshi.sfzc.org/dharma-talks/ and in Suzuki, 1984.

[10] J. Tōzan Ryokai (807–869).

[11] Dongshan Liangjie (807–869) and his disciple Caoshan Benji (840–901) are traditionally viewed as co-founders of Caodong Chan (J., Sōtō Zen).

[12] *Prajñāpāramitā Hridaya Sūtra.*

[13] The Rinzai Zen (C. Linji Chan) master Haukin Ekaku (1685–1768) also uses this deconstructive move in his demolition of any possible reification or objectification of the Heart Sūtra. His answer: 'Well, I have eyes, ears, nose, tongue, body and mind! And forms, sounds, smells, tastes, touch, and dharmas do exist!' (Waddell, 1980, p. 94).

[14] We must be careful of the nuance here: Sri Ramana's emphasis is always non-dual in nature. Hence his teaching on the grace and intentions of the *guru* will always come from a non-dual perspective and not necessarily conform to linear, cause-and-effect-type relationships between categories. His answer to the following question is instructive as to his absolute non-dual perspective on the grace of the *guru*: 'Q: Does Bhagavan [Ramana Maharshi] feel for us and show grace? M: You are neck-deep in water and yet cry for water. It is as good as saying that one neck-deep in water feels thirsty, or that a fish in water feels thirsty, or that water feels thirsty' (Godman, 1992, p. 99; see also part three of the same title, pp. 89–107, for a comprehensive selection of Ramana Maharshi's teachings on the *guru*–disciple relationship).

[15] Isaac Shapiro and Vartman, (now called Sandford) are contemporary Advaita teachers. Isaac Shapiro is a disciple of H. W. L. Poonja, Vartman is a disciple of another Poonja disciple Gangaji (the teacher in this dialogue). Both teach widely in the West.

Chapter 2

[1] The three principal schools of Vedāntic philosophy are Śaṅkara's Advaita (non-dualistic); Rāmānuja's Viśiṣṭādvaita (qualified non-dualism); and, Madhva's Dvaita Vedānta (dualistic).

[2] In Advaita, the success of any theory of meaning arises from its ability to illuminate the *mahāvākyas* in accordance with Advaita teachings (Potter, 1981, p. 59). The number of *mahāvākyas* is sometimes four, one from each Veda (the four quoted minus 'One without a second'), sometimes six. Pannikar identifies six: the five quoted here plus Om *(Prañava)* (Pannikar, 1977, pp. 653– 671) and Sharma, 2000, includes 'All this, verily, is Brahman' (*sarvam khalvidam Brahma*) *Ch. Up.* III:14.1 excluding 'One without a second' and 'Brahman is intelligence' from the four (p. 174).

3 For example, Śaṅkara held that the self who has gained *apavarga* (completely free from difference) is liberated upon hearing the 'great sentences' such as 'that art thou' (see Potter, 1981, p. 51) and the Vivaraṇa school of Vedānta (post-Śaṅkara) held that an encounter with any of the *mahāvākyas* was sufficient in itself for the realization of the identity between the self and Reality. See Deutsch and Van Buitenen, 1971, p. 242.

4 *ekam evādvitīyam.*

5 *prajñānam brahma* (or 'knowing' as translated in Olivelle, 1996).

6 *ayam ātmā brahma.*

7 *aham brahmāsmi.*

8 *Bṛ. Up.* II:3.6.

9 Unless otherwise indicated all quotations from the *Bṛhad-āraṇyaka Upaniṣad* are from Radhakrishnan, 1994.

10 Unless otherwise noted, the *GK* translation used here is Nikhilananda, 1987.

11 Here Gauḍapāda is using 'nature' in the same sense as self-nature (*svabhāva*) in Mādhyamika.

12 Deutsch and Van Buitenen, 1971, p. 120.

13 Ramana Maharshi would later extend Gauḍapāda's identity of the dream and waking states by using the analogy of the cinema screen. Ramana:

> Existence or consciousness is the only reality. Consciousness plus waking, we call waking. Consciousness plus sleep, we call sleep. Consciousness plus dream, we call dream. Consciousness is the screen on which all the pictures come and go. The screen is real, the pictures are mere shadows on it ... There is no difference between the dream and the waking state except that the dream is short and the waking long. (Godman, 1992, pp. 14–15)

14 As regards later Advaita, it is important to note here that Śaṅkara does not use *vikalpa* in the same sense as Gauḍapāda but Śaṅkara's related theory of superimposition (*adhyāsa*) can be seen as a further analysis of how 'wrong interpretation' (*vikalpa*) occurs.

15 Ramana Maharshi:

> The state of Self-realisation, as we call it, is not attaining something new or reaching some goal that is far away, but simply being that which you always are and which you always have been. All that is needed is that you give up your realisation of the not-true as true. All of us are regarding as real that which is not real. We have only to give up this practice on our part. Then we shall realise the Self as the Self; in other words, 'Be the Self'. (Godman, 1992, p. 11)

16 In particular Sri H. W. L. Poonja, whose emphasis on 'you have to do nothing to be who you are' because nothing needs to be produced for realization, i.e., how one 'really' is, i.e. one's 'real' nature, is non-originated, beginningless, hence no finite, conditioned practice can have any meaningful relation to this pure, non-originated nature. In this sense, Poonjaji's emphasis on this 'nothing to do' can be said to be an attempt to experientially ignite Gauḍapāda's theory of *ajātivāda.*

17 In many ways this remarkable negation is analogous (in its deconstructive intent) to one of the most extraordinary discourses in Buddhism: Chan master Linji's famous 'Kill the Buddha' wherein he strips away all that could be held near and dear to a spiritual aspirant and argues for complete independence from all conceptualization and reifications of innate spiritual understanding.

> Followers of the Way, if you want the kind of understanding that accords with Dharma, never be misled by others. Whether you're facing inward or facing outward, whatever you meet up with, just kill it! If you meet a buddha, kill the buddha. If you meet a patriarch, kill the patriarch!

For the full quote see Watson, 1993, p. 52.

[18] A large number of works have been attributed to Śaṅkara and there is not a uniform scholarly consensus as to their authenticity, but the two texts that we are most concerned with here, the *Brahmasūtrabhāṣya* and the *Upadeśasāhasrī*, are, according to 'common scholarly consent', authentic. For a description of the controversy regarding works attributed to Śaṅkara and the complete 'agreed upon' list see Potter, 1981, p. 116 and Deutsch and Van Buitenen, 1971, pp. 123–124.

[19] Unless otherwise noted, the *BSB* translation used here is Thibaut, 1904, as found in Deutsch and Van Buitenen, 1971, pp. 150–203.

[20] Unless otherwise noted, the *Upadeśasāhasrī* translation used here is by Sengaku Mayeda as found in Deutsch and Van Buitenen, 1971, pp. 122–150.

[21] Ramana Maharshi to a student: 'Think 'I, I', and hold on to that one thought to the exclusion of all others' (Godman, 1992, p. 71).

[22] Ramana Maharshi, for example, when pressed for a definition of *brahman* would use *sat-cit-ānanda* but always in the Śaṅkaric undifferentiated sense. To the question 'Brahman is said to be *sat-chit-ānanda*. What does that mean?' Ramana responds: 'Yes. That is so. That which is, is only *sat*. That is called Brahman. The lustre of *sat* is chit and its nature is *ananda*. These are not different from sat. All three together are known as *sat-chit-ānanda*' (Godman, 1992, p. 16).

[23] This 'qualified *brahman*' is *saguṇa brahman*, *brahman* with attributes. From the perspective of *avidyā* (or *māyā*) the world must be seen as having an intelligent principle as its creative source which is *īśvara* (lord) or *saguṇa brahman*. Again, once the 'qualityless reality' (*nirguṇa brahman*) is realized, all qualifications and differentiations are seen to be mere superimpositions and therefore ultimately false. See Deutsch and Van Buitenen, 1971, pp. 308–310.

[24] In his *Mūlamadhyamakakārikā* (*MMK*) Nāgārjuna identifies and explains the importance of the 'two truths' to a complete understanding of the Buddha's teaching. He writes: 'The teaching of the *Dharma* by the various *Buddhas* is based on the two truths; namely, the relative (worldly) truth and the absolute (supreme) truth.' And 'Those who do not know the distinction between the two truths cannot understand the profound nature of the Buddha's teaching' (*MMK* XXIV:8–9; Inada, 1970, p. 146).

[25] Deutsch renders the Sanskrit term *bādha* (literally contradiction, often translated in Advaita terminology as cancellation or sublation) as *subration* which he defines as

> an axio-noetic process that involves, psychologically, a withdrawal of attention from an object as it was originally judged to be and the fastening of attention either to the same object as reappraised or to another object that replaces the first object as a content of consciousness; and the placing of a higher value upon the content of the new judgement. (Deutsch, 1969, p. 16)

[26] Śaṅkara made a sharp distinction between two kinds of teachings found in Vedic literature, the *karmakāṇḍa* and the *jñānakāṇḍa*. *Karmakāṇḍa* is concerned with action in the world, ethical directives etc., and it is there for those who are not at a high enough state of spiritual development to reach the highest truth. *Jñānakāṇḍa* pertains

to the sections of the Veda that specifically focus on *mokṣa* and, as such, is a source of knowledge independent of the injunctive context provided in the *karmakāṇḍa*.

27 Also to determine the purport of any scriptural passage, i.e., that their purport (*tātparya*) be only the revelation of *brahman*, Advaita makes use of the hermeneutical strategy of the sixfold criteria (*ṣaḍlinga*) which are: *Upakramopasaṁhara* (beginning and end); *abhyāsa* (repetition); *apūrva* (novelty); *phala* (fruit); *arthavāda* (commendation); and, *upapatti* (demonstration). See Rambachan, 1991, pp. 63–65.

28 Deutsch gives a variant listing of the traditional six *pramāṇas*: perception (*pratyakṣa*); inference (*anumāna*); comparison (*upamāna*); noncognition (*anupalabdhi*); postulation (*arthāpatti*); and testimony (*śabda)* (Deutsch and Van Buitenen, 1971, p. 311).

29 In traditional Hindu thought, the Vedas and the Upaniṣads are *śruti,* that is scripture that is directly revealed or 'authorless' (literally 'that which is heard directly'). *Śruti* is considered spiritually superior to *smṛti*, which is considered to be 'authored'. The Bhagavadgīta is, arguably, the most important and influential example of *smṛti.*

30 This is in marked contrast to later Advaita, or neo-Advaita, where direct experience is held to be the self-evident proof of *brahman*-knowledge.

31 This is the point behind Ramana Maharshi's answer in the following dialogue:

> A man asked Sri [Ramana]: 'Sri Bhagavan [i.e., Ramana] can know when I shall become a jnani [knower of *brahman*]. Please tell me when it will be.' Ramana replies: 'If I am Bhagavan then there is no one apart from me to whom jnana [*brahman*-knowledge] should arise or to whom I should speak. If I am an ordinary man like the others then I am as ignorant as the rest. Either way your question cannot be answered.' (Maharshi, 1984, p. 519)

32 *Bṛ. Up.* II:3.6.

33 *Bṛ. Up.* III:9.26.

34 *Bṛ. Up.* III:8.8.

35 *Bṛ. Up.* II:5.19.

36 *satyam, jñānam, anantam, brahma.*

37 Here we can note Advaita's tendency to prize *jñāna-yoga* as the discipline best suited for the seeker of 'true knowledge'. Several 'yogas' (path, way or discipline) that lead to spiritual experience are articulated in the Indian tradition: *karma-yoga*, the discipline of disinterested action as emphasized in the *Bhagavadgītā*; *rāja-yoga*, the 'psychological' path codified by Patañjali; *bhakti-yoga*, the way of devotion as found in the various sects of Śaivism and Vaiṣṇavism; and *jñāna-yoga*, the discipline of knowledge that is associated with Advaita Vedānta.

38 The three stages of *jñāna-yoga* have their textual source in Yājñavalkya's instructions to his wife Maitreyī in the *Bṛhad-āraṇyaka Upaniṣad* (*Bṛ. Up.* II:4.5 and IV:5.6).

39 Rambachan accords priority to Listening (*śravaṇa*). See Rambachan, 1991, p. 116.

40 For the list of Śaṅkara's examples and indicators of *brahman*, see Deutsch and Van Buitenen, 1971, pp. 125–126.

41 This is reiterated in the teachings of the modern Advaita master, H. W. L. Poonja, when he admonishes a student with: 'Yes. Even parrots can be taught to say "Who am I? Who am I? Who am I? The inquiry I speak of is Self with the Self' (Poonja, 1993, p. 34).

42 'Brahman is not an object of the senses, it has no connection with … other means of knowledge. For the senses have, according to their nature, only external things for their objects, not Brahman' (*BSB* I.1.2; Deutsch and Van Buitenen, 1971, p. 156).

[43] Deutsch and Van Buitenen, 1971, pp. 137–148.

[44] This is a very similar dilemma to the objector in *BSB* II.1.14 (Deutsch and Van Buitenen, 1971, p. 180) who asks: 'If all distinctions are not real, then how is *brahman*-knowledge known?'

[45] Compare Gauḍapāda's point on the reality of duality and the 'fact' that duality is seen for what it is once the Real is known: 'Although dualists may think that they disagree with us, there is no real conflict; we both admit duality, but we, unlike them, hold that duality is confined to the realm of appearances and is not found in reality' (*GK* III, 17–18, summarized in Potter, 1981, p. 109).

[46] Fort also classifies Swami Vivekananda, Sarvepalli Radhakrishnan and the previous *Śaṅkaracārya* of Kanchipuram, Candrasekharendra Sarasvati as 'neo-Vedantins'. See Fort, 1998.

[47] The Ramanasramam publishes numerous booklets of Ramana's writings edited and translated by various devotees. The 'standard' work is Arthur Osborne's *The Collected Works of Ramana Maharshi*, which brings together all of Ramana's writings in one slim volume. It is not used in this research because of the various hermeneutical problems in Osborne's methods of editing and compilation. He writes that he 'improves' some of the translations and merges certain teachings with other dialogues, a strategy which proved problematic for the purposes of this study. See Osborne, 1996.

[48] Godman reports that 'Sri Ramana usually answered questions in one of the three vernacular languages of South India: Tamil, Telugu and Malayalam. No tape-recordings were ever made and most of his answers were hurriedly written down by his official interpreters' (Godman, 1992, p. 5).

[49] Also known as Swami Ramanananda Saraswati.

[50] In particular the biography and interviews with one of Ramana's longest surviving disciples, Annamalai Swami. See Godman, 1994 and 2000.

[51] For Ramana's teachings, also see www.sriramanamaharshi.org. Poonjaji's teachings can also be found online: www.avadhuta.com/avadhuta.html.

[52] For traditional biographies of Ramana see Osborne, 1970, Mahadevan, 1977 and Narasimha, 1993. These well-known works lean towards the hagiographic and for this reason were not consulted for interactions with students; however, Arthur Osborne's biography of Ramana is used as the source for the traditional account of Ramana's transformative 'death experience'. The account is very similarly described in all three.

[53] For example Yājñavalkya to Uṣasta Cākrāyaṇa in the *Bṛ. Up.* III:4.1–III:4.2 and Yājñavalkya to Maitreyī in the *Bṛ. Up.* IV:5.1–IV:5.15.

[54] I am *brahman*: *aham brahmāsmi, Bṛ. Up.* I:4.10.

[55] Not this! not this! *neti, neti, Bṛ. Up.* II:3.6.

[56] For an insightful discussion and examples of misconceptions of Ramana's teachings see the chapter 'Self-enquiry – misconceptions' in Godman, 1992.

[57] With the emphasis on experience and the move away from scripture, the terminology employed also changes. Ramana and Poonjaji after him tend to use the expression 'self-realization' rather than *brahmajñāna,* or 'self' rather than *ātman-brahman*-identity.

[58] Ramana Maharshi claimed that silence was the true teacher and teaching. Much has been written about Ramana's silent gaze, as his presence seemed to have a profound effect on some seekers. Ramana himself claimed no disciples and, in his view, passed

on no lineage even though his lineage is claimed by several contemporary teachers; hence, in many senses it is problematic to call him an Advaitin. The description 'neo-Advaitin', following Fort, is perhaps more accurate. See Fort, 1998, pp. 129–130.

59 Interestingly Mahadevan interprets this exchange as Ramana expressing 'complete identity' with Śaṅkara's teaching while Fort notes that it could be interpreted as an avoidance on Ramana's part of positing such an identity. See Mahadevan, 1977 and Fort, 1998.

60 *Satsang* could also be a group of devotees gathering without a teacher to perform *pūja*, sing devotional songs or hold discussions on spiritual topics.

61 See descriptions of the ashram routine in Godman, 1994 and Narasimha, 1993, and the numerous descriptions of Ramana's interaction with seekers in Godman, 1992 and Maharshi, 1984.

62 Generally dated as around 1935. See the texts referred to in the note above.

63 Perhaps Ramana's most famous Western follower was Paul Brunton, who described his first meetings with Ramana in 1934; see Brunton, 1994. There are also dialogues in Maharshi, 1984 with the Buddhist scholar W. Y. Evans-Wentz. Several Westerners were long-term residents at the ashram during Ramana's lifetime: Arthur Osborne, Major A. W. Chadwick (Sadhu Arunchala), S. S. Cohen and Grant Duff, to name a few.

64 For a full account of this experience see Godman, 1998a, pp. 24–29. The word 'experience' is used for convenience, as Poonjaji reports that

> I wouldn't call it an experience, because to have an experience there needs to be an experiencer and something that is experienced. Neither was present. Something was pulling me inside, and that thing that pulled me had no form. I don't know what it was. (Godman, 1998a, p. 28)

65 The grip of a 'need' for spiritual practice appears to be one of the most difficult 'barriers' or 'attachments' to undo. A contemporary Advaita practitioner reports a similar 'need' for practices even though his teacher at the time negated the idea of practice. 'I was seeing Wu Wei and he was a pure Advaitin, no practices at all, but I needed my practices even though I knew he was right' (InterviewDO2, 2002).

66 In the ever-growing literature on Ramana Maharshi, much has been written about his 'silent gaze'. Most commentators, both traditional and contemporary, agree that Ramana's 'deepest' and most 'direct' teaching was silently transmitted, although, for the benefit of those (most people) who were incapable of receiving this 'transmission', he advised various practices – with self-inquiry being regarded as the most effective. See Godman, 1992, and Osborne, 1970.

67 After the Maharshi telling Poonjaji that 'you alone are God' and giving him the instruction to 'find out who the seer is', Poonjaji notes that his first thought was: 'It is not good to be chocolate. I want to taste chocolate.' He later saw this as an indication of the powerful hold that his devotional practices had over him (Godman, 1998a, p. 107). It is not unreasonable to assume that the emphasis that Poonjaji later placed on undoing his student's attachments to rigid practice routines and schedules was based on his experience with his own practices.

68 Poonjaji's response is mirrored in Chan master Fayan Wenyi's (855–958) refusal to be pinned down to conceptual explanation. Master Fayan was once asked: 'What is the First Principle?' To which he answered: 'If I were to tell you, it would become the second principle' (Fung, 1948, p. 246).

[69] David Godman makes an interesting comparison between Poonjaji's and Ramana Maharshi's teachings on effort:

> Ramana Maharshi realized the Self without any effort, without being interested in it, and without any practice, and then spent the rest of his life telling people that they must make continuous effort up till the moment of enlightenment. Papaji [Poonjaji] spent a quarter of a century doing *japa* and meditation prior to his climactic meetings with Ramana, but when he began teaching, he always insisted that no effort was necessary to realize the Self. Papaji's attitude to self-inquiry was, 'Do it once and do it properly.' Ramana's was, 'Do it intensively and continuously until realization dawns.' Although you could never get Papaji to admit that there were differences between his teachings and those of his Guru, they clearly didn't agree on the question of effort. (Godman, Interview, p. 3)

[70] Ramana makes a similar non-dual point with this answer to this devotee's desire:

> *Q*: Swami, I have only one desire, namely to put my head on Bhagavan's [Ramana Maharshi's] foot and do *namaskar* [ritual devotion]. Bhagavan must grant me this favour.
> *Ramana*: Oh, is that the desire! But then which is the foot and which is the head? (Godman, 2003, p. 1)

[71] Also, it is an inquiry possessed of existential urgency and force. See note 41 above.

[72] In *BSB* II.1.14 Śaṅkara reminds his objector of the 'fact' that, according to Advaita, liberation cannot be an effect – as effect, it is unreal.

[73] Other well-known Western disciples of Poonjaji include, Arjuna Nick Ardagh (an Irish-American who incorporates Advaita teachings in his psychology practice; see www.livingessence.com) and Isaac Shapiro (a South African who gives regular *satsang* in Europe and Australia; see www.isaacshapiro.de).

[74] For Gangaji's biography see www.gangaji.org and Gangaji and Moore, 2003.

[75] Contemporary Western Advaita admits of a variety of influences and hence some significant spiritual differences, both in practices and teachings, to the Advaita of Ramana and Poonjaji. Many contemporary teachers who claim the Ramana-Poonjaji lineage have branched off into quite different approaches (for example, the Australian Advaita teacher Vartman (now called Sandford) a disciple of Gangaji currently teaches 'spirituality through sexuality'; see www.whenIawoke.com/sages/Vartman) and Andrew Cohen (an American, who broke with Poonjaji in the 1990s and now teaches 'Evolutionary Enlightenment'; see www.andrewcohen.org). Despite the differences, the common thread in these Advaita variants appears to be 'you are freedom' and 'you have to do nothing to be who you are'. Although outside the scope of this study, the contemporary Western branchings and departures from classical Advaita and modern neo-Advaita would make a fascinating and valuable study.

Chapter 3

[1] *Laṇkāvatāra Sūtra* (Suzuki, 1999, pp. 67–68). Unless otherwise indicated, the *Laṇkāvatāra Sūtra* (*Discourse on the Descent into Laṇkā*) translation used here is by D. T. Suzuki, 1999.

[2] John R. McRae makes the point that there is no direct historical evidence that

Bodhidharma and the second Chan patriarch Huike taught from the *Laṇkā*. He argues that early Chan interest in the *Laṇkā* seemed to be strongest from the end of the sixth century to the beginning of the seventh (McRae, 1986, p. 29). The Tang master Mazu Daoyi is said to have used it for the basis of his 'one mind' teaching (Chang, 1969, p. 149) and David Kalupahana identifies the metaphysical teachings of the *Laṇkā* with the philosophical foundations and practices of the Caodong School (J. Sōtō) (Kalupahana, 1992, pp. 228–236).

3 *Diamond Sūtra*. Unless otherwise noted, the *Vajracchedikā Prajñāpāramitā Sūtra* translation used here is by Edward Conze, 1958.

4 David Kalupahana identifies the metaphysical teachings of the *Vajra* with the philosophical foundations and practices of the Linji School (J. Rinzai) (Kalupahana, 1992, pp. 228–236). However, in the Japanese Sōtō school the *Vajra*'s deconstructive 'formula' is also employed by Dōgen.

5 This is not to suggest that these are the only sūtras of importance to Zen. The *Prajñāpāramitā Hridaya Sūtra* (*The Heart Sūtra*) and the *Vimalakīrti Nirdeśa Sūtra* are but two examples of other Zen scriptural touchstones which, for reasons of space, cannot be considered here.

6 D. T. Suzuki describes the *Laṇkā* as being 'a highly chaotic text' (Suzuki, 1999, p. li) and the 'frequent repetition and violent transitions' of the *Vajra* led Conze to believe that 'reciters at various times added a passage here or there and that ... scribes at one time misplaced some of the palm leaves' (Conze, 1958, pp. 51–52).

7 A common instruction of Zen masters is to "forget my words but remember their meaning'. Sōtō Zen master Shunryu Suzuki expressed this point as: 'You should forget what I say, but be sure you know the real meaning of the words' (Chadwick, 1999, p. 181).

8 In the classical Indian languages 'quotes' are expressed by the phrase '*iti*' placed at the end of a term or sentence. See Kalupahana, 1992, p. 157.

9 *MMK* XXV:19.

10 *Laṅkā*, p. 140.

11 The form of spiritual inquiry that Nāgārjuna developed in the *MMK* was subsequently refined by Tibetan meditators into a meditative method of deconstructive paradoxical analysis largely based on the commentaries of Candrakīrti (c. 7th century).

12 Inada (1970, p. 16) comments that *pratītyasamutpāda* has been variously translated as 'twelve-fold causal chain', 'dependent existence', 'conditioned origination', 'dependent origination', and 'dependent co-origination'. He notes that most of these renderings come from understandings formulated in early Buddhism and advances 'relational origination' as an alternative. In this study, the standard translation 'dependent co-origination' and Inada's 'relational origination' are used interchangeably.

13 Based on the *MMK* XV:7, Kalupahana (1986) advances the view that the *MMK* is a 'grand commentary on the *Kaccāyanagotta-sutta*' (p. 81); a view not shared by Garfield (among others), who notes 'while this *sutta* is clearly important for Nāgārjuna, nothing in the text justifies such a global interpretation. The range of topics that Nāgārjuna considers far exceeds the scope of that *sutta*' (Garfield, 1995, p. 223).

14 Sprung notes that etymologically the Sanskrit term *svabhāva* 'embraces, but does not extinguish, both what we call essence or nature and being or existence'. Hence it can be given in English as 'self-existence', 'self-being' 'self-nature', or 'self-essence' (Sprung, 1978, p. 131). Another oft-used translation is 'own-being'.

[15] A rather succinct definition of the Advaita *brahman*.

[16] In the *Vajra*, the Bodhisattva Subuti confronts a similar problem by refusing to claim Arhatship, because such a claim would posit Arhatship as an entity to be attained and consolidated.

[17] Here Garfield makes the important distinction between grasping for *nirvāṇa* and an aspiration to attain buddhahood: 'It is central to Mahāyāna Buddhist practice to develop the altruistic aspiration to attain buddhahood for the sake of all sentient beings ... But this aspiration can be cultivated without reification of self, of the goal, or of the objects of compassion or action and, hence, without grasping of the kind at issue' (Garfield, 1995, p. 230).

[18] Inada (1970, p. 98) gives two translations of *parabhāva*: 'extended nature' in the sense of an entity having the existential character of extending or reaching over into the nature of other entities, and 'other-nature' in contrast to 'self-nature'.

[19] For example: Yasutani-rōshi, in response to the American Zen student Philip Kapleau: 'Can you show me this enlightened nature of yours?' (Kapleau, 1989, p. 226) and Zen master Kusan Sunim: 'Throw it away! To awaken your mind ... ask with all your strength, "What is it?"' (Batchelor, 1990, p. 22).

[20] In the previous chapter, compare Ramana Maharshi's instruction to 'Find the I!'

[21] Nāgārjuna's use of the tetralemma in the *MMK* has come under considerable scholarly scrutiny, with readings ranging from denying it much significance at all (Sprung, 1979) to locating it at the heart of Mādhyamika thought (e.g. Garfield, 1995; Ruegg, 1977). There is also much dispute over the purport of the tetralemma, ranging from nihilistic readings, in which Nāgārjuna is claimed to be denying all existence, such as Wood (1994), to interpretations that read Nāgārjuna employing the tetralemma as positing emptiness as an almost transcendental form of absolute, such as Murti (1973).

[22] Ruegg cites the examples of Āryadeva's *Catuḥśataka* and Candrakīrti's *Prasannapadā* (Ruegg, 1977, p. 3).

[23] Kalupahana rejects the thesis that Nāgārjuna had no views of his own to advance as a Vedāntic interpretation or as Nāgārjuna read through Candrakīrti (Kalupahana, 1986, p. 86).

[24] Dōgen wrote *Fukanzazengi* immediately upon his return from China, when he was 28 years old. At the end of *Shōbōgenzō Bendōwa*, he states that 'the forms and standards for sitting in zazen may be practiced following *Fukanzazengi* ...' (Nishijima and Cross, 1994, p. 22). Waddell and Abe note that *Fukanzazengi* has long been the Sōtō School's single most cherished writing, being recited at the regular night sitting in Sōtō temples and at other appropriate occasions. For a full discussion of the textual status and influence of *Fukanzazengi* see Waddell and Abe, 1973, pp. 115–120. In a commentary given for this study, Sōtō Zen master Ekai Korematsu referred to *Fukanzazengi* as 'the key to all of Dōgen ... contain[ing] everything that Dōgen Zenji wanted to say' (Korematsu, 2000).

[25] The young Dōgen's doubt was initiated by a passage on the Buddha-nature in the *Mahāparinirvāṇa sūtra* that was read as 'Śākyamuni Buddha said: "All sentient beings everywhere possess the Buddha-nature; the Tathāgata exists eternally and is without change"' (Kodera, 1980, p. 25). This passage also proved to be important in Dōgen's reinterpretation of Buddha-nature.

[26] Heine notes that the term *datsuraku* is a compound of *datsu* which means 'to remove, escape, extract', and *raku*, 'to fall, scatter, fade'. *Raku* implies a passive occurrence

that 'happens to' someone or something, as in the scattering of leaves by the breeze ... *Datsu* seems to be the more outwardly active term, though it refers to the distinctive occasion of the withdrawal from, omission or termination of activity: it is the act of ending activity. Yet, the ceasing of action suggested by *datsu* is the consequence of a more deliberate decision than the surrender or acquiescence of *raku*' (Heine, 1991, p. 5). The term is variously translated as 'moulting', 'shedding', 'falling', 'dropping off', and 'casting off'. In this discussion 'dropping off' and 'casting off' are used interchangeably.

27 Sanbōkyōdan (Three Treasures Association) is a contemporary Zen lineage founded by Yasutani Hakuun (1885–1973) in 1954. The defining feature of Sanbōkyōdan Zen is a single-minded emphasis on the experience of *kenshō* (literally: seeing into one's own nature), which differs significantly from the more traditional forms of Zen in Japan as found in Sōtō, Rinzai and Ōbaku training halls. For accounts of Sanbōkyōdan Zen practice under Yasutani-rōshi see Kapleau, 1989. For a more critical account in the context of Japanese 'New Religions', see Sharf, 1995. It is one of the most influential Zen lineages in the West.

28 Unless otherwise indicated, the translations of the *Shōbōgenzō* are by Norman Waddell and Masao Abe, published in *The Eastern Buddhist* from 1971–1977.

29 Both Kasulis (1985, p. 78) and Ekai Korematsu (2000) note that Dōgen most often used the term '*shō*' (authentication) when referring to enlightenment or awakening rather than *satori* (realization) or *kaku* (awakening). According to Kasulis, 'for Dōgen, proper sitting authenticates the sitting already there. Conversely, the student never reaches a point when zazen is suspended' (Kasulis, 1985, p. 78).

30 Compare Nāgārjuna *MMK* XXIV:10: 'Without relying on everyday practices (i.e., relative truths), the absolute truth cannot be expressed. Without approaching the absolute truth *nirvāṇa* cannot be attained.'

31 In terms of describing Dōgen's writings as phenomenological, Kasulis cautions that the term phenomenological should not be taken in the strict Husserlian sense as 'Dōgen has no clear position vis-à-vis intentionality.' But in terms of 'another mainstay of phenomenology, bracketing', Dōgen has a clear stance. In Kasulis' opinion, 'Dōgen is neither a naïve realist insofar as he is sensitive to the contribution of mind in the constituting of experience nor is he a subjective realist.' For Dōgen, 'although mind cannot be separated from reality, reality cannot be reduced to mind. Dōgen's tack is to concern himself only with what is experienced. Limiting himself to this, he is not concerned with notions of reality outside of this experiencing consciousness.' In the *Shōbōgenzō*,

> Dōgen frequently takes a metaphysical statement from the Tendai or Huayan traditions and interprets it as a descriptive statement about the structure of a specific experience; in effect, he suspends metaphysical and epistemological commitments outside the realm of things as experienced.

Accordingly, for Kasulis, 'Dōgen is implicitly carrying out his own form of bracketing and the term phenomenological is surprisingly appropriate to characterize the nature of this methodology' (Kasulis, 1985, p. 69 fn.).

32 The mutual interpenetration of all phenomena derives from the Huayan school of Buddhism and is articulated in the *Avataṃsaka Sūtra*.

33 The three distinctions – thinking, not-thinking and non-thinking – are taken from a traditional *mondō* (Zen dialogue) between a questioning monk and Master Yakusan

Gugō (C. Yueshan, 745–828) that Dōgen quotes at the beginning of *Shōbōgenzō Zazenshin* (*A Needle For Zazen*):

> While the great Master Yakusan … is sitting, a monk asks him, 'What are you thinking in the still-still state?' The Master says, 'Thinking the concrete state of not thinking.' The monk says, 'How can the state of not thinking be thought?' The Master says, 'It is non-thinking.' (*Shōbōgenzō Zazenshin*; Nishijima and Cross, 1996, p. 91)

[34] Kasulis translates *hishiryō* as 'without thinking'. However, for reasons of consistency I have replaced this with 'non-thinking', following Waddell and Abe (1973) and an oral commentary given for this study by Ekai Korematsu (2000).

[35] In explaining this, there is a cognitive paradox here that was nicely summed up by a Zen practitioner: 'It seems that not-thinking generates a lot of thinking!' (InterviewJ20, 2001).

[36] According to his own writings and the traditional biographies, Dōgen actually had three meetings with two *tenzos*. All were deconstructively important but, for reasons of focus and space, the first meeting has been selected as it best illustrates the young Dōgen's shift from an intellectual search for the way to the notion of 'wholehearted practice' that includes 'words and letters'. For full details of all three meetings see Kodera, 1980, and Kim, 1987. For Dōgen's own account in translation see Leighton, 1996.

[37] *Shōbōgenzō 'Buddha-nature'*.

[38] Some translators say 'distortion'. See Kim, 1985, p. 64 for such an example.

[39] *Shōbōgenzō 'Total Dynamic Working'*.

[40] For Ekai Korematsu's teachings and Zen community see www.jikishoan.org.au.

[41] For Hōgen Yamahata's teachings and Zen community see www.openway.org.au.

[42] Personal communication, 1999a.

[43] For examples see Yamahata, 1998, pp. 26, 228 and 234.

Chapter 4

1. Here it should be noted that these aspects are not the only facets of Advaita and Zen practice. Both Advaita and Zen practices have devotional and ritualistic aspects (among others). For example, ritual is an important aspect of Zen monasticism and is claimed to be an inseparable part of overall Zen practice, while devotion to the teacher and the lineage is often stressed in Advaita. For a discussion and overview of these aspects in Zen, see Faure, 1991, and for the devotional aspects of Advaita practice, see Godman, 1998.
2. *Points to Watch in Practicing the Way.*
3. All Zen interviewees stressed the importance of the teacher with terms such as 'essential' (InterviewB00, 2000) and 'absolutely necessary' (InterviewH10, 2000) being representative.
4. Other Advaita interviewees made similar observations about the teacher 'holding the space' i.e., in their terms, representing the 'energy' that 'drives' the inquiry in *satsang* (InterviewDO2, 2002).
5. The teacher here is Hōgen Yamahata's teacher, Sōtō master Harada Tangen-rōshi, abbot of Bukokuji Monastery, Japan.

[6] A long flat stick carried in the meditation hall and used to strike the shoulders of sleeping practitioners or at the request of practitioners for releasing stiffness. Its use has been discarded in many modern Sōtō temples both in Japan and the West. See Leighton, 1996. However, Zen teachers often carry a smaller version that they use for emphasis while teaching rather than striking. Ekai Korematsu-oshō and Augusto Alcalde-rōshi are two contemporary teachers that carry a 'teaching stick'.

[7] Compare Dōgen's reported experience of being 'stunned' in his encounter with the *tenzo* where he immediately responded with the 'beginner's mind' question 'What are words and phrases? What is wholeheartedly engaging the Way?' whereas here the practitioner reports that his 'mind was crazily trying to figure out the situation'. In trying to epistemologically frame the experience, that is, to 'make sense' out of it, the practitioner compounds his frustration and pushes for an 'unfindable answer'. The difference is that Dōgen responded directly from a 'not-knowing space' while the practitioner's attempt to 'figure out' a response was predicated on dualistic epistemological structures of thought. His later description of the practice of *zazen* feeling like 'stewing in your own juice' is illustrative of the experience of being entangled or embroiled in one's own oppositional thought structures and processes.

[8] A description of the process of *shikantaza* given by contemporary Sōtō teacher Ekai Korematsu (Korematsu, 2000).

[9] This aspect of experiential undoing will be outlined and explored in the next chapter wherein a phenomenological 'space' is identified and explored as part of the dynamics of experiential undoing.

[10] The teacher is Yasutani Hakuun (1885–1973), founder of the contemporary Zen Sanbōkyōdan (Three Treasures Association) lineage. Sanbōkyōdan teachers employ elements from both Rinzai and Sōtō practice. The Zen teachings of Dōgen, however, are taken as foundational. See Yasutani, 1996.

[11] Another practice that is given if practitioners are having difficulty with *shikantaza* is 'counting the breath', which serves to steady practitioners and enable them to establish their practice. Interestingly, practitioners report that such practices (*kōan*, counting the breath, etc.) all seem to dissolve into an objectless type of practice akin to *shikantaza*. Indeed, experientially speaking, one practitioner maintains that 'fundamentally there is no difference between *kōan* practice and *shikantaza* because in my experience in doing *mu* practice [the *kōan mu*] it tends to fade away and then you're left with a *shikantaza*-type practice' (InterviewJ00, 2000).

[12] Here, it is interesting to compare Ramana Maharshi's answer to a student: 'You are neither *That* nor *This*. The truth is "I am". "I AM that I AM" ... Mere *Being* is alone natural. To limit it to "being a man" is uncalled for' (Maharshi, 1984, pp. 555–556). Ramana is instructing that mere being as in 'I Am', not 'I am *something*', is what the student must realize, while in Zen the *rōshi* is pointing to the ultimately unsubstantial 'I' which cannot be an 'entity' that is defined by 'What?' 'Who?' and 'How?' In Advaita, being is all; in Zen being is nothing; in both cases 'I' cannot be reduced to any 'thing'.

[13] Ekai Korematsu further remarks that 'sitting still is like a prerequisite for deconstruction business!' (Korematsu, 2001a).

[14] Compare the Advaita master Poonjaji:

> Objects exist in time, through time. The perception of them is ignorance. The ultimate reality is not an object of thinking. When you perceive objects you are in

ignorance, you are in time. The mind is time. It is past and present appearing to you as objects of perception. The present cannot be shown. It cannot be perceived. It has nothing to do with time or mind. (Godman, 1998c, p. 32)

15 *Shōbōgenzō Uji.*

16 Here it is also important to note that Poonjaji's question utilizes two deconstructive techniques: unfindability analysis and bringing everything back to the here and now.

17 These transcripts were taken from *satsangs* given by Poonjaji in Lucknow from August–December 1992. They were transcribed by devotees and published on Arjuna Nick Ardagh's (a disciple) website www.livingessence.com from which I downloaded them (accessed in August 2001). Unfortunately, they are no longer available on this website. However, excerpts from them are posted on Poonjaji's site: www.avadhuta.com.

18 In an interview (*dokusan*) Hōgen tells his student: 'The most advanced moment is now. Why not now?'

19 Compare Dōgen in *Shōbōgenzō Zenki*: 'Life is not a coming and it is not a going; it is not an existing and it is not a becoming' (Waddell and Abe, 1972a, p. 74).

20 Here Wright is referring to Huayan Buddhism but his analysis is applicable to the dynamics of both Zen and Advaita dialogues.

21 Dōgen describes the turning of *dharma* in *Shōbōgenzō Genjōkōan*: 'When they realize one side the other is in darkness' (Waddell and Abe, 1972b, p. 134).

22 This teaching is a corollary to the Advaita instructions of 'turning awareness to the source of awareness' or 'allowing thought formulations to dissolve back into their unformulated states' (Gangaji, 1995, p. 116).

23 *Total Dynamic Working.*

24 Compare Dōgen in *Shōbōgenzō Hokke-Ten-Hokke*: 'When the mind is in a state of delusion the Flower of Dharma turns. When the mind is in the state of realization, we turn the Flower of Dharma' (Nishijima and Cross, 1994, p. 215).

25 Compare *Bṛ. Up.* II:5.19: 'This Brahman is without an inside and without an outside.'

26 For examples of such encounters see Chang, 1969, especially parts three and four.

27 The *locus classicus* of this dialogue in Zen is *Mumenkuan*, Case 30, 'This very mind is Buddha', and Case 33, 'Not mind, not Buddha' – both from Chan master Mazu Daoyi (709–788). See Aitken, 1991, pp. 189, 204.

28 Compare Dōgen's poem: 'Mind itself is buddha – difficult to practice, but easy to explain; No mind, no buddha – difficult to explain, but easy to practice' (Heine, 1997, p. 134).

29 See pp. 249–251.

30 *Shōbōgenzō Bukkōjōji:* 'Ongoing Enlightenment'.

Chapter 5

1 The full dialogue of Chan master Wenyi (885–958) is: '"What are you looking for, going here and there?" Luohan asked Wenyi. "I don't know", he answered. "Not-knowing is most intimate", approved Luohan, precipitating Wenyi's awakening' (Loy, 1988b, p. 141).

2 The full dialogue of Chan masters Nanjuan (748–834) and Zhaozhou (778–897) is:

> Nanjuan: 'If you try to turn towards the Way, it will turn away from you.'
> Zhaozhou: 'If I do not try to turn towards it, how can I know the way?'
> Nanjuan: 'The Way is not a matter of knowing or not-knowing. Knowing is delusion; not-knowing is blank consciousness. When you have really reached the true way beyond all doubt, you will find it vast and boundless as outer space.'
> (*Wumenkuan*, Case 19; Loy, 1988b, p. 141)

3 Poonjaji: 'Undo and where do you arrive? A distance between thought and thought. This dive is the same as nothingness ...' (Poonja, 1992b, pp. 23–24).

4 In a commentary on the above point, Ekai Korematsu identifies non-thinking as 'the empty point' (Korematsu, 2000) and further identifies the alternating non-thinking 'space' between thinking and not-thinking as the turning dynamic that constitutes Dōgen's 'essential art of *zazen*'. 'In actual practice, thinking comes and not-thinking arises – in the dynamic, in the space that they alternate, is non-thinking' (Korematsu, 2000).

5 Compare Dōgen in *Shōbōgenzō Kokū* (Space): 'The mutual encounter and mutual realization in the moment of the present between a person facing a wall and the wall facing the person' (Nishijima and Cross, 1999, p. 59).

6 *Shōbōgenzō Gyōji*.

7 In Śaṅkara's thought, questions as to the existence of the self are a non-issue, for to doubt one's own existence is logically impossible, that is, self-contradictory, 'for everyone is conscious of the existence of (his) self and never thinks, "I am not"' (Thibaut, 1904, p. 9).

8 Robert Aitken (b. 1917), one of the first American Zen teachers, Dharma heir of Yamada Kōun-rōshi in the Sanbōkyōdan lineage, and founder of the Diamond Sangha in Honolulu.

9 Private interview with the teacher.

10 In Case one of the *Mumenkuan* entitled 'Zhaozhou's Dog', a monk asked Zhaozhou, 'Has the dog Buddha nature or not?' Zhaozhou said, '*Mu*' (Aitken, 1991, p. 7) – one of the most famous *kōans* and often the first *kōan* assigned by a teacher. Literally *mu* (C. *wu*.) means 'there-is-not', 'to-have-not', 'the not', 'nothing', 'the empty'. It is most often translated as 'No'. For a masterly modern commentary on the *kōan mu* by Yasutani-rōshi, see Kapleau, 1989, pp. 76–88.

11 Another Zen practitioner reported that she sometimes experienced *shikantaza* as 'a sense of vastness or space that's large, there's room for everything ... You can just let things be' (InterviewB00, 2000).

12 This insight is reiterated by another practitioner, who observes:

> Sōtō practice is interesting. Earlier, I was doing *kōan* practice [and] I didn't get a feel at first for what *shikantaza* was and then ... I spoke to Hōgen-san about it once and I said, 'I'm not sure about *shikantaza*, what it is exactly?' and he said 'well, one day you'll discover that there's no difference [between practices]'. And I think I've got a sense of that now which is a little bit like one side tends to negate the other and then laugh at it ...' (InterviewJ00, 2000)

13 Compare the exchange on Dōgen's non-duality of practice and realization between Ekai Korematsu and a student: 'It's like a case of which came first, the chicken or the egg!' To which Ekai-oshō replied: 'What about if they both come together?' (Korematsu, 2001b).

[14] In psychology 'flow states' have been described by Csikszentmihalyi as being 'so absorbed in action there is 'no thinking' of what one is doing' (Csikszentmihalyi, 1975). This could also be a Zen description of non-duality in action.

[15] An apt comparison to the potential reification of 'presence' and 'being present' in Zen occurs in Theravāda practice when practitioners adhere to the concepts of 'mindfulness' and 'being mindful'.

[16] According to the Buddha, the thought of perfect enlightenment 'is unsupported by forms, sounds, smells, tastes, touchables, or mind-objects, unsupported by dharma, unsupported by no-dharma, unsupported by anything and why? All supports have actually no support' (Conze, 1958, p. 54).

[17] In another two other examples, when asked 'Are you doing anything when you sit?' A second long-term practitioner replied: 'Certainly not in *shikantaza* – you're making effort to some degree.' [Q]: 'Making effort to do what?' [Practitioner]: 'To be present …' (InterviewJ00, 2000). While a third replied: 'It's a funny thing sitting – you just sit there doing nothing and that's just it … I do nothing and nothing happens and you create the whole world from that!' (InterviewB00, 2000). All Zen practitioners interviewed said that the practice of *shikantaza* was 'doing nothing' but not 'doing nothing' in the 'usual' way. Most 'didn't know how to explain it'.

[18] Meditation hall.

[19] Head cook.

[20] Nāgārjuna demonstrated this logically and Dōgen phenomenologically.

[21] Inada, 1970, p. 158.

[22] Green Gulch Farm is a part of the San Francisco Zen Center. Reb Anderson and Norman Fischer are Sōtō Zen teachers in the lineage of Shunryu Suzuki-rōshi.

Conclusion

[1] Although outside the scope of this study, the experiential undoing of reified 'bottom-line' ontologies, whether they are 'full' or 'empty', highlights a possible broader application of experiential deconstruction outside of the context of spiritual practice. The radical questioning of duality – no matter what the underlying ontology – offers a potential framework for understanding how the human mind gets caught up in beliefs and ideologies both religious and secular and how it might liberate itself from them. In the sense that this process is self-reflexive, i.e., it continually works to undo its own reified structures, experiential deconstruction can be said to operate like a dynamic meta-perspective through which we can see 'where [our minds] get caught on things' and how we shape and 'hold on' to beliefs and ideas.

[2] For other research approaches on the deconstructive processes underlying non-dual spiritual experience see Nelson (2000); Puhakka (2000); and Rothberg (1990 and 2000).

Bibliography

Abe, M. (1985), 'The oneness of practice and attainment: Implications for the relation between means and ends', in La Fleur, W. R. (ed.), *Dōgen Studies*, University of Hawaii Press, Honolulu, pp. 99–111.

— (1992), 'The oneness of practice and attainment: Implications for the relation between means and ends', in *A Study of Dōgen: His Philosophy and Religion*, State University of New York Press, Albany, New York.

Aitken, R. (1991), *The Gateless Barrier: The Wu-Men Kuan (Mumonkan)*, North Point Press, San Francisco.

Batchelor, S. (1990), *The Faith to Doubt: Glimpses of Buddhist Uncertainty*, Parallax Press, Berkeley.

Behari, B. (1991), *Sufis, Mystics and Yogis of India*, Bharatiya Vidya Bhavan, Bombay.

Bilimoria, P. (1989), 'Self, not-self and the ultimate: Śaṅkara's two-tiered definition-cum-description revisited', *Journal of Indian Council of Philosophical Research*, 6 (2), 155–167.

Brunton, P. (1994), *A Search in Secret India*, B. I. Publications, New Delhi (originally published 1934).

Bugault, G. (1983), 'Logic and dialectics in the Mādhyamakakārikās', *Journal of Indian Philosophy*, 11, 7–76.

Chadwick, D. (1999), *Crooked Cucumber: The Life and Zen Teachings of Shunryu Suzuki*, Broadway Books, New York.

Chang, C.-Y. (1969), *Original Teachings of Ch'an Buddhism*, Pantheon Books, New York.

Cheng, C.-Y. (1973), 'On Zen (Ch'an) language and Zen paradoxes', *Journal of Chinese Philosophy*, 1 (1), 77–102.

Clark, S. R. L. (1986), *The Mysteries of Religion: An Introduction to Philosophy through Religion*, Basil Blackwell, Oxford.

Cleary, J. C. (1986), *Zen Dawn: Early Zen Texts from Tun Huang*, Shambhala, Boston.

Conze, E. (1958), *Buddhist Wisdom Books*, George Allen & Unwin, London.

— (1977), *Buddhist Scriptures*, Penguin, Harmondsworth (first published 1958).

— (1983), *Buddhist Thought in India*, George Allen & Unwin, Boston (first published 1962).

Csikszentmihalyi, M. (1975), *Beyond Boredom and Anxiety*, Jossey-Bass, San Francisco.

Dasgupta, S. (1992a), *A History of Indian Philosophy*, Vol. 3, Motilal Banarsidass, Delhi

(original publication, Cambridge, 1922), 5 vols.
— (1992b), *A History of Indian Philosophy*, Vol. 1, Motilal Banarsidass, Delhi (original publication, Cambridge, 1922), 5 vols.
Davis, L. S. (2005), 'Deconstructive spiritual inquiry: Experiential undoing in Advaita & Zen', PhD Thesis, Deakin University, Australia.
Deutsch, E. (1969), *Advaita Vedānta: A Philosophical Reconstruction*, East-West Center Press, Honolulu.
Deutsch, E. and Van Buitenen, J. A. B. (1971), *A Source Book of Advaita Vedānta*, The University Press of Hawaii, Honolulu.
Doherty, G. (1983), 'Form is emptiness: Reading the Diamond Sutra', *The Eastern Buddhist*, 16 (2), 114–123.
Faure, B. (1991), *The Rhetoric of Immediacy: A Cultural Critique of Ch'an/Zen Buddhism*, Princeton, New Jersey, Princeton University Press.
— (2004), *Double Exposure: Cutting across Buddhist and Western Discourses*, trans. Lloyd, J., Stanford University Press, Stanford (originally published by Flammarion, Paris, 2000 as *Bouddhismes, Philosophies et Religions*).
Fort, A. O. (1998), *Jīvanmukti in Transformation: Embodied Liberation in Advaita and Neo-Vedānta*, State University of New York Press, Albany, New York.
Fost, F. F. (1998), 'Playful illusion: The making of worlds in Advaita Vedānta', *Philosophy East and West*, 48 (3), 387–405.
Fung, Y.-L. (1948), *A Short History of Chinese Philosophy*, The Free Press, Macmillan, New York.
Gangadean, A. K. (1993), *Meditative Reason: Toward Universal Grammar*, Peter Lang, New York.
Gangaji (1995), *You Are That! Satsang With Gangaji*, Vol. 1, Satsang Press, Boulder, Colorado, 2 vols.
— (1999), 'Public Satsang Melbourne 1999', unpublished typescript.
— (2001), *Find the Meditator*, www.gangaji.org.
Gangaji and Moore, R. (2003), *Just Like You: An Autobiography*, DO Publishing, USA.
Garfield, J. L. (1995), *The Fundamental Wisdom of the Middle Way*, Oxford University Press, New York.
Garfield, J. L. and Priest, G. (2003), 'Nāgārjuna and the limits of thought', *Philosophy East and West*, 53 (1), 1–21.
Godman, D., *An Interview with David Godman by Rob Sacks*, http://www.davidgodman.org/ (accessed 29 November 2009).
— (ed.) (1992), *Be As You Are: The Teachings of Sri Ramana Maharshi*, Penguin, New Delhi.
— (1994), *Living by the Words of Bhagavan*, Sri Annamalai Swami Ashram Trust, Tiruvannamalai.
— (1998a), *Nothing Ever Happened*, Vol. 1, Avadhuta Foundation, Boulder, Colorado.
— (1998b), *Nothing Ever Happened*, Vol. 2, Avadhuta Foundation, Boulder, Colorado.
— (1998c), *Nothing Ever Happened*, Vol. 3, Avadhuta Foundation, Boulder, Colorado.
— (ed.) (2000), *Annamalai Swami: Final Talks*, Sri Annamalai Swami Ashram Trust, Tiruvannamalai.
— (2003), *Padamalai*, http://www.davidgodman.org/ (accessed 29 November 2009).
Grimes, J. (1991), 'Some problems in the epistemology of Advaita', *Philosophy East and West*, 41 (3), 291–301.

Heine, S. (1982), 'Multiple dimensions of impermanence in Dōgen's "Genjōkōan"', *Journal of the International Association of Buddhist Studies*, 4 (2), 44–62.

— (1991), *A Dream Within a Dream: Studies in Japanese Thought*, Peter Lang, New York.

Hiriyanna, M. (1994), *Outlines of Indian Philosophy*, Motilal Banarsidass, Delhi.

Hongzhi (1991), *Cultivating the Empty Field: The Silent Illumination of Zen Master Hongzhi*, trans. Leighton, T. D., North Point Press, San Francisco.

Inada, K. K. (1970), *Nāgārjuna: A Translation of his Mūlamadhyamakakārikā with an Introductory Essay*, The Hokuseido Press, Tokyo.

InterviewB00 (2000), 'Zen interview', unpublished typescript, Melbourne.

InterviewDO2 (2002), 'Advaita interview', unpublished typescript, Melbourne.

InterviewH10 (2000), 'Zen interview', unpublished typescript, Melbourne.

InterviewJ00 (2000), 'Zen interview', unpublished typescript, Melbourne.

InterviewJ20 (2001), 'Zen interview', unpublished typescript, Melbourne.

InterviewKC9901 (2000), 'Zen/Advaita interview', unpublished typescript, Tiruvannamalai, South India.

Kalupahana, D. J. (1986), *Nāgārjuna: The Philosophy of the Middle Way*, State University of New York Press, Albany, New York.

— (1992), *A History of Buddhist Philosophy: Continuities and Discontinuities*, University of Hawaii Press, Honolulu.

Kapleau, P. (1989), *The Three Pillars of Zen*, Doubleday, New York.

Kasulis, T. P. (1985), *Zen Action, Zen Person*, University of Hawaii Press, Honolulu.

Kim, H.-J. (1985), 'The reason of words and letters: Dōgen and kōan language', in La Fleur, W. (ed.), *Dōgen Studies*, University of Hawaii Press, Honolulu, pp. 54–82.

— (1987), *Dōgen Kigen: Mystical Realist*, University of Arizona Press, Tucson, Arizona.

King, R. (1995), *Early Advaita and Buddhism: The Mahāyāna Context of the Gauḍapādīya-kārikā*, State University of New York Press, Albany, New York.

Kodera, T. J. (1980), *Dōgen's Formative Years in China: An Historical Study and Annotated Translation of the Hōkyō-ki*, Routledge & Kegan Paul, London.

Korematsu, E. (1999a), 'Dharma talks: Practice meetings', unpublished typescript, Melbourne.

— (1999b), 'Personal interview: Zen workshop', unpublished typescript, Melbourne.

— (1999c), 'Retreat teachings (Teishō), May 1999', unpublished typescript, Melbourne.

— (2000), 'Dōgen commentaries', unpublished typescript, Melbourne.

— (2001a), 'Personal interview: Deconstruction/reconstruction', unpublished typescript, Melbourne.

— (2001b), 'Retreat teachings (Teishō), April 2001', unpublished typescript, Melbourne.

Kusan, S. (1985), *The Way of Korean Zen*, trans. Fages, M., Weatherhill, New York.

Leighton, T. D. (1996), *Dōgen's Pure Standards for the Zen Community: A Translation of Eihei Shingi*, State University of New York Press, Albany, New York.

Lindtner, C. (1997), 'Nāgārjuna', in Carr, B. and Mahalingam I. (eds), *Companion Encyclopedia of Asian Philosophy*, Routledge, London.

Loori, J. D. (ed.) (2002), *The Art of Just Sitting: Essential Writings on the Zen Practice of Shikantaza*, Wisdom Publications, Boston.

Loy, D. (1988a), *Nonduality: A Study in Comparative Philosophy*, Yale University Press, New Haven.

— (1988b), 'The path of no-path: Śaṅkara and Dōgen on the paradox of practice', *Philosophy East and West*, 28 (2), 125–146.
McRae, J. R. (1986), *The Northern School and the Formation of Early Ch'an Buddhism*, Kuroda Institute University of Hawaii Press, Honolulu.
Mahadevan, T. M. P. (1977), *Ramana Maharshi: The Sage of Arunacala*, George Allen & Unwin, London.
Maharshi, R. (1984), *Talks with Sri Ramana Maharshi*, Sri Ramanasramam, Tiruvannamalai (originally published 1955).
Moustakas, C. (1990), *Heuristic Research: Design, Methodology, and Applications*, Sage Publications, London.
Murti, T. R. V. (1955), *The Central Philosophy of Buddhism*, Allen & Unwin, London.
— (1973), 'Saṃvṛti and Paramātha in Mādhyamika and Advaita Vedānta', in Sprung, M. (ed.), *The Problem of Two Truths in Buddhism and Vedānta*, Reidel, Dordrecht.
Narasimha, B. V. (1993), *Self Realization: The Life and Teachings of Sri Ramana Maharshi*, Sri Ramanasramam, Tiruvannamalai (originally published 1931).
Nelson, P. L. (2000), 'Mystical experience and radical deconstruction: Through the ontological looking glass', in Hart T., Nelson P. L. and Puhakka K. (eds), *Transpersonal Knowing: Exploring the Horizon of Consciousness*, State University of New York Press, Albany, New York, pp. 55–84.
Nikhilananda, S. (1987), *The Māṇḍūkya Upaniṣad with Gauḍapāda's Kārikā and Śaṅkara's Commentary*, Advaita Ashrama, Calcutta.
Nishijima, G. and Cross, C. (1994), *Master Dōgen's Shōbōgenzō*, Vol. 1, trans. Nishijima, G. and Cross, C., Windbell, Surrey, UK, 4 vols.
— (1996), *Master Dōgen's Shōbōgenzō*, Vol. 2, trans. Nishijima, G. and Cross, C., Windbell Publications, London, 4 vols.
— (1999), *Master Dōgen's Shōbōgenzō*, Vol. 4, trans. Nishijima, G. and Cross, C., Windbell Publications, London, 4 vols.
Odell, D. (2004), *A Rushed Quality: Observations on Living*, www.blackjelly.com/Mag2/features/rushed.htm.
Olivelle, P. (1996), *The Upanishads*, Oxford University Press, New York.
Osborne, A. (1970), *Ramana Maharshi and the Path of Self-Knowledge*, Jaico Publishing House, Bombay (repr. 1994).
— (1996), *Collected Works of Ramana Maharshi*, Sri Ramanasramam, Tiruvannamalai.
Pannikar, R. (1977), *The Vedic Experience*, Motilal Banarsidas, Delhi.
Poonja, H. W. L. (1992a), *Satsang Transcripts August–December 1992*, www.livingessence.com and www.poonjaji.org.
— (1992b), *Wake Up and Roar: Satsang with H. W. L. Poonja*, Vol. 1, Satsang Foundation, Boulder, Colorado, 2 vols.
— (1993), *Wake Up and Roar: Satsang with H. W. L. Poonja*, Vol. 2, Satsang Foundation, Boulder, Colorado, 2 vols.
Potter, K. H. (ed.) (1981), *Encyclopedia of Indian Philosophies: Advaita Vedānta up to Samkara and His Pupils*, Princeton University Press, Princeton, New Jersey.
Powell, W. F. (1986), *The Record of Tung-shan*, trans. Powell, W. F., Kuroda Institute, University of Hawaii Press, Honolulu.
Puhakka, K. (2000), 'An invitation to authentic knowing', in Hart, T., Nelson, P. L. and Puhakka, K. (eds), *Transpersonal Knowing: Exploring the Horizon of Consciousness*, State University of New York Press, Albany, New York, pp. 11–30.

Radhakrishnan, S. (1994), *The Principal Upaniṣads*, trans. Radhakrishnan, S., Indus, HarperCollins India, New Delhi.

Rambachan, A. (1991), *Accomplishing the Accomplished: The Vedas as a Source of Valid Knowledge in Śaṇkara*, University of Hawaii Press, Honolulu.

Reat, N. R. (1983), 'Insiders and outsiders in the study of religious traditions', *Journal of the American Academy of Religion*, 51 (3), 459–476.

Robinson, R. H. (1972), 'Did Nāgārjuna really refute all philosophical views?', *Philosophy East and West*, 22, 325–331.

Rothberg, D. (1990), 'Contemporary epistemology and the study of mysticism', in Forman, R. K. C. (ed.), *The Problem of Pure Consciousness: Mysticism and Philosophy*, Oxford University Press, New York, pp. 163–210.

— (2000), 'Spiritual inquiry', in Hart, T., Nelson, P. L. and Puhakka, K. (eds), *Transpersonal Knowing: Exploring the Horizon of Consciousness*, State University of New York Press, Albany, New York, pp. 161–184.

Ruegg, D. S. (1977), 'The uses of the four positions of the catuṣkoṭi and the problem of the description of reality in Mahāyāna Buddhism', *Journal of Indian Philosophy*, 5, 1–71.

Sharf, R. H. (1995), 'Sanbokyodan: Zen and the way of the new religions', *Japanese Journal of Religious Studies*, 22 (3–4), 417–458.

Sharma, A. (2000), 'Sacred scriptures and the mysticism of Advaita Vedānta', in Katz, S. T. (ed.), *Mysticism and Sacred Scripture*, Oxford University Press, New York, pp. 169–183.

Smart, N. (1977), *The Religious Experience of Mankind*, Collins, Fountain Books, London, repr. edn.

Sprung, M. (1978), 'Being and the middle way', in Sprung, M. (ed.), *The Question of Being: East-West Perspectives*, The Pennsylvania State University Press, University Park, Pennsylvania.

Stafford Betty, L. (1983), 'Nāgārjuna's masterpiece – logical, mystical, both or neither?', *Philosophy East and West*, 33 (2), 123–138.

Stambaugh, J. (1990), *Impermanence is Buddha-Nature: Dōgen's Understanding of Temporality*, University of Hawaii Press, Honolulu.

Streng, F. J. (1967), *Emptiness: A Study in Religious Meaning*, Abingdon Press, New York.

— (1971), 'The Buddhist doctrine of two truths as religious philosophy', *Journal of Indian Philosophy*, 1 (3), 262–271.

— (1987), 'Sunyam and sunyata', in Eliade, M. (ed.), *The Encyclopedia of Religion*, Vol. 14, Macmillan Publishing Company, New York, pp. 153–159.

Suzuki, D. T. (1999), *The Laṅkāvatāra Sūtra*, trans. Suzuki, D. T., Motilal Banarsidass, Delhi.

Suzuki, S. (1984), *Zen Mind, Beginner's Mind*, Weatherhill, New York.

Thibaut, G. (1904), *Vedanta-Sutras with the Commentary of Sankaracarya*, Sacred Books of the East, Vol. 34, Oxford University Press, Oxford.

Valle, R. and Mohs, M. (1998), 'Transpersonal awareness in phenomenological inquiry: philosophy, reflections, and recent research', in Braud, W. and Anderson, R. (eds), *Transpersonal Research Methods for the Social Sciences: Honoring Human Experience*, Sage Publications, Thousand Oaks, California, pp. 95–113.

Vireswarananda (1993), *Brahma-Sutras with the Commentary of Sri Śaṅkara*, Advaita Ashrama, Calcutta.

Waddell, N. (1979), 'Being Time: Dōgen's *Shōbōgenzō Uji*', *The Eastern Buddhist*, 12 (1), 114–129.
— (1980), 'Zen master Hakuin's poison words for the heart', *The Eastern Buddhist*, 13 (2), 73–114.
Waddell, N. and Abe, M. (1971), 'Dōgen's *Bendōwa*', *The Eastern Buddhist*, 4 (1), 124–157.
— (1972a), 'Dōgen's *Shōbōgenzō Zenki*: Total working time and *Shōji*: Birth and death', *The Eastern Buddhist*, 5 (1), 70–80.
— (1972b), '*Shōbōgenzō Genjōkōan*', *The Eastern Buddhist*, 2 (2), 129–140.
— (1973), 'Dōgen's *Fukanzazengi* and *Shōbōgenzō Zazengi*', *The Eastern Buddhist*, 6 (2), 115–128.
— (1975), '*Shōbōgenzō* Buddha-nature: Part 1', *The Eastern Buddhist*, 8 (2), 94–112.
Watson, B. (1993), *The Zen Teachings of Master Lin-chi*, Shambhala, Boston.
Wood, T. E. (1994), *Nāgārjunian Disputations: A Philosophical Journey through an Indian Looking-Glass*, Honolulu, University of Hawaii Press.
Wright, D. S. (1982), 'The significance of paradoxical language in Hua-yen Buddhism', *Philosophy East and West*, 32 (3), 325–338.
Yamahata, H. (1998), *On the Open Way: Zen Here-Now*, Open Way Zen Centre, Byron Bay, Australia.
— (1999a), 'Personal interview: Zen retreat Greyfrair's Mt Eliza', unpublished typescript, Melbourne.
— (1999b), 'Teishō: Zen retreat Greyfrair's Mt Eliza', unpublished typescript, Melbourne.
— (2001), 'Public talk', unpublished excerpts, Kagyu E-vam Buddhist Institute, Melbourne.
— (2004a), *Autobiography*, www.openway.org.au.
— (2004b), *On Progress*, www.openway.org.au.
Yanagida, S. (1983), 'The "recorded sayings" texts of Chinese Ch'an Buddhism', in Lai, W. and Lancaster, L. (eds), *Early Ch'an in China and Tibet*, Berkeley Buddhist Studies Series, Berkeley, California.
Yasutani, H. (1996), *Flowers Fall: A Commentary on Zen Master Dōgen's Genjōkōan*, Shambhala, Boston.

Index

(Page numbers in italics denotes reference in the Notes)

Abe, M. 94, 95–98, 100, 102, 105, 106, 144, 158, 159, *200*, *201*, *202*, *204*
abhāva (negation) 32
Abhidharma corpus 77, 80
abhyāsa (repetition) *195*
absence
  and presence *see* presence: and absence
    74, 87, 92
absolutism 80
adhyāropa (superimposition – a word-manipulation teaching technique used in conjunction with *apavāda* (desuperimposition)) 36–37
adhyāsa (superimposition – mistaking something for what it is not) 26–27, 31–32, 35–36, 39–40, 42–43, 46, 53–57, 65, 67, 69, 123, 126–127, 147, 168, *193*, *194*
advaitavāda (non-different) path 5, 65, 113, 156, 184
advaya (not-two) 5, 80, 85, 99, 111–112
  advayavāda (non-two path) 5, 113, 156, 184
affirmation–negation–affirmation 'formula' 19–20, 52, 73, 76–79, 93, 100–101, 119, 121, 145, 149, 153–154, 158, 169, 172, 175–176, 179, 182, 186–187
  see also negation
Aitareya Upaniṣad (III:1.3) 19
Aitken (Aitken-rōshi), R. 170, *204*, *205*
ajātivāda (non-origination) 22–23, 25, 27, 61, 70, 81, 86, *193*
all-accepting compassion xvii
all-self, ontology of 3–4, 7, 184, 187
anādi (beginningless) 31
anātman 3–4, 90
anatta (no-self) ontology of 4, 7, 69, 71, 72, 184, 187
Anderson, R. 184, *206*
anirvacanīya (indescribable) 31
anitya (non-substantiality/impermanence) 71, 75
Annamalai Swami 49, *196*
anubhava (immediate/direct intuition) 34–35, 38, 40–41, 51, 65
anumāna (inference) 32, *195*
anupalabdhi (noncognition) *195*
apavāda (desuperimposition) 36–37
apavarga (complete freedom from difference) *193*
apprehension, Śaṅkara's concept of 27–47
apūrva (novelty) *195*
Ardagh, Arjuna N. *198*, *204*
arthāpatti (presumption/postulation) 32, *195*
arthavāda (commendation) *195*
Āryadeva *200*
asat (absolutely unreal) 30–31, 126
ātman (non-dual self) 3–4, 6, 9–12, 18–28, 36–40, 51–53, 57, 63, 81, 90, 123–124, 150
  ātman-brahman identity 24–25, 28,

30, 34, 38–47, 52, 55–56, 60–61, 65–66, 68–70, 125–127, 142, 148, 154, 158, 160, 166, 184, 187, *196*
ātman vichara 9, 117
avaitavāda (non-difference) 27
Avataṃsaka Sūtra *201*
avidyā (ignorance) 25–27, 29, 31–33, 41–42, 46, 51, 65, 69, 83, *194*
awakening, spiritual xiv, 13, 16, 58, 62, 63, 96–97, 99, 102, 105, 144, *201*, *204*
acquired (*shikaku*) 95
original (*hongaku*) 93–94

Bādarāyaṇa 28
bādha (contradiction) *194*
Baker, R. 10
Batchelor, S. 12, *200*
Behari, B. 27
Being xvii, 5, 29, 57, 64, 165, *203*
Being-Consciousness-Bliss (*sat-cit-ānanda*) 29, *194*
Bhagavadgītā, the *195*
bhakti (devotion) 58
bhakti-yoga 195
Bhattacharya 5
bifurcation, dualistic
of entities 7, 65, 80, 82, 118, 133, 142, 146–147, 149, 152–155, 157, 159, 175, 185–187
of linear ideas of time xv, xx, 8, 61–62, 72, 113, 118, 133–138, 154–155, 184, 186
Bilimoria, P. 29, 38
bi-negation, technique of 35, 89, 90
blurring, of boundaries 146, 169
bodhi 93
Bodhidharma 73, *199*
bondage and liberation (*mokṣa*) 22–27
both/and configuration 90, 143, 150, 151
'bottom-line' ontologies *206*
brahmajñāna (liberating knowledge) 32–33, 35–36, 38, 40, 41–42, 63, 65, 69, 86, 126, 147, 153, 158, 160, 169, *196*
brahman (ultimate reality) 4–6, 11, 14, 18–22, 26, 29–31, 36–39, 46, 48, 52–53, 85–86, 98, 117, 119, 128, 142, 144, 146, 149, 153–154, 167, 184, 189, *191*, *192*, *194*, *195*, *200*, *204*
brahman-knowledge 34–35, 44, *196*
brahmaniṣṭham 35
nirguṇa brahman 27–28, 32–33, 41
see also *ātman-brahman* identity
Brahmasūtrabhāṣya 28–30, 31, 33, *194*, *195*, *196*, *198*
Brahmasūtrabhāṣya adhyāsa bhaṣya 31
breathing 10, 20, 177, 179
counting the breath 179, 182, *203*
Bṛhad-āraṇyaka Upaniṣad 6, 17, 19–21, 23, 28, 37, 52, 66, 68, *191*, *193*, *195*, *196*, *204*
Bṛhad-āraṇyaka Upaniṣadbhāṣya 37, 52–53
Brunton, P. *197*
Buddha, the 3, 71–84, 90, 105, *192*, *194*, *206*
see also Buddha-nature (*buddhatā*); *dharma*: Buddha-*dharma*
Buddha-nature (*buddhatā*) 72, 94–99, 105–106, *200*
Bugault, G. 82, 86–87, 88, 89

Candrakīrti *199*, *200*
Caoshan Benji *192*
Catuḥśataka *200*
causation 7–8, 151, 186
see also ends and means (cause and effect) dualism
centring, of body and mind 162, 167, 177, 178
Chadwick, D. 10, *199*
Chadwick, Major A. W. (Sadhu Arunchala) *197*
Chan tradition 73–74, 76, 102, 149, *193*, *197*, *204*, *205*
Chāndogya Upaniṣad 19, 23, 32, 66, *191*, *192*
Chang, C.-Y. *199*, *204*
Cheng, C.-Y. 152
Clark, S. 12
Cleary, J. C. 146
'clouds' and clarity, Gangaji's dualism of 67–68

Cohen, A. *198*
Cohen, S. S. *197*
'coming back' 108, 177
'concrete this', the 110–111
continuous practice (*gyōji*) 96–97, 102, 159, 169, 184
conventional truth *see* two truths, the (*saṃvṛti-satya* and *paramārtha-satya*)
Conze, E. 71, 72, 73, 77, 78, 79, 93, *199*, *206*
cornered, (experience of) being 55, 125, 131, 133, 137–138
Cross, C. 153, *200*, *202*, *204*, *205*
Csikszentmihalyi, M. *206*
cutting away, of dualistic ideas 161

darshan 57
Dasgupta, S. 22, 189
datsuraku *200–201*
Davis, L. S. *191*
death 9, 11, 33, 49–52, 120, *196*
  birth–death cycle 91, 93–94
Deutsch, E. 22, 28, 31–33, 36, 38, 39–46, 50, 119, *193*, *194*, *195–196*
dharma 12, 78–79, 84, 105, 145–146, *194*, *204*, *206*
  Buddha *dharma* 6
  dharma talks 107, 121, 135
dialoguing, as means to spiritual insight 8–12, 118, 157
  see also teacher–student dialogues
Diamond Sūtra see *Prajñāpāramitā Sūtras*
differentiation
  denial of 4, 23–25, 28–34, 38–43, 56, 65, 69, 81, 86, 98, 127, 143–144, 153–154, 160, 164–168, 172–173, 184, 187, *194*
  identity and difference 5–6, 81, 86–88, 93, 98–99, 106, 112–113, 144–146, 154, 172–174 *see also* identity
doer, objectivization of 43, 53, 124–127
Dōgen (Eihei Dōgen Zenji) xiii, 9, 76, 79–80, 93–106, 107, 108, 110, 111, 112, 119, 132, 134, 136, 140–141, 144–145, 152, 153, 154, 158, 159, 169, 172, 173, 176, 178, 183–184, *191*, *199*, *200*, *201*, *202*, *203*, *204*, *205*, *206*
Doherty, G. 78
'doing nothing' 176–177, *206*
doing/not doing dichotomy xxi, 150–151, 153–154
dokusan (interview) 9, 121, 170, 173, *204*
  see also teacher–student dialogues
Dongshan Liangjie 15, *192*
doubt xv–xvi, 8–11, 15, 28, 34, 94–95, 105, 128, 138, 161–164, *200*, *205*
dream states (internal illusion) 23–25, 33–34, 45–46, *193*
ḍṛṣi (views) 80
Duff, G. *197*
duḥkha (suffering) 71
Dvaita Vedānta school of Vedāntic philosophy *192*
dynamics, of experiential undoing xx, 156–185

'eight negations', the 81
emptiness (*śūnyatā*) 4, 74–75, 81–87, 89, 92–93, 98, 112, 143, 145, 149, 158, 168, 189, *200*
ends and means (cause and effect) dualism xv, xx, 8, 33, 97, 106, 108, 111, 113, 118, 137, 147, 151, 155
enlightenment 9, 63, 71–75, 79, 84, 93–106, 110, 112, 135, 144, 146, 152, 154, 159, *198*, *201*, *206*
eternalism (permanence) 81, 99, 112
Evans-Wentz, W. Y. *197*
experiential mapping xx–xxi, 156, 159–185
experiential tension xv, 15–17, 124, 141, 173

'falling apart' ('disassembling') 132, 141
Faure, B. 149, *202*
Fayan Wenyi *197*, *204*
'feedback that teaches' 103
'find out', admonition to 13–14, 15, 52, 59, 124, 137, 140, *197*
Fischer, N. 184, *206*
'flow states', psychology of *206*

Fort, A. O. 48, *196*, *197*
Fost, F. F. 29
Four Noble Truths (*āryasatya*) 71–72, 81, 84
Fukanzazengi (*The Universal Promotion of the Principles of Zazen*) 93, 99–100, 158, *200*
Fung, Y.-L. 149, *197*

Gakudō-yōjinshū 119
Ganga (Ganges) 63–64, 66
Gangadean, A. K. 157
Gangaji 17, 66–69, 120, 124, 125–128, 150, 158, *192*, *198*, *204*
Garfield, J. L. 88, 89, 90, 91, 92–93, *199*, *200*
Gauḍapāda 8, 22–27, 30, 32, 47, 61, 70, 86, *193*, *196*
Gauḍapādīya-kārikā 4, 8, 22, 24–27, *193*, *196*
'getting the turn between things' 173, 187
Godman, D. 16, 49, 52, 53, 54–55, 58, 59, 61, 62, 63, 64, 70, 122, 126, 128, 141, 147, 157, 162, 169, *192*, *193*, *194*, *196*, *197*, *198*, *202*, *204*
Govinda 22, 27
great chain of being 72
Grimes, J. 29, 30, 46
guru's grace 17

habits of mind (*vasanas*) 139
Harada Tangen-rōshi *202*
Haukin Ekaku *192*
Heart Sūtra see *Prajñāpāramitā Sūtras*
Heine, S. 144, 145, 173, *200–201*, *204*
'here and now'
- 'bringing everything back to xviii, xx, 105, 113, 117–118, 123, 125, 133–139, 143, 186, *204*
- 'right here' and 'right now' 93, 133–134, 183
- 'Why not now?', in teaching of Hōgen Yamahata 109–111
- 'Why not now?', in teaching of Poonjaji 137–138

hermeneutical-phenomenological analytical strategy xvii–xx, 117, 188, *191*, *195*
heuristic research design xvi–xviii, xx, 156, 159, 182
Hiriyanna, M. 154
hishiryō (non-thinking) xxi, 95, 100–101, 105, 108, 112, 146, 153, 156–158, 173, 176, 178, *201*, *202*, *205*
hongaku (awakening) 94
Hongzhi Zhengjue xvi
Huike *199*

'I'-force, the 55
identity 6, 12–13, 19, 23–24, 27, 31, 70, 97, 123, 133, 159, 167, 170, 188, *193*, *197*
- and difference 5–6, 81, 86–88, 93, 98–99, 106, 112–113, 144–146, 154, 172–174
- *see also ātman-brahman*-identity

immediacy 10, 16, 20–21, 34, 36, 38, 48, 60, 62, 65, 110, 125, 132, 134, 137–138, 144–146, 153–154, 171, 177, 185
Inada, K. K. 29, 81, 85, *192*, *194*, *199*, *200*, *206*
'insider/outsider' approaches *191*
interdependent existence 85
Interviews
- B00 (Zen) 119, 132, 145, 175, 178, *202*, *205*, *206*
- DO2 (Advaita) 120, 159, 161–168, *197*, *202*
- H10 (Zen) 15, *202*
- J00 (Zen) 120–121, 131, 138, 154, *203*, *205*, *206*
- J20 (Zen) 119, 131, 159, 169–184, *202*
- KC9901 (Advaita) 12, 119, 133

intra-psychic dynamics of non-dual forms of inquiry and transformations xxi, 159, 188

jīva (empirical self) 12, 24–28, 51
jīvanmukta (liberated being) 49, 57
jñānakāṇḍa portions of *śruti* 32, 35, 40, *194–195*
jñāna-yoga 28, 38–39, 42, 48, 54, *195*

juxtaposition, technique of 35–37, 88, 119, 122, 144

Kaccāyanagotta-sutta (*Discourse to Kātyāyana*) 82
Kalupahana, D. 73, 77, *199*, *200*
Kapleau, P. 94, 130, 176, *200*, *201*, *205*
karmakāṇḍa *194*, *195*
karma-yoga *195*
Kasulis, T. P. 99, 100–101, 102, 105, 176, *201*, *202*
kenshō (seeing one's own nature) *201*
'Kill the Buddha', Linji's injunction to *193–194*
Kim, H.-J. 101, 106, 119, 134, 149, 154, *202*
King, R. 4
knower, objectivization of 34, 43–44, 65, 124–127
kōan practice 129, 171, *203*, *205*
Kodera, J. 102, 103, 105, *200*, *202*
Korematsu (Korematsu-oshō), Ekai 11, 101, 103–104, 106–109, 110, 111, 132, 134, 140–141, 145, 158, 172, 173, 174, 176, 177, 180–181, 182–183, *200*, *201*, *202*, *203*, *205*
koṭi (four alternative positions) 26, 88
  see also tetralemma
Kṛṣṇa 58, 61
Kusan Sunim 6, 12, 13, *200*
kyōsaku stick 121, 129, 180, *203*

lakṣaṇā (implication) 35, 37–38
Laṇkāvatāra Sūtra 73–79, 80, *198–199*
Leighton, D. 102, 103, 104, 144, *202*, *203*
liberation (*mokṣa*) 3, 15–16, 19, 22–27, 32–33, 38–41, 61, 63–65, 76, 83–84, 92–93, 134, 142–143, *198*
  of words and letters 95, 102, 105
linear causality 94, 98, 107–108, 111–112, *192*
linear conceptions of space and time xv, xx, 8, 61–62, 72, 113, 118, 133–138, 154–155, 184, 186
Linji 105, 193
'look directly', admonition to xiii–xiv, 14, 15
Loori, J. D. 144
Loy, D. 5, 7–8, 189, *204*, *205*
Luohan 157, *204*

madhyamā pratipad (middle way) 71, 99, 112
Mādhyamika school 4–6, 80–82, 85–86, 88–89, 149, *191*, *193*, *200*
Mahadevan, M. P. 10, *196*, *197*
Mahāparinirvāṇa sūtra 105, *200*
mahāvākyas 19, 40, 42, 66, *192*, *193*
Mahāyāna Buddhism 95, 105, *191*, *192*
  deconstructive strategy 76, 98, 149
  Mahāyāna sūtras 66, 72–80, 172, 176, *198–199*, *200*
  ontological differences and non-duality in 3–8
Maitreyī 6, *195*, *196*
'making effort' 101, 176, *206*
manana (reflection) 38, 39, 42
Māṇḍūkya Upaniṣad 4, 22
masters (modern and contemporary)
  Advaita Vedānta 47–79
  Zen Buddhism 106–11
māyā (illusion) 22, 23–25, 31, 47, 69, *194*
Mayeda, Sengaku *194*
Mazu Daoyi 149, *199*, *204*
McRae, John R. *198–199*
meditative awareness, non-dual characteristics of xvii–xviii
meditative enquiry, as means to spiritual insight xv, 8–12, 72, 112, 117, 128, 157, 160, *199*
methodology xvi–xx
mithyā (illusory) 22, 30–31
Mohs, M. xvii
Moore, R. *198*
mountain, sitting like 101, 140
  see also shikantaza
Moustakas, C. xvii
movement
  in experience of practitioner xvii, xx–xxi, 118, 155, 158, 162–163, 174–175, 181, 185
  in stillness 145

mu, practice of 171, *203*, *205*
Mūlamadhyamakakārikās (Fundamental Verses of the Middle Way) 4, 6, 74, 76, 80–93, 112, 183, *192*, *194*, *199*, *200*, *201*
Mumenkuan *204*, 205
mumukṣutvam (desire for freedom alone) 38
Muṇḍaka Upaniṣad III:2.9 60
Murti, T. R. V. 3, 5, 200

Nāgārjuna 4, 6, 29, 74, 76, 79, 80–93, 94, 98, 99, 111, 112, 134, 169, 183, 189, *191*, *194*, *199*, *200*, *201*, *206*
nāma rūpa ('name and form') 19, 21, 29
Nanjuan 157, *205*
Narasimha, B. V. *196*, *197*
negation
  abhāva, as means of valid knowledge 32
  bi-negation 35, 89, 90
  deconstructive techniques of 70, 117–118, 123, 139, 142, 146–155, 161, 186, *193*
  of dualistic conceptual thinking xx, 6–7, 16, 24, 27, 63, 73, 112–113
  'eight negations', the 81
  interplay with affirmation *see* affirmation–negation–affirmation 'formula'
  negations of the Heart Sūtra 15, 68, 69
  neither/nor negation 90, 149–153, 157–158, 172
  neti, neti (not this, not this) 19, 35–37, 52–53, *196*
  of presence and absence 141
Nelson, P. L. *206*
neti, neti (not this, not this) 19, 35–37, 52–53, *196*
  see also negation
nididhyāsana (contemplation) 38–39, 42
nihilism (impermanence) 81–82, 99, 112
niḥsvabhāvatā (independent existence) 81
Nikhilananda, S. 22, 24, 25, 26, *193*
nirvāṇa (absolute, unconditioned Reality) 6, 76, 80–85, 91–93, 99, 118, 134, 183, *200*, *201*
nirvikalpaka (construction-free) awareness 34, 41
Nishijima, G. 153, *200*, *202*, *204*, *205*
Noble Eightfold Path 82
non-being 31, 74–75, 80, 99, 111
non-duality
  in Advaita Vedānta and Zen Buddhism, overview 3–17
  non-dual experience 4, 7, 18, 167, 169–170, 174, 188
  non-dual experiential 'space' 129, 133, 152, 157–159
non-emptiness 85
nonexistence 5, 22, 30, 61, 81–82, 84–86, 88–89, 137
non-phenomenal ground, *brahman* as (*nirviśeṣa-vastu*) 154, 187
non-thinking (*hishiryō*) xxi, 95, 100–101, 105, 108, 112, 146, 153, 156–158, 173, 176, 178, *201*, *202*, *205*
no-self (*anatta*) ontology of 4, 7, 69, 71–72, 184, 187
'not-knowing space' 103–104, 124–125, 128, 130–133, 138, 155, 157, 160, 185
not-thinking (*fushiryō*) 100–101, 105, 153, 156, 158, *201*, *202*
'Not this, Not this' (*neti, neti*) 19, 37, 52–53
'not two' 6, 85, 90, 93, 99, 113, 118, 134
'nothing ever happens', as summary of Advaita Vedānta 69–70, 126, 142–144, 187, *206*
'now' *see* 'here and now'

Odell, D. 138, 144
Olivelle, P. *193*
'open mind' 128
Osborne, A. 50, 51, 126, *196*, *197*

Pannikar, R. *192*
parabhāva (other/extended nature) 83, *200*
paradoxical problems xv–xvi, xx, 113,

117–118, 123, 139–142, 186
in Advaita Vedānta 142–144
paradox of expressibility 79, 91–92
in Zen Buddhism 144–146
paramārtha-satya (ultimate/supreme truth) 29, 81, 84, 90
see also two truths, the (*saṃvṛti-satya* and *paramārtha-satya*)
pāramārthika (absolutely real) xix, 29–31, 44, 46–47, 53, 69, 70
parīkṣā (critical investigation) 80
participant-observation fieldwork, overview xvi
Patañjali *195*
phala (fruit) *195*
philosophical foundations
of Advaita Vedānta 18–70
of Zen Buddhism 71–113
Poonja (Poonjaji), H. W. L. 47–48, 49, 54, 58–66, 69, 70, 122, 136–137, 138, 141–142, 143, 147, 148, 150–153, 157, 158, 159, 162, 163, 168, *192*, *193*, *195*, *196*, *197–198*, *203–204*, *205*
Potter, K. H. 8, 25, 26, 30, 32, 34, 39, *191*, *192*, *193*, *194*, *196*
Powell, W. F. 15
practice
and realization 63, 94–99, 102, 106–111, 145, 152–153, 169, 182, *193*, *198*, *205*
wholehearted 95, 102–105, *202*
see also shikantaza
Prajñāpāramitā Sūtras 81, 119, 183, *192*
Prajñāpāramitā Hridaya Sūtra (Heart of Perfect Wisdom Sūtra) 15, 66, 68, 69, *192*, *199*
Vajracchedikā Prajñāpāramitā Sūtra (Diamond Sūtra) 73–79, 172, 176, *199*, *200*
pramāṇas (means of valid knowledge) 32–34, *195*
pramātṛ (knower) 34, 46, 65
Prasannapadā *200*
pratītyasamutpāda (dependent co-origination) 4, 71, 75, 81, 83, 86, 107, *199*
pratyakṣa (perception) 32, 34, *195*
predication 40, 89, 142
presence
and absence 122–123, 138, 141–142
of *guru* 57, 58, 64, 119, 122, *206*
pure 100, 101, 158, 181
reifying of 176
Priest, G. 90, 91, 92–93
Puhakka, K. 158, *206*
pūjās (ritual worship) 58, *197*

questioning, as means to spiritual insight xv–xvi, 8–12, 32, 48, 50, 51, 52, 55, 59, 64, 71, 73, 110, 118, 123, 124, 126, 128, 131, 132, 138, 149, 151, 161, 162, 188, *201–202*, *206*
see also teacher–student dialogues

Radhakrishnan, S. *191*, *193*, *196*
rāja-yoga *195*
Ramana Maharshi 9, 10, 11, 13, 14, 16, 17, 47, 48, 49–59, 60–61, 64, 70, 124, 126, 128, 139–140, 160, 162, 165–166, 169, *192*, *193*, *194*, *195*, *196–197*, *198*, *200*, *203*
Rambachan, A. 35–37, 39, 53, *195*
reaffirmation 78
reality-as-it-is xv, 13, 73, 76, 183
Reat, N. R. *191*
reification 63, 80, 82, 87, 99, 105–106, 136, 145, 147, 149–150, 163, 172, *192*, *193*, *200*, *206*
of awareness, deconstruction of 186–90
of Buddha-nature 94
of *dharma* 79
of dichotomies 62, 112, 144
of emptiness 85
of entities 16, 99, 123
of the path 88, 92, 111
of practice, and realization 104, 160
of self 56, 82, 129
of the teacher–student relationship 118, 122–123
of *zazen* 110
religion, Ninian Smart's six dimensions of *191*
resolution-practice 97

'right here' and 'right now' 93, 133–134, 183
ritual, in Zen monasticism *202*
Robinson, R. H. 92
rope-snake mistake 25–26, 45
Rothberg, D. *206*
Ruegg, D. S. 81, 88–89, 152, *200*
Rujing, Tiantong (J. Tendō Nyojō) 94, 102
Ryokai (J. Tōzan) *192*

śabda (verbal testimony) 32, 34–35, *195*
śabda-pramāṇa 35
sadasadbhyamanirvacanīyà (indescribable as either real or unreal) 30–31, 126
sadasatvilakṣaṇa (other than real or unreal) 30–31, 33, 98, 126
sādhana (spiritual practice) 19, 52
    sādhana catuṣṭaya 38–39
ṣaḍlinga, sixfold criteria of Advaita *195*
śamādisādhanasampatti (mental tranquillity 38
saṃsāra (relative, conditioned reality) 6, 76, 80–83, 91–93, 99, 118, 134, 183
saṃvṛti-satya (conventional relative truth) 29, 81, 83–84, 90
    see also two truths, the (*saṃvṛti-satya* and *paramārtha-satya*)
San Francisco Zen Center *192*
saṅgha 84
Śaṅkara 18, 22, 27–47, 48, 50, 51, 52, 53, 65, 70, 85, 98, 119, 126, 165, 168, 186, 189, *192*, *193*, *194*, *195*, *197*, *198*, *205*
Sarasvati, C. *196*
sat (real) 30–31, 51, 57–58, 126, *194*
satsang (*sat-sanga)* (meeting of truth with reality) 49, 57–59, 64–66, 119, 136, *197*, *198*, *202*, *204*
savikalpaka (construction-filled) awareness 34
'seek within', admonition to 55
seer, enquiring into nature of 21, 59, 68, 124, *197*
self
    'absorption of', Ramana Maharshi's experience of 49–58, 126
    'doing nothing' to be who we are 58–66
    Gangaji's understanding of 66–69
    'I'-thought, the 52–54
    and other (subject and object) dualism xv, xvii–xviii, 8, 24, 65, 113, 118, 138, 155, 187
    self-nature (*svabhāva*) 4, 46, 72, 74–75, 77, 82–89, 92–93, 98, *193*, *199*, *200*
    self-realization 48, 53, 58, 60, 62–63, 65, 124, 126, 128, 150, 166, *196*
    self-recognition 59, 62
    'Who am I?' – question of 9–10, 13–14, 24, 49–60, 64, 70, 124, 128–130, 133, 136–138, 160–164, *195*
    see also brahmajñāna (liberating knowledge)
Sengzhao 149
sesshin (retreat) 110, 170, 178, 181
Shapiro, I. *192*, *198*
Sharf, R. H. *201*
Sharma, A. *192*
'shift', deconstructive xvii, xx–xxi, 118, 129, 155
shikaku (acquired awakening) 95
shikantaza ('just sitting') 9, 95–96, 99–102, 106–112, 117, 121, 129–133, 138, 140, 144–145, 152–154, 157, 169–189, *203*, *205*, *206*
shinjin-datsuraku (casting off of body and mind) 94–99, 102
Shōbōgenzō 80, 95, 99, 105, 106, 119, 172, *201*
    Bendōwa 96, 97, *200*
    'Buddha-nature' *202*
    Bukkōjōji 204
    Busshō 97, 105
    Genjōkōan 153, *204*
    Gyōji 97, 102, *205*
    Hokke-Ten-Hokke *204*
    Kokū *205*
    'Total Dynamic Working' *202*, *204*
    Uji *204*
    Zazenshin *202*
    Zenki 106, 144, *204*

Shōgaku, Wanshi *191*
showing, in relation to proving 86–88
shushō-ittō 94, 144
silence 54, 57, 109, 122, 152, *196*
Smart, N. *191*
smṛti (authored scripture) *195*
sources of the tradition
  Advaita Vedānta 18–47
  Zen Buddhism 73–106
space
  experiential 159–185
  'not-knowing space' 103–104, 124–125, 128, 130–133, 138, 155, 157, 160, 185
spine, return to 107–109
Sprung, M. *199*, *200*
śravaṇa (listening) 38–39, 42, *195*
śruti (scripture) 32, 35–36, 39–41, *195*
Stafford Betty, L. 92
stick
  teaching (*kyōsaku*) 121, 129, 180, *203*
  used for stirring funeral pyre 54, 55, 70, 128
stillness, importance of 127, 132, 145, 180, 182, *203*
  stillpoint of being xvii, 131, 152, 157, 189
straight back, having 177, 178
Streng, F. J. 79, 82, 85, 91, 92
stuck, experience of being 104, 131, 133, 138–140, 143, 149, 157, 174, 182
student–teacher encounters *see* teacher–student dialogues
subject–object dualism 24–26, 28–29, 34, 41, 44, 46, 55, 65, 138, 158–159, 177, 181
substance-view of reality 3–4, 7–8, 27, 29, 46
substantialism 80
Subuti *200*
śūnyatā (emptiness) 4, 74–75, 81–87, 89, 92–93, 98, 112, 143, 145, 149, 158, 168, 189, *200*
superimposition
(as teaching technique) *see adhyāropa*
  apavāda (desuperimposition used in conjuction with superimposition (*adhyāropa*))
  superimposition (mistaking something for what it is not) *see adhyāsa*
Suzuki, D. T. 73, 74, 75, 76, 80, *198*, *199*
Suzuki (Suzuki-rōshi), Shunryu 10, 183, 187, *191*, *192*, *199*, *206*
svabhāva (self-nature) 4, 46, 72, 74–75, 77, 82–89, 92–93, 98, *193*, *199*, *200*
svaprakāśa (self-luminous) consciousness 28
svarūpalakṣaṇa (Śaṅkara's primary definition of *brahman*) 29
Śvetaketu 19

Taittirīya Upaniṣad II:1.1 37
taṭasthalakṣaṇa (Śaṅkara's secondary definition of *brahman*) 29, 37, 40
tathāgata (fully enlightened one) 81, 105, *200*
teacher–student dialogues xviii, xix, 8–12, 19, 28, 39, 47, 50, 64, 118–123, 129, 131, *192*, *202*
tenzo, Dōgen's pivotal meeting with the 102–106, 183, *202*, *203*
tetralemma (*catuṣkoṭi*) xix, 88–91, *200*
'That art thou' (*tat tvam asi*) 18–21
Thibaut, G. *194*, *205*
'things-as-they-are' (*yathābhūtam*) 8, 72, 153, 169, 175
'things coming together' 108
'things just being present' 176
thinking
  dualistic (oppositional) 7, 18, 69–73, 83, 105–106, 111, 113, 118, 136, 139–142, 146, 152, 156, 173
  dynamic between thinking and not-thinking 187, *205*
  either/or thinking 148, 150
  non-oppositional 174
  ordinary ways of 17, 170, 172
  or reflection (*manana*) 38
  shiryō 100–101, 108, 112, 153, *201*
  thinker of 21
Three Treasures (*buddha*, *dharma* and *saṅgha*) 84
Three Treasures Association (Sanbōkyōdan) *201*

transpersonal orientation xvii
turning space between thinking and not-thinking 158
two truths, the (*saṃvṛti-satya* and *paramārtha-satya*) 29, 53, 81, 84–85, 90–94, 99, 112, 119, 139–140, 173–174, *194*

Uddālaka 19
ultimate truth *see* two truths, the (*saṃvṛti-satya* and *paramārtha-satya*)
unborn nature of all things 26, 74–75, 146
undoing of dualistic conceptual structures xiv–xv, 7, 12–17, 39, 54, 60, 69–70, 79, 108–109, 113, 117–190, *203*
  in Advaita Vedānta 160–169
  in Zen Buddhism 169–185
unfindability analysis xx, 70, 88, 113, 117–118, 138, 141, 152, 186, *204*
  in relation to Advaita Vedānta 123–129
  in relation to Zen Buddhism 129–133
Upadeśasāhasrī (A Thousand Teachings) 3, 7–12, 13, 28, 32–33, 36, 39–46, 49, 50–51, 64, 93, 103, 108–110, *194*
Upakramopasaṁhara (beginning and end) *195*
upamāna (comparison) 32, *195*
Upaniṣads see Aitareya Upaniṣad; *Bṛhad-āraṇyaka Upaniṣad*; *Bṛhad-āraṇyaka Upaniṣadbhāṣya*; *Chāndogya Upaniṣad*; *Māṇḍūkya Upaniṣad*; *Muṇḍaka Upaniṣad*; *Taittirīya Upaniṣad*
upapatti (demonstration) *195*
Uṣasta Cākrāyaṇa 20–21, *196*

vairāgya (renunciation) 38
Vajracchedikā Prajñāpāramitā Sūtra 73–79, 172, 176, *199*, *200*
Valle, R. xvii
Van Buitenen, J. A. B. 22, 28, 31, 32, 33, 36, 39–40, 41, 42–45, 46, 50, 119, *193*, *194*, *195–196*
Vartman (Sandford) 17, *192*, *198*
Venkataraman *see* Ramana Maharshi
vidyā (non-dual knowledge) 29, 32, 42, 46, 51, 69
vikalpa (wrong interpretation) 23, 25–27, 32, 47, 81, *193*
Vimalakīrti Nirdeśa Sūtra *199*
viṣaya (known) 34, 46, 65
Viśiṣṭādvaita school of Vedāntic philosophy *192*
Vivekananda, Swami *196*
vyavahāra xix
vyāvahārika (empirically real) 29–30, 44, 46–47, 53, 66

Waddell, N. 94, 96, 97, 100, 105, 106, 136, 144, 158, *192*, *200*, *201*, *202*, *204*
waking states (external illusion) 23–24, 45, *193*
Watson, B. *105*, *194*
We Wei *197*
Wood, T. E. *200*
'working on' and 'working out', in teaching of H. W. L. Poonjaji 59–60
Wright, D. S. 139, *204*
Wumenkuan *205*

Yājñavalkya 6, 20–21, 68, *196*
Yakusan Gugō (C. Yueshan) *201–202*
Yamada Kōun-rōshi *205*
Yamahata, Hōgen (Hōgen-san) 107, 109–111, 120–121, 122, 134–135, 148–149, 150, *202*
Yanagida, S. *192*
Yasutani (Yasutani-rōshi) Hakuun 94, *200*, *201*, *203*, *205*
yathābhūtam (things-as-they-are) 8, 72, 153, 169, 175

zazen (seated meditatation) 15, 93, 99–103, 105, 107–110, 121–122, 134, 140, 144, 157–158, 169, 172, 176–177, 182, *200*, *201*, *203*, *205*
Zhaozhou *205*

25034948R00140

Printed in Great Britain
by Amazon